AMERICAN HOMELESSNESS

A Reference Handbook

AMERICAN HOMELESSNESS

A Reference Handbook

Second Edition

Mary Ellen Hombs
Director
Legal Services Homelessness Task Force

CONTEMPORARY WORLD ISSUES

ABC-CLIO

Santa Barbara, California
Denver, Colorado
Oxford, England

Library of Congress Cataloging-in-Publication Data

Hombs, Mary Ellen.
American homelessness : a reference handbook / Mary Ellen Hombs.
—2nd ed.
  p.   cm.—(Contemporary world issues)
Includes bibliographical references and index.
  1. Homelessness—United States—Handbooks, manuals, etc.
I. Title. II. Series.
HV4505.H647 1994   362.5′0973—dc20   94-33788

ISBN 0-87436-725-5 (alk. paper)

00 99 98 97 96 95 94   10 9 8 7 6 5 4 3 2 1

ABC-CLIO, Inc.
130 Cremona Drive, P.O. Box 1911
Santa Barbara, California 93116-1911

*To Simone Weil, who said that the only real question to be asked of another is "What are you going through?",
and to Elliot Liebow, who has listened so well to what homeless people have answered.*

Contents

Preface

THE PROBLEM OF HOMELESSNESS HAS GROWN and changed dramatically since it first became very visible during the 1980s. Whereas people once gleaned most of their knowledge about homelessness from special media reports during winter months and holiday periods, now many Americans acknowledge that they see homeless people in their daily travels between home and work or school. We have become somewhat accustomed to seeing the indications of homelessness around us, to hearing of fund-raising events for local shelters and soup kitchens, and to finding less media coverage than before. What once seemed to be an emergency now appears to be a chronic problem. Although the problem is more commonplace, it is becoming even more difficult to solve. Individuals question whether they should give money to apparently homeless people, because they have doubts about whether this helps. More people understand that effective solutions require examining many complex national factors, including the housing market, the labor market, national policies on health care and mental health care, and welfare programs.

In December 1993, a dramatic event occurred in Washington, D.C., that underscored the role that homelessness plays in our everyday lives today. A woman who had been chronically mentally ill and in and out of homeless assistance programs was found dead one morning in the bus shelter where she had been sleeping. The bus shelter was located outside the U.S. Department of Housing and Urban Development (HUD), the federal agency charged with the responsibility to administer federal homeless programs. HUD secretary Henry Cisneros, who recently had said that ending homelessness would be his top priority, declared the woman's death to be "a wake-up call" to do more and to prove that people were not tired of trying to solve the problem. He ordered emergency spending for the winter months and told his employees to assist any homeless person they saw, including bringing him or her into the HUD building for shelter. The individual toll of homelessness was recalled for many people in an urgent way by this event.

The deep roots of homelessness are reflected not only in the dimensions of the problem itself but in the resources that have evolved to deal with it. Many service and advocacy organizations now exist; virtually every state has a homeless organization addressing state policy. We know a good deal more about homelessness, and our information resources have developed. Specialized newsletters and databases are available. National student organizations have formed, holding weekend and summer sessions on homelessness, including direct contact with homeless people, for interested young people. Some of these responses have been institutionalized in college and religious programs.

This book gives an overview of these and other resources, as they have developed over time. It is no longer possible to list all the resources available, because they have proliferated so rapidly and in so many directions. Instead, this book provides the tools to identify some of the proven resources and supplies the locations of information that will keep the reader current.

Chapter 1 provides an introduction to the fundamentals of the problem. It offers a framework for answering some basic questions including: Who is homeless, and why? How many people are homeless, and what role does poverty play in their lives? Chapter 2 looks at important events in contemporary homelessness and provides a picture of how organizational efforts and national response have developed. Chapter 3 profiles individuals who have had a significant impact on homelessness, either in the national public eye or because of their local efforts.

Chapter 4 presents some of the available factual material about homelessness and poverty, including information on public assistance programs, health issues, and use of services. Chapter 5 includes excerpts and material from published documents and reports that reflect the range of problems within homelessness, such as children's education and homeless people with HIV/AIDS. Some of these are first-person accounts by homeless people. Chapter 6 summarizes significant federal legislation on homelessness, including the original McKinney Act and the proposals made for its reorganization in mid-1994. Chapter 7 provides an overview of important litigation affecting the homeless.

Chapter 8 is a directory of major nonprofit organizations and government agencies that work on a range of issues including shelter, housing, and health. Chapter 9 offers references to some of the earliest written material on the problem, as well as more recent data and government reports. Chapter 10 highlights videos on homelessness and related topics, as well as computer databases and other resources and is followed by a glossary of useful definitions common to the wide variety of issues that need to be understood, such as welfare programs and housing assistance.

It is hoped that this book will make the problem of homelessness more understandable. Some readers may admire the efforts of those they read about, or agree with the theories presented, but it is important to remember that the "problem" of homelessness is the problem of individuals: men, women, and children. Homeless people are human beings—hungry, tired, hurting, crying, sweating in summer, freezing in winter. Whatever understanding comes from reading this book should be applied to ending homelessness and setting aright the lives of those who experience it.

The intractability of homelessness has also been recognized by Clinton administration officials at the Department of Housing and Urban Development, which in early 1994 proposed not only doubling federal budget resources for homelessness, but revamping the approach of McKinney Act programs designed to address it. The proposals, expected to be passed by Congress in late 1994, realign the federal programs to be consistent with the "continuum of care" concept aimed at moving homeless people from emergency to permanent resources.

1

Introduction

BEGINNING IN THE EARLY 1980S, the problem of homelessness[1] received increasing attention across the country; the sheer visibility of contemporary homelessness is perhaps its most identifiable attribute. Whether it is the sight of a person begging on the corner, a family living in a car, the countless homeless people in the streets and subways of big cities, or the ragged men and women silhouetted against the monuments and memorials of the nation's capital, striking images of this utmost poverty are inescapable for most Americans.

Researchers interested in homelessness have examined social science literature to see how many articles appeared on this topic. As of mid-1992, their research shows the following chronology:

1972:	11	1983:	14
1973:	6	1984:	35
1974:	8	1985:	23
1975:	13	1986:	61
1976:	10	1987:	78
1977:	3	1988:	112
1978:	12	1989:	135
1979:	6	1990:	176
1980:	12	1991:	195
1981:	7	mid-1992:	62[2]
1982:	15		

Insofar as public concern is driven both by personal experiences of seeing people who are apparently homeless and by seeing homelessness represented in press accounts, this chronology gives a good indication of the parabolic curve that gradually built up during the 1980s and then suddenly dropped off. Replacing the heavy coverage of the mid-1980s were the more intermittent and less sympathetic stories of the "truth" about homelessness, including the reported incidence of drug use, prevalence of HIV/AIDS, disinterest in employment, and exploitation of available resources (such as stories about people entering shelters in order to receive a preference for permanent housing). Gone—except for the traditional Thanksgiving and Christmas press coverage—were the stories asserting that "homeless people are just like us except they've had a few bad breaks."

The less sympathetic coverage also has contributed to policy debate and proposals that revolve around a historic dilemma: Are there homeless and very poor people who are simply victims of bad luck and deserve our help and support, and are there also people whose own personal undesirable behavior—whether alcohol or drug related, whether laziness or lack of thrift—could be rectified by their own efforts and contribute to their more stable, more "normal" future? In other words, as the dilemma is more usually phrased, aren't some of the poor deserving and some not?

But news coverage and other articles again began to increase in number in late 1993, due to several factors. Shortly after U.S. Secretary of Housing and Urban Development Henry Cisneros declared homelessness to be his agency's top priority, a homeless woman died at a bus stop outside the agency. Her death was highly publicized and analyzed as a symbol of a larger social problem. Just a few months later came the release of the Federal Plan on homelessness, prepared as a result of President Clinton's 1993 Executive Order; this news was also carried around the nation. During the same period, more and more communities passed new laws or undertook enforcement campaigns of existing laws to regulate the behavior of homeless people in public spaces, by prohibiting acts such as sleeping, storing belongings, or distributing food. These actions also brought new and increased press coverage, though seldom of a sympathetic nature.

Coming as it has on the heels of the record-breaking 1989 national demonstration for housing and the passage of ambitious bipartisan legislation to help homeless people, this type of media coverage does portray one segment of the public's sentiment. Increasingly, communities express their frustration with a problem that doesn't seem to go away and, in fact, is ever-present in just those areas where people seek respite from the everyday: shopping districts, restaurants, and entertainment areas.

Increasingly, that frustration is also fiscal, as local communities and states struggle with a declining economy and drastically shifting federal dollars for social services, even as they have spent sometimes staggering sums for shelters. Thus, as the 1980s drew to a close, communities responded to homelessness by trying to move it: zoning out of lucrative downtown areas any services or shelters that would draw in homeless people, criminalizing sleeping in public and begging, trying to push homeless people away.

Polls do not always back up what seems to be the public push for punitive measures. Some even characterize the change of winds as reflecting hopelessness rather than callousness; taxpayers are concerned about homelessness, but don't like the heavy and apparently fruitless expenses of public programs.

If some truth is to be known about homelessness at this point, it is this rather complex realization: From coast to coast during the 1980s, communities of all sizes discovered within their own borders a new version of a problem many Americans previously associated only with the Depression years or with certain stereotypes. Yet the images shown on the evening news of the ragged individual behaving bizarrely on a downtown street corner are not the figures either of the Depression and dust bowl years or, more recently, of the 1950s and 1960s, when the common idea of a homeless person was a middle-aged white male alcoholic undoubtedly homeless by choice. They describe a more recent version of very poor people, one that involves families with children, homeless youth, and single adults.

So, while homelessness itself is not new, what is new is the size and scope of the problem, how it has come about, whom it affects, what our individual and collective attitudes toward it are, and how inseparable it is from deepening poverty. In the 1980s, homelessness reached epidemic proportions in this country. As the numbers of those affected continued to increase, service providers and public officials alike recognized that the problem is complex, touching on many issues of poverty such as public assistance, wage levels, and affordable housing. Nor are these issues neatly confined to our borders any longer, as larger economic shifts are driven by global influences.

The nation faces a significant challenge: Not only do people continue to be pushed to the streets, but for some of them, escape seems nearly impossible. Reports show that homelessness is growing around the nation—in communities large and small—and families with children represent a rapidly expanding segment of that population, as do racial and ethnic minorities, who are disproportionately poor.

What Is Homelessness?

What are we talking about when we talk about homelessness? Are homeless people just those we see lying outside on our streets, begging, sleeping in front of national monuments? What about people in emergency shelters? What if an individual has a nearby relative and chooses not to stay with that person? Is someone homeless when friends or family offer temporary accommodations on a sofa? When we say a person is "homeless," do we really mean he or she is "houseless"? Does homelessness mean more than the mere absence of shelter in its most fundamental form?

This question has been the focus of much debate. There is no one generally accepted definition of homelessness, although it should be apparent that the choice of definition has significant influence when estimating the size of the problem of homelessness. Various agencies of the federal government have even used several different definitions during the last decade. Among the major definitions are these:

> A person is homeless if his or her residence at night is "in public or private emergency shelters, which take a variety of forms—armories, schools, church basements, government buildings, former firehouses and, where temporary vouchers are provided by private and public agencies, even hotels, apartments, or boarding homes"; or "in the streets, parks, subways, bus terminals, railroad stations, airports, under bridges or aqueducts, abandoned buildings without utilities, cars, trucks, or any of the public or private space that is not designed for shelter."[3] This definition, it should be noted, does not include people in halfway houses or long-term

detoxification residences, or incarcerated persons who would otherwise be in shelters or on the streets. However, battered women are included, if they are on the streets, in a shelter, or in a group house.

A homeless person is "anyone who lacks adequate shelter, resources, and community ties."[4]

A homeless individual (1) lacks a fixed, regular, and adequate nighttime residence and (2) has a primary nighttime residence that is (a) a supervised, publicly or privately operated shelter designed to provide temporary living accommodations (including welfare hotels, congregate shelters, and transitional housing for the mentally ill), (b) an institution that provides a temporary residence for individuals intended to be institutionalized, and (c) a public or private place not designed for, or ordinarily used as, a regular sleeping accommodation for human beings.[5]

Persons seeking assistance from federal homeless housing programs are defined as homeless if they are sleeping in places not fit for humans, sleeping in homeless shelters, or about to sleep in one of these places because they are being evicted or discharged and have no other place to go and have no other resources or support.[6]

Persons who are living "doubled up" with friends or family in precarious, makeshift housing arrangements lack the "fixed, regular, and adequate nighttime residence" described above and should be considered homeless;[7] they are some of the people included in the term "hidden homeless."

While not seeking to define homelessness, the U.S. Bureau of the Census combined two categories of "transient" persons in its census count: "(a) all persons at missions, flophouses, and other transient accommodations renting for less than $4 per night; local jails and similar short-term detention centers; and places such as all-night theaters, railroad stations, and bus depots"; as well as "(b) transient persons (i.e., 'street people') missed in all other housing units and found on street corners, bus and train stations, welfare offices, food stamp centers, and so on."[8]

These definitions do not reflect the other, less tangible aspects of homelessness, as described in this statement by the National

Coalition for the Homeless: "Being homeless means more than not having a place to sleep. Being homeless means having no place to save the things that connect you to your past, losing all contact with friends and family, uprooting your children from school. It means suffering the frustration and degradation of living hand to mouth, depending on the generosity of strangers or the efficiency of a government agency for your survival, for your children's survival."[9]

Who Is Homeless?

At the beginning of the 1980s, the prevailing stereotype of a homeless person was that of a middle-aged white urban male alcoholic, a transient who either wandered the country (as a "vagrant," "tramp," or "hobo") or inhabited downtown "skid row" areas characterized by low-cost hotels and bars. Most of all, this person was viewed as "shiftless" for not living a "responsible" life with job and family, and blameworthy for whatever poverty, misery, or suffering accompanied this voluntarily chosen lifestyle.

Traditionally, the only services available to this homeless person were church services, those of the "mission" establishments, such as the Salvation Army and the Gospel Mission, which offered overnight sleeping space and meals in exchange for a small fee and a sincere desire to rehabilitate one's life by attending mandatory sermons and renouncing alcohol. In proportion to the numbers who might seek this path to help, few of the available beds were for homeless women.

No longer does this description of homeless people hold true. As the causes of homelessness have broadened and become more tied to fundamental economic changes in our nation, homelessness has become both a symptom of chronic poverty and an event that cuts across traditional defenses of income, education, and geography. The population of the streets has been democratized correspondingly.

Many studies of homeless people find these trends:

- More and more, these are young people.

- Racial and ethnic minority groups are disproportionately represented.

- Families with children constitute approximately 35 percent of homeless people.

- In most areas, working people account for an average of 30 percent of the homeless population.

- Homelessness is becoming a chronic and recurring event, reflecting the inadequacy of existing solutions in the face of low public-benefits levels and wages and high housing costs.

Not only families are homeless. Single adults may be homeless because of a job loss, trouble at home, or a health problem. Veterans are discharged from the military; prisoners are released after serving sentences; young adults "graduate" from the foster-care system. Any of the people in these categories can and often do become homeless. In addition, significant minorities of homeless people are mentally ill, alcohol/drug–dependent, or HIV/AIDS–infected.

Literal homelessness, however, is only the most extreme manifestation of a more generalized, growing, and enduring poverty caused by drastic cuts in federal low-income housing programs and state cash assistance programs, and exacerbated by a combination of factors and personal difficulties: rising housing costs, safety-net program cuts, and a minimum wage that has not kept pace with the cost of living.

For each individual or household that actually reaches the streets or shelters, many more are living on the edge of homelessness, doubled- or tripled-up in precarious housing arrangements with friends or family. Further, in some areas, people resort to living in structures not intended to be used as housing—garages, for example.

How Many People Are Homeless?

From the difficulty revealed in arriving at a definition of homelessness, it should be apparent that there is no adequate way to arrive at an estimate of the size of the population. There has been enormous controversy over this point since the problem began to burgeon in the early 1980s—just as the economy was on an upswing—and advocates, researchers, and government officials remain greatly divided over estimates. Figures offered range from a low of 250,000 people to at least 3 million.[10]

Substantial problems of methodology exist in trying to count homeless people, not the least of which is that many homeless people work very hard to obscure their homelessness by dress, appearance, and daily schedule. They try to make their homelessness "invisible" to those who might not otherwise recognize it. Still others achieve invisibility by sleeping in abandoned buildings, in cars parked behind shopping malls, or in a tent in the woods. As revealed by the definitional problem, the homelessness of many others is "hidden" by precarious housing arrangements with friends or families, circumstances that can be ended in a moment. As previously pointed out, others make do in structures not intended as living quarters, including in rural areas.

What Causes Homelessness?

Several major contributing causes have been identified by researchers examining the growth of homelessness.

Lack of Community-Based Care

While the deinstitutionalization of mental patients was widely viewed as the primary cause of homelessness in the early 1980s, deinstitutionalization itself was not to blame. The rationale behind releasing mental patients from long-term hospital care when they did not require such a setting was a good one. What resulted, however, was the careless depopulation of state institutions without the necessary community-support facilities, housing, and services that would allow former patients to live securely in the community. When combined with tightened readmission standards at the same hospitals, the wave of vulnerable dischargees was characterized by one psychiatrist as akin to being "dumped amid the broken promises."[11]

General agreement exists as to the national prevalence of serious mental illness, including schizophrenia and manic depression, among homeless people. Experts state that there are twice as many mentally ill homeless persons as there are institutionalized patients. Increasing numbers of incarcerated people suffer from mental illness; many were homeless when jailed and will be homeless upon their release.[12] As long as little provision is made for released patients and adequate housing is unavailable in the community, the plight of the mentally ill homeless will be dismal.[13]

The impact of a lack of community-based care extends to the need for residential facilities for homeless persons in recovery from alcohol and drug abuse, for persons with HIV/AIDS and their families, and for the increasing numbers of homeless people with tuberculosis, which can require lengthy treatment. Homelessness of all these groups is frequently caused by a shortage of available affordable housing units, which themselves are in short supply because of a lack of funds and a continuing wave of community opposition to racial and socioeconomic residential integration.

Increasing Poverty and Decreasing Assistance

The economic recovery of the early 1980s did not reach everyone in the nation; homeless people and those at risk ended the decade in worse shape than before. Hit hardest by poverty were children and youth: Almost half of the poor were children under 18. The 1987 poverty rate for white Americans was 10.5 percent, representing a very slight drop from the previous 11 percent. But for African-Americans the rate was 33.1 percent and for Hispanics 28.2 percent; poverty in both groups has been increasing.

In the 1980s inequalities in American income distribution reached their greatest extremes—for both rich and poor households—for the entire period in which such data have been collected.[14] The wealthiest 20 percent of the population received the highest percentage of income ever recorded (43.7 percent), while the poorest 40 percent received 15.4 percent, the lowest ever recorded.[15] Clearly, the rich got richer and the poor got poorer. The poverty gap (the amount by which poor people's income falls below the poverty line) widened, and despite general economic recovery, the poverty rate failed to drop significantly.

While the numbers of poor people increase and their economic position in society worsens, qualitative changes in their ranks suggest that the problem may be more widespread than in the past. The face of poverty increasingly reveals minorities, women who are heads of households, and younger married couples. These groups are not the temporary poor likely to be well served by emergency measures in either the public or private sector. Instead they include victims of lingering racial discrimination and sexism, individuals educationally unprepared for the vast structural changes in the nation's economy, and people trapped in decaying inner-city environments whose energies are sapped by the basic struggle to survive.

Working but Not Making Enough

More and more, the ranks of the homeless poor include working people, because housing costs are rising beyond the reach of low wages. More than 75 percent of new jobs in the 1980s paid only minimum wage.[16] When coupled with the rising costs of housing, it is not difficult to see why many shelters are populated with workers who have nowhere else to live. Reports from major cities bear out the urgency of employment issues for homeless people. An annual mayors' survey in 1992 found that in 29 major cities, up to 50 percent of homeless people were employed. The mayors repeatedly cite employment-related problems as contributing to local homelessness, and employment-related solutions as the way to end it.[17]

Fewer Safety-Net Programs and Less Available Affordable Housing

The benefits programs that once would have constituted a final protection from the streets have been greatly eroded. Programs designed to help people out of poverty or ease its misery have been cut or have failed to keep up with the cost of living. Cuts often occur in the form of tightened eligibility standards.

The influence of income problems on the search for housing is very real, because the critical shortage of low-cost housing makes the difference between chronic hardship and outright homelessness. The 1980s witnessed a radical reversal of the federal government's 40-year commitment to providing low-income housing, with the dire consequence that assisted housing availability does not begin to meet demand.

Unsubsidized low-rent housing in the private sector is also in crisis. Between 1970 and 1982, many cities lost from 50 to 85 percent of their single-room-occupancy (SRO) rooms.[18] The General Accounting Office (GAO) estimated that 1.1 million of these units were lost between 1970 and 1982.[19] These hotels, a traditional source of low-cost housing for single people, have recently been federally funded on a small scale to meet a continuing need.

The Response to Homelessness

The growth of the problem of homelessness nationally and the federal budget cuts of the 1980s caused a number of sectors of society to respond. Volunteer organizations offering food, shelter, and other services have expanded dramatically, with both religious and civic groups playing a role. State and local governments sometimes provide shelter and services. Foundations and religious organizations are addressing the serious health care needs of those who live outdoors in all kinds of weather without adequate protection.

Some individuals and organizations with access to the media have made the problem visible to the public through routes as diverse as cartoons and television movies. Books have been written, newspaper articles published. Dramatic public events, such as funerals and memorials, have brought the grim reality of suffering to television news. Demonstrations have led citizens to the doorstep of the White House to demand assistance for those in need.

Community nonprofit organizations, along with state and local government—and even business—have tried in some areas to meet the growing demand for affordable housing. Renovation of old buildings, creation of new housing units, adaptation of other facilities—including former military bases—have all been tried as people seek to answer the need of those around them. The federal government, after several years of involvement, has launched new initiatives aimed at consolidating and redirecting existing programs. In his first year in office, HUD Secretary Henry Cisneros made homelessness his agency's top priority, sought a doubling of homeless funds, and proposed reorganizing homeless spending.

Homelessness is a complex problem, and one that cannot be solved quickly. The material in this book demonstrates the fundamental need for housing to solve the most pressing of the problems facing homeless people, but also the need for all the health care, income, and social supports that can move people away from crisis and out of poverty.

Notes

1. Portions of this introductory material were previously published as "Federal Policy for the Homeless" in Volume I of the *Stanford Law and Policy Review* of Stanford Law School. They are used here by agreement with the Board of Trustees of Leland Stanford Junior University.

2. Beth D. Jarrett and Wes Daniels, *Law and the Homeless: An Annotated Bibiliography* (Miami: University of Miami School of Law, 1992), 4.

3. The Department of Housing and Urban Development (HUD), *A Report to the Secretary on the Homeless and Emergency Shelters,* May 1984, 7–8.

4. Irene Shifren Levine, "Homelessness: Its Implications for Mental Health Policy and Practice." Prepared for the Annual Meeting of the American Psychological Association, 30 August 1983, 1.

5. Stewart B. McKinney Homeless Assistance Act (P.L. 100-77).

6. *Council Communique,* Interagency Council on the Homeless, July/August 1992. Under this definition, a person in substandard housing is not eligible for aid, unless the housing has been condemned. A person living doubled up is not considered homeless, nor is a person being discharged from a mental health facility unless it is the institution's policy to discharge people without a housing placement. Persons being discharged from correctional institutions, even under "compassionate discharges" for persons with HIV/AIDS and/or tuberculosis and other serious illnesses, are not eligible for aid.

7. United States General Accounting Office (GAO), *Homeless Children and Youth: About 68,000 Homeless and 186,000 in Shared Housing at Any Given Time* (Washington, DC: U.S. GAO, June 1989), 8.

8. Statement of William Hill, April 1986, Regional Director, New York Regional Office, Field Division, Bureau of the Census, Before the Subcommittee on Census and Population, New York City.

9. National Coalition for the Homeless, *Homelessness in America: A Summary* (New York: National Coalition for the Homeless, 1989), 1.

10. The 250,000 figure was first asserted in the 1984 study released by the U.S. Department of Housing and Urban Development. Then HUD Assistant Secretary of Community Planning and Development, S. Anna Kondratas, was one of the chief public defenders of this figure, which was criticized as low by advocates. In September 1989, however, Kondratas stated during her Senate confirmation hearings that she endorsed the 650,000 figure offered in the National Academy of Science's 1988 report, *Homelessness, Health and Human Needs.* Advocacy organizations, however, continue to state that they believe at least 3 million people are homeless. Among these groups are the Community for Creative Non-Violence, which first announced this figure in 1983, and the National Coalition for the Homeless.

11. E. Fuller Torrey, *Nowhere To Go* (New York: Harper & Row, 1988), 3.

12. Ibid., 5.

13. Ibid.

14. Center on Budget and Policy Priorities, "Poverty Remains High Despite Economic Recovery" (Washington, DC: Center on Budget and Policy Priorities, 1988).

15. Martin Tolchin, "Minority Poverty on Rise but White Poor Decline," *New York Times,* 1 September 1988.

16. U.S. Conference of Mayors, "The Continuing Growth of Hunger, Homelessness and Poverty in America's Cities: 1987. A 26-City Survey" (Washington, DC: U.S. Conference of Mayors, January 1987), 87.

17. U.S. Conference of Mayors, "A Status Report on Hunger and Homelessness in America's Cities: 1992" (Washington, DC: U.S. Conference of Mayors, December 1992), 49, 76, 96–99.

18. David C. Schwartz, Richard C. Ferlauto, and Daniel N. Hoffman, *A New Housing Policy: Recapturing the American Dream* (Philadelphia: Temple University Press, 1988), 204.

19. Ibid., 23.

2

Chronology

1976 **December.** The Community for Creative Non-Violence (CCNV) begins a local campaign to offer shelter to all who need it in Washington, D.C.

1978 **November.** CCNV starts two-week occupation of the National Visitors Center (Union Station) as a shelter for homeless people in Washington, D.C., to dramatize the number in need in the city.

1979 **October.** *Callahan v. Carey* lawsuit filed in New York City by volunteer Wall Street attorney Robert M. Hayes, to establish a right to shelter for homeless men.

1980 **April.** CCNV burns census forms to protest inadequate measures for counting homeless people in the 1980 national census.

May. *Williams v. Barry* lawsuit filed in Washington, D.C., to prevent closing of city-run men's shelters with only 48 hours' notice.

July. Coalition for the Homeless formed in New York City as a result of public activities in response to removal of homeless people from the area around Madison Square Garden, site of the Democratic National Convention.

September. "A Forced March to Nowhere," an initial CCNV survey of homelessness and services around the nation, presented to House District Committee hearing on urban problems.

1981   **February.** Demonstrators block Pennsylvania Avenue in response to the cuts in federal programs for poor people announced in the first Reagan Administration budget the previous evening.

March. *Private Lives/Public Spaces* released in New York City, after researchers Kim Hopper and Ellen Baxter complete a lengthy survey of homeless people in that city.

June. "Call to Prayer" begins at White House: six weeks of daily demonstrations against the impact of the Reagan budget on the poor.

August. Consent decree signed in *Callahan v. Carey* lawsuit, providing overnight shelter for single homeless men in New York City, as well as court-ordered standards for the operation and expansion of shelters for men.

September. *The Long Loneliness in Baltimore* released as a survey of homelessness in Baltimore.

October. Massachusetts Coalition for the Homeless formed.

November. Building commences on "Reaganville" demonstration tent encampment in Lafayette Park, across from the White House by members of CCNV, who serve a traditional Thanksgiving meal in the park; protest is to recall the "Hooverville" homeless settlements of the Depression. Demonstrators are arrested, but tents remain until spring.

December. Memorial service for the nation's homeless people is held in Lafayette Park, across from the White House in Washington, D.C.; service attended by hundreds of advocates from around the country, who plant over 400 crosses bearing names and dates of death for homeless people.

1982   **February.** *Eldredge v. Koch* filed in New York City to extend right to shelter to homeless women.

March. Crosses removed from Lafayette Park by homeless advocates, who carry them to Capitol Hill and present one to each member of Congress.

April. National Coalition for the Homeless formed.

1982   **May.** *Klosterman v. Carey* filed, seeking housing for former state
cont.   psychiatric patients who are homeless.

July. Luncheon for members of Congress to highlight use of
salvaged food and level of food waste in the nation; an entire
meal is prepared by CCNV from usable food salvaged from
dumpsters, including quiche, raspberry tarts, crab, and more.

September. Central City Shelter Network formed, San
Francisco.

September. *The Homeless of Phoenix: A Profile* released.

October. Consortium for the Homeless formed, Phoenix.

November. Homeless Caucus formed, San Francisco.

Koster v. Webb filed in Long Island's Nassau County, as a federal
challenge to shelter conditions for homeless families.

December. *Homelessness in America: A Forced March to Nowhere,* by
Mary Ellen Hombs and Mitch Snyder, released as national survey of homelessness and responses to it in cities around the
nation, as well as an examination of Reagan Administration
policies. The book is released in conjunction with congressional
hearings on the same day.

"Homelessness in America," which were the first congressional
hearings on homeless people since the Depression, are convened by the Housing Subcommittee led by Representative
Henry B. Gonzalez (D-TX). Homeless people, shelter providers,
and elected officials from around the nation testify on the growing problem of homelessness.

1983   **January.** People's State of the Union Address: 163 homeless
people, shelter providers, and civil rights and peace movement
leaders are arrested for occupying the Capitol rotunda, demanding food, shelter, and jobs for the poor.

"The Emergency Jobs Appropriations Act of 1983" is passed
in Congress, providing $100 million for emergency food and
shelter.

April. Soup line held in U.S. capitol building to protest the
shortage of resources for hungry and homeless people.

1988   **February.** Ten thousand homeless people, their supporters, and civil rights leaders march in Atlanta just prior to the "Super Tuesday" presidential primaries.

April. Grand opening of newly renovated Federal City Shelter, operated by CCNV in Washington, D.C., as comprehensive service model.

July. *Mixon v. Grinker* filed in New York City, to seek "medically appropriate" housing for homeless people infected with HIV.

September–November. Daily protests demanding congressional action to house homeless people occur at the U.S. capitol, while fasters hold vigil on the capitol steps, calling for more housing for the poor.

December. Ten thousand march in New York City for action to house homeless people.

1989   **January.** Two hundred homeless people and activists meet for two days in Atlanta to form a national agenda to end homelessness and provide affordable housing.

February. President Bush calls for full funding of the McKinney homeless assistance programs in his first budget message to Congress.

June. *Palmieri v. Cuomo* filed in New York, seeking residential drug treatment on demand for homeless addicted persons.

October. HOUSING NOW!, a historic and broad-based coalition to end homelessness and secure affordable housing, brings hundreds of thousands of marchers to Washington, D.C.

November. Eleven men and women arrested after taking over vacant government-owned housing in Tucson, Arizona, are acquitted by a city magistrate on the grounds that their trespassing constituted a lesser evil than the imminent harm posed by homelessness. This legal theory is known as a "defense of necessity." The group acted as part of nationwide demonstrations for housing in July, after the federal government failed to make surplus properties available as required by law.

1989 **December.** A federal district court judge in Washington, D.C.,
cont. rules that the federal government must make available thousands of vacant federal buildings for homeless people during
the coming winter. The judge found that the federal government had made "pitifully few" properties available as required
under the McKinney Act, and ordered a strict schedule for
compliance.

1990 **March.** The U.S. Census conducts "S Night," a count of
"selected components" of the homeless population. The count
and its procedures are controversial among advocates and service providers, because some agree to assist census officials and
others, most prominently Mitch Snyder, call for massive resistance to the effort.

July. Mitch Snyder, regarded as the most visible and controversial advocate for homeless people, commits suicide in the CCNV
shelter in Washington, D.C. Thousands of people from all walks
of life attend his funeral at the shelter and march down Pennsylvania Avenue to the city hall.

November. Voters in the District of Columbia narrowly defeat a
ballot measure that would have preserved the city's right to
overnight shelter for homeless people, six years after its initial
overwhelming passage on the ballot. Polls show that voters are
sympathetic to homeless people, but frustrated with the city
government's handling of services.

1991 **January.** Five coalitions for the homeless in the Midwest an-
nounce that they have jointly applied for foreign aid from 22
countries. The coalitions, representing Illinois, Ohio, Indiana,
Michigan, and Wisconsin, take the step to draw attention to the
lack of assistance from the federal and state governments for
meeting the needs of poor people.

HUD establishes formal eligibility criteria for McKinney programs by creating a definition of homelessness to be used in
determining who would be served. The definition causes several groups previously served—including institutionalized mentally ill persons, persons living doubled up in housing, and
homeless persons living in rural areas—to become ineligible.

February. The National Institute of Mental Health (NIMH)
releases a congressionally mandated study of deinstitutionalization, which finds that the problem has contributed to homelessness but is not a primary cause.

1991
cont.

April. The National Coalition for the Homeless issues a report sharply criticizing the census count of some homeless people conducted in 1990. According to the coalition, the count missed at least two-thirds of the limited number of people who were the object of the effort. Missing from any census plan for the "Street and Shelter Night" count were domestic-violence shelters, persons living doubled up, and homeless people living in boxes, railcars, or abandoned buildings. Two-thirds of the nation's local jurisdictions made no attempt at a count.

June. The new National Coalition To Eliminate Tuberculosis meets in Atlanta to discuss a strategic plan to halt the spread of the reemerging disease.

November. The National Coalition for the Homeless releases the report "Heroes Today, Homeless Tomorrow?" examining the growing problems faced by homeless veterans.

December. Over 25 communities participate in National Homeless Persons' Memorial Day on the first day of winter. Vigils, services, and marches commemorate those who have died because of a lack of shelter.

The U.S. Department of Health and Human Services withdraws the most recent of its regulatory attempts to crack down on the use of welfare hotels as shelters for homeless families. The agency had sought to limit the time period for which state government could be reimbursed for the cost of sheltering families in the often dirty and dangerous facilities.

1992

January. The federal government releases its implementation plan for ending homelessness. It calls for better coordination among programs, increased participation in mainstream programs, improved targeting to homeless people, more support services, enhanced access to permanent housing, new strategies for preventing homelessness, and increased knowledge on how to address homelessness. The plan is criticized by advocates for restating existing knowledge and for being vague.

March. The Federal Task Force on Homelessness and Severe Mental Illness releases its report "Outcasts on Main Street." The report calls for more appropriate and integrated services and housing for those in need, estimated at 200,000 persons.

July. The first national day of voter registration for homeless people is held, as part of the "You Don't Need a Home To Vote"

1992
cont.
campaign of the National Coalition for the Homeless and the Community for Creative Non-Violence.

September. Congress votes to fund 500 housing units for persons with HIV/AIDS. This is the first such spending for specifically AIDS-related housing.

October. President George Bush signs into law a new program aimed at homeless persons in rural areas, and a new demonstration program called "Safe Havens," intended to reach seriously mentally ill homeless people who are unwilling or unable to participate in other programs. New laws also require service-providing organizations to create employment opportunities for homeless people and to include homeless people on their boards.

The first nationwide mock-ballot election for homeless people is held. Over 1,500 homeless people in 16 states cast ballots. Preferences are: Bill Clinton: 61 percent; George Bush: 17 percent; Ross Perot: 11 percent.

November. On Veterans Day, President George Bush signs P.L. 102-590, the Comprehensive Services for Homeless Veterans Act. The new law makes grants and services available to programs serving homeless veterans.

December. President-elect Bill Clinton calls for a national summit on homelessness and housing. (Homelessness was not a topic in the election campaign.)

1993
January. New Department of Housing and Urban Development Secretary Henry Cisneros walks around downtown Washington, D.C., to talk with homeless people.

A new case definition for AIDS takes effect. Expansion of the definition, which now includes manifestations exclusive to women as well as pulmonary tuberculosis, is expected to double reported cases.

March. A New York City judge rules in the *Mixon* lawsuit (seeking adequate housing for homeless persons with HIV/AIDS) that the city must offer safer living conditions for such persons because their systems are weakened by the virus and they are susceptible to tuberculosis and other infections. As many as 15,000 homeless New Yorkers are estimated to have HIV infection.

1993
cont.

May. President Clinton signs an Executive Order calling for a Federal Plan To End Homelessness within nine months.

June. Advocates in Atlanta, Georgia, picket the ground breaking for the city's Olympic stadium for the 1996 games, citing the planned destruction of public housing units and the city's increasing use of criminal laws to control homeless people by making it illegal to beg, wash windshields for money, or sleep in parks.

HUD secretary Cisneros announces the D.C. Initiative, a $20 million federal plan to give additional aid to the nation's capital for ending homelessness.

September. San Francisco mayor Frank Jordan announces that the city will begin taking shopping carts away from homeless people, in yet another step to crack down on homeless people in public places. Local supermarkets claim losses of $1 million from carts being removed.

October. HUD secretary Cisneros announces that homelessness will be his agency's number one priority; he unveils a model program to help end homelessness and says that it will operate in several cities where homelessness has been a chronic problem.

The U.S. Senate prevails in its budget appropriations recommendation and the federal Interagency Council on the Homeless is defunded. The council, charged with developing a federal plan to end homelessness, is subsequently absorbed into the White House Domestic Policy Council, but remains staffed by HUD.

November. A new study of homeless people in New York City and Philadelphia finds that the size of their homeless populations has been vastly undercounted in the past, with much larger percentages having been homeless at some point during the previous several years than had been shown in other studies.

1994

January. In the wake of a devastating earthquake, HUD secretary Cisneros announces a $20 million award to Los Angeles to fight homelessness.

February. HUD secretary Cisneros announces a proposed doubling of federal spending on homelessness and says he hopes to reduce the number of homeless people on the streets by one-third over the next three years. A draft copy of the Interagency Council's federal plan to end homelessness is leaked to the press during February and it supports the finding of late 1993 reports that homelessness is much more widespread than previously thought and requires large increases in federal spending on housing, mental health, and income supports.

Also in February, Clinton administration officials, speaking at an unprecedented federal summit meeting on homeless veterans, say government must do more for an estimated 250,000 homeless veterans in the nation.

March. In one of a number of such opposition moves across the country, local opponents of a planned reuse of surplus military property react angrily to a proposal announced to shelter homeless people at Long Beach Naval Station when it closes in September 1994. Homeless persons have first priority for such property under the McKinney Act.

Also in March, New York City mayor Rudolph Giuliani's administration announces that it will release a new policy on homelessness within two months, and that the policy will probably include new limits on shelter use and changes in the unconditional right to shelter in effect under the *Callahan* court case since the early 1980s.

3

Biographical Sketches

Richard Appelbaum

Richard Appelbaum is currently an associate professor of sociology at the University of California at Santa Barbara. He holds a Ph.D. from the University of Chicago. Appelbaum has written numerous books and articles on housing and has been involved in a number of large-scale survey research projects. He was the chief witness to discredit the methodology of the 1984 Department of Housing and Urban Development (HUD) report before Congress. He is a member of the national task force on housing policy associated with the Institute for Policy Studies.

Ellen Bassuk

Ellen Bassuk, M.D., is president of The Better Homes Foundation, established in 1988 in Newton, Massachusetts. She is an associate professor of psychiatry at Harvard Medical School, and is an expert on psychiatric emergency care and related policy issues such as deinstitutionalization. Since 1982 she has conducted clinical research projects on the needs of the homeless mentally ill and mothers and children.

Ellen Baxter

Ellen Baxter is director of The Heights, a model SRO project for the homeless in the Washington Heights neighborhood of Manhattan. She holds a Master of Public Health degree from

Columbia University. With Kim Hopper, Baxter wrote the ground-breaking study *Private Lives/Public Spaces* about the homeless in New York City while she was a researcher at the Community Service Society.

Robert Callahan

Robert Callahan, a 53-year-old Irishman, was the named plaintiff in the landmark right-to-shelter suit *Callahan v. Carey* in New York City. Callahan was a former short-order cook who became homeless for the first time at age 49 and was scared away from the existing Men's Shelter when he went there for help. He met attorney Robert Hayes at the Holy Name Center for Homeless Men, a Catholic day center on the Bowery, and agreed to be part of the suit.

Henry G. Cisneros

Henry G. Cisneros is Secretary of Housing and Urban Development in the Clinton Administration and responsible for federal homeless housing programs. Cisneros was previously mayor of San Antonio, Texas, from 1981 to 1989; he was the first Hispanic mayor of a major U.S. city. As HUD secretary, Cisneros announced that homelessness would be his agency's top priority; he proposed doubling spending for homeless programs in 1994, as well as a major legislative realignment of McKinney programs.

Andrew M. Cuomo

Andrew M. Cuomo is HUD Assistant Secretary for Community Planning and Development in the Clinton administration and responsible for operation of the HUD homeless programs. Cuomo came to HUD from New York City, where he headed the New York City Commission on the Homeless under Mayor David Dinkins. The commission's report first defined the "continuum of care" concept that Cuomo applied to HUD programs as the model for relating emergency, transitional, and permanent housing resources and services for homeless people. Cuomo had previously founded and operated a large nonprofit housing organization for homeless families, Housing Enterprises for the Less Privileged (HELP) in New York.

Cushing Dolbeare

A consultant on housing and public policy, Cushing Dolbeare has been associated with several major housing and homeless organizations, including the National Low Income Housing Coalition, the Low Income Housing Information Service, the National Rural Housing Coalition, and the National Coalition for the Homeless. She has written extensively on national housing policy.

Henry B. Gonzalez

Representative Henry B. Gonzalez was first elected to the U.S. House of Representatives in 1961; he represents the 20th Congressional District in San Antonio, Texas. He is currently chairman of the House Banking, Finance, and Urban Affairs Committee, and has been chairman of its Housing and Community Development Subcommittee since 1981. In 1982, Gonzalez chaired the first congressional hearings on homelessness since the Great Depression, and has subsequently convened dozens of other hearings on related issues.

Chester Hartman

Chester Hartman has been active in community housing and neighborhood struggles and has taught planning at several universities. He is the executive director of the Poverty and Race Research Action Council (PRRAC) and chairs the Planners Network. He is a Fellow at the Institute for Policy Studies in Washington, D.C. Hartman is the author of numerous books on housing policy, and has been a consultant to many federal, state, and local government agencies. He was an expert witness at the congressional hearings on the May 1984 HUD report.

Robert M. Hayes

Robert M. Hayes filed the landmark New York City right-to-shelter case *Callahan v. Carey* in 1979, while he was an attorney at the Wall Street firm of Sullivan and Cromwell. He subsequently left the firm in 1982 and founded both the Coalition for the Homeless, oriented to New York City issues, and the National Coalition for the Homeless. Hayes also filed or assisted numerous other homelessness-related legal actions and remains associated with the organizations he started. He returned to private law practice in 1989.

Kim Hopper

Kim Hopper, an anthropologist, was previously a research associate at the Community Service Society, where he coauthored with Ellen Baxter the landmark study *Private Lives/Public Spaces*. He is a founder and member of the board of directors of the New York City Coalition for the Homeless and the National Coalition for the Homeless. Hopper is the author of numerous monographs and articles, and has been an expert witness in many civil suits concerning the rights and needs of the homeless.

S. Anna Kondratas

S. Anna Kondratas was assistant HUD secretary for community development and planning under the Bush Administration. She was previously administrator of the Food and Nutrition Service of the U.S. Department of Agriculture, responsible for the Food Stamp and Women, Infants, and Children (WIC) nutrition programs. Kondratas was formerly the Schultz senior policy analyst in health and urban affairs at the Heritage Foundation, from which position she was a public spokesperson on homelessness and government policy.

Stewart B. McKinney

Representative McKinney, for whom the McKinney Homeless Assistance Act was named, was a Republican member of the House of Representatives at the time of his death from AIDS in 1987. McKinney represented Connecticut's 4th Congressional District for over 16 years. From 1983 until his death, he was the ranking Republican member of the Banking Subcommittee on Housing and Community Development, where he fought to preserve domestic programs. It is believed that he contracted fatal AIDS-related pneumonia from being outdoors in the cold during the demonstrations for the homeless that occurred at the U.S. capitol during the winter of 1987.

Rebecca Smith

Rebecca Smith, a homeless woman, froze to death in a box on a New York City street corner in 1982. Her death received extensive press coverage after it was discovered that the 61-year-old woman, hospitalized repeatedly for schizophrenia, had been visited by at least 50 people who sought to give her food and shelter during the last weeks of her life. Smith, a mother and the valedictorian of her college class, was declared an "endangered adult" under the city's protective services law; she died before the order could take effect and remove her from the street.

Mitch Snyder

Mitch Snyder was a member of the Community for Creative Non-Violence (CCNV) in Washington, D.C., which he joined in 1973 to open a small shelter for homeless people who would otherwise be held in jail because they lacked a home address. Snyder had previously spent 27 months in federal prison, where he was influenced by many antiwar activists. Snyder committed numerous acts of nonviolent civil disobedience, fasted, and lived on the streets for extended periods of time. He coauthored *Homelessness in America: A Forced March to Nowhere*; he was well known as an activist and speaker on poverty and homelessness. Snyder committed suicide in 1990.

Chris Sprowal

Chris Sprowal is a founder and first president of the National Union of the Homeless. He is a cofounder of the Committee for Dignity and Fairness for the Homeless in Philadelphia, a self-help advocacy and service organization managed and operated by homeless and previously homeless people, formed in October 1983. He is a graduate of New York University in engineering. Sprowal was an organizer of the 1984 convention of the homeless, whose motto was "Homeless but not helpless."

Louisa Stark

Louisa Stark is a founder and former president of the National Coalition for the Homeless, serving from 1984 to 1989. She chaired the Consortium for the Homeless in Phoenix. Stark has been an adjunct professor in the department of anthropology at Arizona State University in Phoenix. She served on the Committee on Health Care for Homeless People of the Institute of Medicine, National Academy of Sciences.

John Talbot

John Talbot, M.D., is a professor of psychiatry at Cornell University Medical College and associate medical director of the Payne Whitney Psychiatric Clinic at the New York Hospital in New York City. He has written widely on the problems of the mentally ill homeless.

E. Fuller Torrey

E. Fuller Torrey is an author as well as a clinical and research psychiatrist in Washington, D.C., specializing in schizophrenia. For five years in the early 1970s, Torrey was special assistant to the director of the National Institute of Mental Health; subsequently he spent eight years as a staff psychiatrist at St. Elizabeths Hospital in Washington. He has extensive professional experience with homeless women.

4

Facts and Statistics

SEVERAL AREAS OF INFORMATION are useful in trying to understand contemporary American homelessness, and this chapter looks at a few of the most critical topics. The material in this chapter provides a context for understanding the relationship of homelessness to several important program and policy areas. Some facts about homelessness are presented; also discussed are poverty, cash assistance programs, and housing problems.

Facts about Homelessness

Who Is Homeless?

The U.S. Conference of Mayors Task Force on Hunger and Homelessness 1992 survey of 29 cities found that most of the cities estimated that about 55 percent of the homeless people in their area were single adult men, 11 percent were single adult women, and 2 percent were youths. Families with children accounted for 32 percent of homeless people.

Officials in these cities estimate that the racial makeup of the homeless population is: 52 percent African-American, 33 percent white, 11 percent Hispanic, 3 percent Native American, and 1 percent Asian.

How Long Are People Homeless?

In 58 percent of the survey cities, the length of time people were homeless increased in 1992. The estimated duration of homelessness was two months to one year.

The Causes of Homelessness

The cities surveyed by the Conference of Mayors identified the following causes of homelessness in their area, in order of declining frequency:

- lack of affordable housing
- unemployment and employment-related problems
- poverty
- substance abuse and lack of needed services
- mental illness and lack of available services
- inadequate public assistance benefits
- domestic violence
- the economy
- health care costs

The Demand for Emergency Shelter

The Conference of Mayors found that the demand for shelter increased by about 14 percent in almost all the cities in 1992.

The demand for shelter by homeless families increased by about 11 percent, and 75 percent of the cities turn away both families and individuals for lack of shelter. Over 20 percent of the shelter need is unmet.

Shelter space increased about 7 percent in 1992, and transitional housing increased by about 20 percent.

Some 70 percent of the cities' officials believed that state budget cuts were responsible for increased homelessness.

In 55 percent of the cities surveyed, a single agency is responsible for addressing the problem of homelessness; 79 percent of the cities have either a plan or a policy for addressing homelessness.

What Kind of Shelter Is Available?

Family shelter is not always available where people need it. In 62 percent of the cities surveyed, family members may have to separate in order to receive emergency shelter because married couples may not stay together or older male children may not stay with their mothers.

What Kind of Shelter Is Unavailable?

The Conference of Mayors found that 76 percent of the cities surveyed believed families with children needed more shelter. Other groups in particular need were: substance abusers (72 percent of the cities), mentally ill people (62 percent), persons with HIV/AIDS (38 percent), unaccompanied youth (21 percent), and single men and single women (14 percent).

The services most needed by these groups were found to be:

families with children: affordable permanent housing, emergency shelter, transitional housing, child care, jobs and job training, supportive services and case management, educational assistance.

substance abusers: treatment options, detoxification facilities, supportive housing, shelter, counseling or case management, job training.

mentally ill persons: supportive housing, emergency shelter, case management and counseling, treatment.

persons with HIV/AIDS: emergency shelter, services.

unaccompanied youth: emergency shelter, counseling, education and training.

single adults: housing options, emergency shelter, jobs and job training.

How Is Emergency Shelter Funded?

The Conference of Mayors survey asked cities how they funded their emergency shelter programs. Several sources of federal funds are used:

- 83 percent use funds from the Stewart B. McKinney Homeless Assistance Act

- 62 percent use Community Development Block Grant funds

- 24 percent use Community Services Block funds

- 45 percent use state grants

- 72 percent use local revenue

How Do Shelters Operate?

In 48 percent of the cities surveyed by the Conference of Mayors, homeless people may have to leave their shelters during the day. They may be required or simply encouraged to take part in job searches, employment and training programs, counseling programs, etc., in other locations. In some shelters, such as those operated in church basements or meeting halls, the space may be used for another purpose during the day. If a homeless individual or family member is ill or unusually tired, that person may not be able to stay in the shelter all day and rest, because there is no staff available.

In some places, day shelters provide meals or programs during daytime hours so that homeless people have somewhere to go inside, where they can have coffee, or remain without being asked to leave; they may be able to receive mail, read a newspaper, or store belongings.

Homelessness and Health

While common stereotypes of homeless people would lead one to believe that their health problems consist of mental illness and drug and/or alcohol use, the reality is that health problems are much more complicated. The lack of adequate nutrition, rest, and shelter all contribute to ill health, injury, and death, as does prolonged residence in congregate or other inadequate shelter, which can expose one to infectious disease, including tuberculosis. Life on the street is physically dangerous, too; violence is common, and life and property are under assault from the weather as well as from other people and vehicles. The following section gives a picture of some of the critical health issues facing homeless people.

Little research has been done to examine the health problems of homeless people in nonservice situations; mostly, people are interviewed when they come to service settings such as clinics or soup kitchens. Therefore, the results reflect the health of people who may be sleeping indoors rather than outdoors, or getting a soup-kitchen meal rather than scavenging in garbage cans. Nevertheless, one study that attempted to link location of homeless people to their problems found the following from self-reports of the homeless individuals questioned.[1]

Of those staying in a shelter:

- 20 percent spent at least one day in the past month lying down because of a health problem
- 12 percent had "stomach flu"
- 9 percent had foot sores or ulcers
- 56 percent had been victimized in the past year
- 24 percent had an accident or injury in the past year
- 68 percent smoked cigarettes
- 24 percent used illegal drugs
- 6 percent used alcohol daily
- 50 percent had washed up within the last day

Of those staying outdoors:

- 37 percent spent at least one day in the past month lying down because of a health problem
- 26 percent had "stomach flu"
- 21 percent had foot sores or ulcers
- 75 percent had been victimized in the past year
- 43 percent had an accident or injury in the past year
- 84 percent smoked cigarettes
- 60 percent used illegal drugs
- 34 percent used alcohol daily
- 18 percent had washed up within the last day

The Demand for Emergency Food Assistance

According to the 1992 U.S. Conference of Mayors Task Force on Hunger and Homelessness survey of 29 large and small cities, the demand for emergency food assistance increased by about 18 percent in all but two of the cities surveyed.

The demand for food aid by families increased by about 13 percent.

Seventeen percent of the need for emergency food is unmet.

More than half of the cities use local revenues to help fund emergency food efforts, and 31 percent use Stewart B. McKinney Homeless Assistance Act funds to support this aid.

Facts about Poverty

The Poverty Line

The poverty line is the federal government's official measure of what it takes to support a household. A new set of income standards is released each year by the U.S. Department of Health and Human Services, and the figures for different size households determine eligibility for many assistance programs. The standards set by the poverty line also determine the federal government's official estimates of how many people are living in poverty. Table 4-1 shows the poverty line figures for 1994.

The Poverty Rate

The poverty rate rose to 12.8 percent in 1989. This was higher than at any time during the 1970s, despite the recession of the

Table 4-1
Poverty Line Figures for 1994*

Size of Family Unit	Poverty Guidelines
1	$7,360
2	$9,840
3	$12,320
4	$14,800
5	$17,280
6	$19,760
7	$22,240
8	$24,720
each additional member	$2,480

*(for all states except Alaska, Hawaii, and the District of Columbia)

1980s and subsequent economic recovery. Over 31 million people were living below the poverty line in 1989, and this figure represented an increase of over 5 million people from any year in the 1970s.

Facts about Cash Assistance Programs

Why should the government's cash assistance programs be analyzed when trying to understand homelessness? In virtually all cases, such programs do not bring a person or household up to the poverty line; a crisis requiring funds—a health crisis, the need for transportation, food, or heat—will eat away at funds otherwise available for housing. If the person or family lives in an area of high housing costs, it is even more likely that there will be a continuing risk of homelessness. There is simply not enough income.

Eligibility for Aid Programs

Many states consider a family to be ineligible for assistance if its income is higher than the state's maximum Aid to Families with Dependent Children (AFDC) benefit for a family with no other source of income. Thus, when a state reduces AFDC benefits, it also reduces the number of families who are eligible for the program. States can also use a system in which the family will still be eligible for AFDC if its income remains below the "standard of need," which is the income that the states decide is essential for basic consumption items.

Cash Assistance Programs

Several cash assistance programs at the state and federal level provide funds for different groups of eligible persons or families.

AFDC is the primary cash aid program that serves low-income families with children. It is operated and funded jointly by the federal and state governments. Each state submits a state plan to the U.S. Department of Health and Human Services (HHS), which administers AFDC. The state plans spell out the way in which the program will be operated, payment levels, and other regulations.

At the end of 1991, AFDC caseloads reached record levels, with 4.6 million families receiving benefits; of these, 900,000 families had received benefits since 1989. This represented an average increase of 2,000 children every day during that time period, according to a federal government report.

States pay 46 percent of program costs.

Purchasing power of benefits in the program dropped by 43 percent between 1970 and 1992.

Table 4-2 shows the maximum benefit levels under the AFDC program.

Table 4-2
AFDC Maximum Benefit Levels for a Family of Three as of January 1993

State	Maximum Benefit
Alabama	$164
Alaska	$950
Arizona	$347
Arkansas	$204
California	$624
Colorado	$356
Connecticut	$680
Delaware	$338
District of Columbia	$409
Florida	$303
Georgia	$280
Hawaii	$693
Idaho	$315
Illinois	$367
Indiana	$288
Iowa	$426
Kansas	$429
Kentucky	$228
Louisiana	$190
Maine	$453
Maryland	$359
Massachusetts	$579
Michigan	$489
Minnesota	$532
Mississippi	$120
Missouri	$292
Montana	$390
Nebraska	$364
Nevada	$348
New Hampshire	$516

State	Maximum Benefit
New Jersey	$424
New Mexico	$324
New York	$577
North Carolina	$272
North Dakota	$401
Ohio	$341
Oklahoma	$343
Oregon	$460
Pennsylvania	$421
Rhode Island	$554
South Carolina	$200
South Dakota	$404
Tennessee	$185
Texas	$184
Utah	$402
Vermont	$659
Virginia	$354
Washington	$546
West Virginia	$249
Wisconsin	$517
Wyoming	$360

Notes: Grant levels shown are maximums where the state provides one payment for those in private housing and another level for those in public housing. Some states have different payment levels for different geographic areas, and the payments shown are for the highest payment-level area. The New York State payment shown is the grant level for New York City.

Source: Iris Lav, Edward Lazere, and Robert Greenstein (Center on Budget and Policy Priorities), and Steven D. Gold (Center for the Study of the States). *The States and the Poor: Budget Decisions Hurt Low Income People in 1992*. Washington, DC, and Albany, NY: Center on Budget and Policy Priorities and Center for the Study of the States, 1993, 13–14. (Hereinafter CBPP *The States* report.)

States set benefit levels for their AFDC programs, but the federal government has no minimum benefit.

According to the House Committee on Ways and Means, which analyzes assistance programs, the median benefit in 1992 for a family of three with no other income was $372 monthly, or 41 percent of the poverty line.

In fiscal year 1993, 44 states froze or reduced their AFDC benefit levels. Forty states had taken the same action in fiscal year 1992.

Only five states raised benefits in keeping with the rate of inflation.

Benefit Changes Related to Recipients' Behavior

Several states have changed their AFDC programs to increase or decrease payments to families when certain behavior occurs. For instance, some states will not increase benefits when an additional child is born to a family already in the program. Some states penalize a family when children do not attend school or do not have immunizations.

Some states add penalties for persons who move to the state and apply for AFDC. These are called durational residency requirements; payments are restricted to the level of the state the recipient left. Intended to discourage people from relocating to areas with higher payment levels, the penalties are being challenged in several states as a violation of the individual's right to travel.

Several states provide bonus payments when recipients take part in self-sufficiency improvement such as employment and training programs. Some allow recipients who marry to keep a larger portion of the AFDC grant if they marry a person who is not the natural parent of their children.

Numerous legislative proposals for "welfare reform" were introduced in Congress in 1994; all would closely link benefits and behavior.

Increases in Caseloads

Rising unemployment and other economic troubles generally mean that applications for cash assistance programs will increase, and this has been true over the last several years. AFDC caseloads increased in 44 states in fiscal year 1992.

However, due to the same economic difficulties and resulting drops in state revenues, states were unable to hire the additional needed workers to process increasing numbers of applications; in fact, 22 states decreased their staff. Sixteen states face litigation because of delays in processing applications. Federal regulations require that states take no more than 45 days to process applications, and 17 states allow no more than 30 days for processing.

Every state showed an increased caseload from July 1989 to November 1991. Forty-five states had increases of 10 percent or more, 20 states had 20 percent or more cases, 20 states had 30 percent or more growth, and 10 states had increases of 40 percent or more.

These figures reflect a national average increase of 24.1 percent.

Optional State Programs under AFDC

States may also elect to use either the Special Needs program or the Emergency Assistance to Families (EAF) program under AFDC. A state elects to use one or both of these programs and submits a state plan to the U.S. Department of Health and Human Services (HHS), which administers AFDC. The state plan spells out the specific purposes for which these payments will be made. Table 4-3 shows which states participate in the optional AFDC programs.

Special Needs

The Special Needs program is used by 27 states, often to help prevent or end homelessness.

Some examples of Special Needs payments are: high shelter costs, utility payments, clothing costs, and burial costs.

A family may receive Special Needs payments over a period of time, but the state may also limit the duration of payments. Connecticut reduced the time for emergency housing payments from 80 days to 60 days.

Payments for specific purposes may be limited to specific dollar amounts. For example, Maine has a cap of $75 for a supplemental subsidy payment for high shelter costs.

Table 4-3 shows which states participate in the optional AFDC programs.

Emergency Assistance to Families (EAF)

States may operate an Emergency Assistance to Families (EAF) program, and 47 choose to do so. The Clinton administration's "welfare reform" proposal would cap EAF expenditures to pay for other AFDC changes over a 10-year period. The current program is intended to provide cash assistance to families in crisis situations; as a result, it helps many families who are facing or experiencing homelessness. A family must be AFDC-eligible to receive aid, but the family does not have to be receiving AFDC. The federal government matches state payments in the program.

Table 4-3

States Participating in AFDC Special Needs and Emergency Assistance to Families (EAF) Programs in 1992

State	Special Needs	Emergency Assistance
Alabama	No program	No program
Alaska	No program	No program
Arizona	No program	Increased program
Arkansas	No change	No program
California	No change	No program
Colorado	No program	No program
Connecticut	Reduced program	No program
Delaware	No program	No change
District of Columbia	No program	No change
Florida	No program	No change
Georgia	No change	No program
Hawaii	No change	Reduced program
Idaho	No change	No program
Illinois	Reduced program	No change
Indiana	No program	No program
Iowa	No change	No change
Kansas	No change	No change
Kentucky	No program	No program
Louisiana	No program	No program
Maine	Increased program	Reduced program
Maryland	Increased program	No change
Massachusetts	Increased program	Reduced program
Michigan	No program	No program
Minnesota	No change	No change
Mississippi	No program	No program
Missouri	No program	No program
Montana	No program	No change
Nebraska	No change	No change
Nevada	No program	No program
New Hampshire	No program	No change
New Jersey	No change	No change
New Mexico	No change	No program
New York	No change	No change
North Carolina	No change	No change
North Dakota	No change	No program
Ohio	No change	No change
Oklahoma	No change	Reduced program
Oregon	No change	No change
Pennsylvania	Reduced program	No change
Rhode Island	Increased program	Increased program

State	Special Needs	Emergency Assistance
South Carolina	No program	Increased program
South Dakota	No program	No program
Tennessee	No program	No program
Texas	No program	No program
Utah	No change	No change
Vermont	No program	No change
Virginia	No program	No change
Washington	No change	No change
West Virginia	No change	No change
Wisconsin	No program	No change
Wyoming	No program	Reduced program

Note: Program changes such as reductions or increases are noted for 1992.
Source: CBPP *The States* report, 23–24.

Payments may be made for rent arrears so that a family can stay in its housing, or for utility arrears so that heat or hot water is not shut off. States may pay for first month's rent and security deposit so that a homeless family can relocate to permanent housing.

Supplemental Security Income

Supplemental Security Income (SSI) is fully funded by the federal government for specific low-income individuals and couples with disabilities, as well as the elderly poor. Some 27 states add a further benefit to the program.

The grant level for SSI is set by the federal government and adjusted each year for inflation. The grant level is below the poverty line.

In 1993 a household with no other income could receive a grant of $434 (individual) or $652 (couple) from the federal government.

Some 26 states froze or reduced their state supplements in fiscal year 1993.

Table 4-4 shows the maximum payments made by the states in the SSI program.

General Assistance Programs

General Assistance (GA) programs are operated by some states and counties to provide aid to individuals who are not eligible for

Table 4-4
Maximum State SSI Supplements for Elderly Individuals
per Month in Fiscal Year 1993

State	Maximum
Alabama	none
Alaska	$374
Arizona	none
Arkansas	none
California	$186
Colorado	$56
Connecticut	$313
Delaware	none
District of Columbia	$15
Florida	none
Georgia	none
Hawaii	$5
Idaho	$65
Illinois	case-by-case
Indiana	none
Iowa	none
Kansas	none
Kentucky	none
Louisiana	none
Maine	$10
Maryland	none
Massachusetts	$129
Michigan	$14
Minnesota	$81
Mississippi	none
Missouri	none
Montana	none
Nebraska	$28
Nevada	$36
New Hampshire	$27
New Jersey	$31
New Mexico	none
New York	$86
North Carolina	none
North Dakota	none
Ohio	none
Oklahoma	$60
Oregon	$2
Pennsylvania	$32
Rhode Island	$64

State	Maximum
South Carolina	none
South Dakota	$15
Tennessee	none
Texas	none
Utah	$5
Vermont	$58
Virginia	none
Washington	$28
West Virginia	none
Wisconsin	$93
Wyoming	$10

Note: A household with no other income in 1993 received a grant of $434 per individual or $652 per couple under the SSI program. The amounts shown are for state supplements to this grant.

Source: CBPP *The States* report, 49.

federal income assistance programs. GA programs do not receive any federal funds and are not governed by any federal standards. The state or local government that operates the program determines benefit levels, eligibility criteria, duration of assistance, and other aspects of the program.

GA programs are funded solely by state and local government. These programs are not mandatory, and no federal standards or regulations apply, and they cover different groups of people in different states. Some states offer more coverage than others; for example, some cover all able-bodied adults without children, two-parent families with children, or people with disabilities not severe enough to qualify them for SSI. Other states provide benefits only to those awaiting an eligibility determination for the SSI program.

Because GA programs are often available to single persons, they are a source of income for homeless adults in many places. However, benefits are not adequate to secure housing and other necessities.

Benefit levels under General Assistance are very low.

Many programs have been cut recently, and a number of states have sought to restrict or cut benefits for persons considered "employable."

Some states require recipients to participate in public or private employment to earn the value of their assistance.

In 1991 and 1992, GA programs were reduced more than other low-income programs. Fourteen states cut their programs in 1991, and eight cut programs in 1992. About 450,000 people were affected by these cuts in 1991, and 120,000 more in 1992.

Table 4-5 shows which states operate a General Assistance program, as well as the states' payment levels.

Table 4-5
General Assistance Programs in the States in 1992

State	Program(s)	Benefit*
Alabama	No program	
Alaska	General Relief	$120
Arizona	General Assistance	$173
Arkansas	No program	
California	General Relief	
Colorado	Temporary General Assistance	
Connecticut	General Assistance	$356 (unemployables)
Delaware	General Assistance	$123
District of Columbia	General Public Assistance	$258
Florida	No state program	
Georgia	No state program	
Hawaii	General Assistance	$407
Idaho	General Assistance	
Illinois	Transitional Assistance; Interim Assistance; General Assistance Family and Children; Earnfare	$154
Indiana	Poor Relief	
Iowa	General Relief	
Kansas	General Assistance	$196
Kentucky	No state program	
Louisiana	No program	
Maine	General Assistance	$499
Maryland	Disabled Assistance Loan Program; General Assistance for Pregnant Women	$154
Massachusetts	Emergency Aid to the Elderly, Disabled, and Children	$384
Michigan	Disability Assistance; Family Assistance	$246
Minnesota	General Assistance; Work Readiness	$203
Mississippi	No program	

State	Program(s)	Benefit*
Missouri	General Relief	$80
Montana	General Relief	$229
Nebraska	General Assistance	$225
Nevada	Direct Assistance	
New Hampshire	General Assistance	
New Jersey	General Assistance	$210
New Mexico	General Assistance	$192
New York	Home Relief	$352
North Carolina	No program	
North Dakota	No program	
Ohio	General Assistance; Disability Assistance	$115
Oklahoma	No program	
Oregon	General Assistance	$268
Pennsylvania	General Assistance	$215
Rhode Island	General Public Assistance	$328
South Carolina	General Disability Assistance	
South Dakota	No program	
Tennessee	No program	
Texas	No program	
Utah	General Assistance Self- Sufficiency Program; Emergency Work Program	$233
Vermont	Emergency Assistance	
Virginia	General Relief	
Washington	GA-U for disabled people; GA-S for pregnant women	$339
West Virginia	No program	
Wisconsin	General Relief	$205
Wyoming	No program	

*Fiscal year 1993 maximum monthly benefit for one person

Sources: Marion Nichols, Jon Dunlap, and Scott Barkan (Center on Budget and Policy Priorities) and National Conference of State Legislatures. *National General Assistance Survey, 1992.* Washington, DC: Center on Budget and Policy Priorities and National Conference of State Legislatures, 1992, 9–13. CBPP *The States* report, 40–41.

Facts about Housing

Housing Affordability Problems

The high cost of housing in many areas contributes to homelessness. In the period 1970–1983, the shortage of affordable housing worsened for two reasons. There was a sharp decrease in the supply of low-rent housing and a simultaneous increase in the number of people in poverty due to continuing economic recession and high inflation. Throughout the rest of the 1980s the economy showed growth, but housing problems for poor people did not ease. According to the American Housing Survey for 1989, the number of affordable units in 1989 was the lowest in 20 years.

What does housing affordability have to do with homelessness? Persons on fixed incomes, including those on welfare benefits, may have a difficult time affording housing. Those receiving public assistance already live below the poverty line, and any unexpected expense can cause them to face homelessness again and again. Further, persons who are already homeless may have difficulty finding permanent housing they can afford, so they will be homeless longer.

Following are some facts from the Low Income Housing Information Service about housing affordability problems facing poor people.

Housing Cost Burdens

Federal law sets a standard of affordable housing costs as 30 percent of household income.

Poor Renters

About 39 percent of all renter households in 1990 had incomes less than 50 percent of median. Some 64 percent of poor renters nationwide spent at least half their income on housing costs in 1990.

Low-Cost Rental Housing

There were 6.8 million rental units renting for less than $250 per month (1989 dollars) in 1970. In 1983, there were only 5.9 million such units, and by 1989 this number had declined to 5.5 million.

Housing Costs

Median housing costs for poor renters were $266 per month in 1978. In 1989, this figure had risen to $313 per month.

Housing Assistance to Poor Renters

About 2.7 million, or only about one-third of the 7.5 million poor renters in 1989, received housing assistance from federal, state, or local government. The other 4.8 million poor renters mostly paid full housing costs in the private housing market. Because of the housing-cost burden faced by these renters, many were at risk of homelessness.

According to the U.S. Conference of Mayors Task Force on Hunger and Homelessness 1992 survey of 29 cities, requests for assisted housing increased in 88 percent of the cities.

"Worst Case" Housing Needs

The U.S. Department of Housing and Urban Development (HUD) defines "worst case" housing needs as very low income renters who spend more than 50 percent of their income on housing or live in severely substandard housing. These households receive a priority for federal housing assistance.

In 1989, HUD found that 5.1. million very-low-income renters fell into the category of "worst case" housing needs, and 4.2 million poor renter households had such needs. None received any housing assistance.

Waiting Lists for Housing Assistance

Because there are so few dollars for housing assistance and so many people in need, most local governments have waiting lists on which households can put their name, then wait for a unit or subsidy to become available. In many areas, these lists are very long—usually months or years long—and in some places the government has even stopped taking new names for the list.

The National Association of Housing and Redevelopment Officials found that more than 1 million households were on waiting lists for public housing in 1988. About 800,000 additional households were on waiting lists for subsidized housing.

Large public housing authorities are those that manage more than 2,500 units of housing. Some 16 percent of them have closed their waiting lists. This usually happens in areas where demand is very high and the need for subsidized housing is very great. Waiting times also depend on family size.

The Conference of Mayors survey found that 58 of the cities questioned had closed the waiting list for at least one program.

Large public housing authorities have waiting times of 18–24 months for a unit; small housing authorities have waits up to one year. The Conference of Mayors survey found that housing assistance applicants wait an average of 21 months for public housing, 35 months for Section 8, and 31 months for vouchers. The Section 8 and voucher programs are proposed for merger in 1994.

About 80,000 units of public housing are estimated to be vacant around the country either because they need rehabilitation or are currently being rehabilitated.

For a homeless family, this means that family members may wait in a shelter or transitional housing project—or live outside a shelter—until housing assistance is available. Without adequate housing, homeless families face separation so that adults can go to shelters or live outside, and children can go to foster homes or relatives' or friends' homes.

Poor Homeowners

Poor homeowners are a minority of poor households, but they also face housing cost burdens. In 1990, 53 percent of extremely poor homeowners spent more than 50 percent of their income on housing.

Notes

1. Dr. Lillian Gelberg and Dr. Lawrence S. Linn, "Assessing the Physical Health of Homeless Adults," *JAMA*, vol. 262, no. 14 (13 October 1989): 1976.

5

Documents and Reports

THE HOMELESSNESS THAT BEGAN to burst into the awareness of Americans in the early 1980s was of a kind not seen before; it was more complex, generated from more sources, and affected more people. The first general public and governmental acknowledgment of this new problem came as a result of a series of highly publicized congressional hearings, which also served as some of the first national gatherings of the few advocates, researchers, and service providers working with homeless people.

Homelessness is perhaps best understood in the words of those living closest to it: homeless people themselves. Thus, this chapter—whose goal is to provide a documentary portrait of some major facets of homelessness—draws initially on the first-hand words of some of those seeing and experiencing homelessness up close: in the speeches of advocates; in the testimony of a homeless and disabled chambermaid who was never offered housing assistance; in the impassioned plea of a researcher who frequented the alleys and subway tunnels of New York City to understand the problem; in the somber description of a homeless child forced to live in the violent, drug-infested world of a welfare hotel; in the words of a formerly homeless, now sober mother who is HIV-infected; in the words of perhaps the most stigmatized of homeless people, the minority male drug user.

In one sense, these firsthand offerings describe the "problem." But they are followed by some readings filled with information of a different kind—that generated by congressional committees, research organizations, and official commissions.

These excerpts focus on the realities and obstacles in meeting the basic human needs so eloquently described earlier.

Firsthand Perspectives on Homelessness

Testimony before the Housing Subcommittee

In December 1982, the U.S. Congress convened the first hearing on homelessness since the Great Depression. The first witnesses to testify before the Housing Subcommittee of Representative Henry B. Gonzalez were Mary Ellen Hombs and Mitch Snyder of the Washington, D.C.–based Community for Creative Non-Violence. With their testimony, they released *Homelessness in America: A Forced March to Nowhere,* a ground-breaking look at a new and growing problem. Hombs and Snyder brought with them to the witness table the cremated ashes of "John Doe," one of the many homeless people who had frozen to death in the city. This excerpt is from their testimony.

Americans, more than many people, are severely addicted to some very dangerous myths. Yet, we cannot address reality, or hope to change it, until we free ourselves from the fables that entrap us. Perhaps nowhere is this more true than in regard to homeless people. To see them clearly, to understand what their existence says about us personally and collectively, and to comprehend what their needs are requires this: we must face facts as they are, peel away stereotypical prejudices and delusions, boil off foggy thinking, and listen to the voices of those who have known and seen.

We must work from a single point: this is America, 1982. Homelessness is a national problem of massive and increasing proportions, affecting at least two million people.[1] As a fabric, it is made up of the consequences of a number of elements and conditions basic to the way our nation and our society function. We do not always choose to see these clearly, but we will examine them here in as current, authentic, and nonacademic a fashion as we can.

It is significant that only two years have elapsed since we prepared the report for Congress. In that time, homelessness has begun to smolder and then ignite as a national issue. The signs of our time can be read in a few events.

Big Red used to be a professional country and western guitarist. Now he is middle-aged and an alcoholic. After eight years of living on Washington's outdoor heat grates, Red's hands are so badly burned that his fingers make crackling sounds when he moves them. His usual place of residence is the grate at the Corcoran Art Gallery. Surrounded by billowing clouds of steam, in a scene reminiscent of Dante's *Inferno*, Red needs only to look up to see the home of his nearest neighbor: the President of the United States.

In March 1982, a photo of Red on his grate ran in a two-page story on homeless people in *U.S. News and World Report.* The story was one of several similarly timed accounts. Among others, "60 Minutes," *Newsweek*, "The McNeil-Lehrer Report," and *The Christian Science Monitor* have carried feature pieces. If the winter of 1981–1982 represented anything, it was an incalculable multiplication of media focus on the homeless. Most stories served the useful purpose of throwing a rope into the quicksand of our illusions, offering us a first step out of our ignorance. If we listened and read carefully, we could know that the traditional and persistent picture of street people as "dirty, lazy, drunken bums" bears scant resemblance to today's chronically homeless person. Wino, tramp, hobo: These are images from another era.

Homeless people are a complex group; their identities and the circumstances of their "previous" lives frequently do not match conventional stereotypes. Thus, shock meets the announcement of the opening of a free soupline for destitute children under age twelve in Washington, D.C. Among the first guests was a three-year-old boy accompanying a seventeen-month-old. Within three weeks, "Martha's Table" was serving thirty children a day in a neighborhood that, not surprisingly and not untypically, has seen little change since it hosted the 1968 riots.

If these events awaken us to reality and to action, we must remember that others have paid with their lives to make it so.

> There may be a message in the 34-year-old Chicago man who was killed recently when the out-of-order trash compactor in which he had been sleeping for weeks was mended without his knowing it and the man, having conceived of himself as an ally of refuse and having been for all practical purposes refuse, finally became refuse and was compacted. But if there is a message, I'm not sure that I want to know what it is.[2]

There is indeed a message contained in the life and death of the man from Chicago, just as there is in the story of Big Red and Martha's Table. And, as Ebenezer Hob confesses, most people are not quite certain that they want to know what it is. The discussion, documentation, and reflections on homelessness offered here are for those who realize that they must decipher that message, regardless of where it may lead.

Notes

1. No one can say with certainty how many people in this nation are homeless. Not until they come inside will we know for certain how many there are. However, in 1980, we prepared a report, for a Congressional committee, on the national dimensions of the problem. At that time, we concluded that approximately 1 percent of the population, or 2.2. million people, lacked shelter. We arrived at that conclusion on the basis of information received from more than 100 agencies and organizations in 25 cities and states. That figure has since been widely used by the media, politicos, and organizers. It is as accurate an estimate as anyone in the country could offer, yet it lacks absolute statistical certainty.

In gathering information for this book, we have learned nothing that would cause us to lower our original estimate. In fact, we would increase it, since we are convinced that the number of homeless people in the United States could reach 3 million or more during 1983.

2. From "Confessions," by Ebenezer Hob, printed in *Washingtonian*, July 1978.

Source: *Homelessness in America: A Forced March to Nowhere*, by Mary Ellen Hombs and Mitch Snyder. Washington, DC: Community for Creative Non-Violence, 1983, pp. xvi–xviii.

Testimony of May Ash

On 25 January 1984, members of the Subcommittee on Housing and Community Development of the Committee on Banking, Finance and Urban Affairs, U.S. House of Representatives, held a one-day hearing, "Homelessness in America—II" as a follow-up to the hearing of December 1982, which was the first on homelessness since the Great Depression. The follow-up hearing was held in the basement of the CCNV-operated shelter in Washington, D.C. This excerpt is from the transcript of the hearings, pp. 19–20.

Among those testifying was May Ash, a woman in her late fifties who had worked as a chambermaid at the Waldorf Astoria Hotel in New York City and as a maid for many years. She lost her job and spent six years living in Grand Central Station. At the time of the hearing, she was staying at a church shelter across the street from the Waldorf. May Ash's statement was interrupted several times by her tears. Crying, with a stocking hat pulled over her hair, she was the one whose face was captured by the press and flashed around the nation as the hearing was reported.

My name is May Elizabeth Ash, I am from New York City. I am fifty-six years old. I have been homeless for two years. And I have been living in shelters here and there. Most of my friends that is in the shelters have died and I have seen them come, and been sick at the hospital.

At the age that I am, and with one eye plus other ailments, I am a diabetic, they wouldn't have hired me for work. I wouldn't mind having a job if they would give it to me.

Being homeless is not a thing that I would like. I would rather be somewhere else than to be in a shelter for the rest of my life. . . .

I used to live in Philadelphia before I came to New York. And it was just as rough there as it is here in New York. . . .

In the street there, sleeping in bus stations, train stations, doorways, different places. I go to welfare and they wouldn't help me. They tell me I ain't old enough. . . .

I don't have enough money to pay for the places they would like for me to have. The rent is so high.

Mr. Schumer. The rent was too high for the amount of money that you had?

Ms. Ash. Yes, it was.

Mr. Schumer. Did anyone ever come to you and say you could get some kind of assistance, either public housing or section 8? No one has ever suggested to you or come to you and said they would help you fill out the forms and all of that?

Ms. Ash. Not ever.

Mr. Schumer. Do you receive public assistance? Do you receive welfare?

Ms. Ash. I don't receive welfare. I just started receiving social security disability.

Mr. Schumer. You just started getting that?

Ms. Ash. Yes.

Mr. Schumer. Was there a person that you had to see to fill out all the forms and get the check?

Ms. Ash. Yes.

Mr. Schumer. They never suggested to you, they never tried to give you any help in finding housing?

Ms. Ash. No.

Mr. Schumer. So you really are sort of bereft?

Ms. Ash. Yes, I am.

Testimony of Kim Hopper

Kim Hopper, one of the two New York City researchers who provided the first profiles of homeless people of the 1980s in that city, also testified at the 1984 hearings. With his research colleague, Ellen Baxter, and Robert Hayes, the counsel of the National Coalition for the Homeless, Hopper had testified at the first congressional hearings. This excerpt is from the transcript of the hearing, pp. 192–194.

. . . As you will hear repeatedly today, the plight of our homeless has gone from bad to worse since December 1982. Part of this Nation is now enjoying a modest economic recovery; at the same time legions of this country's men, women, and children suffer the misery of hunger, of homelessness, of acute want among plenty.

Are we helping? A little bit. There are, today, more soup kitchens and more emergency shelters from coast to coast, than at any time since the Great Depression. But even these valiant relief efforts—staffed in large part by volunteers—have not arrested the growth of the vast army of the very poor in America's streets. The mills of homelessness grind on, unabated by our puny efforts at makeshift remedies. Despite tentative signs of an economic upturn, . . . the plain fact is that there are many more Americans homeless today than there were a year ago.

Homelessness in America . . . is no longer a shameful secret. So why isn't something being done? No one doubts that we have the expertise to house the homeless. No one doubts that this Nation's wealth is sufficient to accord the poor, at the very least, the resources needed for survival. The clamor on the streets is a desperate plea for help. So why must the homeless poor continue to plead their case for elementary justice, for decency? Why have we refused to mobilize the minimal reserves needed to alleviate this crisis? . . . [I]n those questions lies an indictment of the state of the moral values of our Nation, of our government, of ourselves.

Last summer Tiffany's, the Fifth Avenue jeweler, put up a window display advertising a fifty thousand dollar necklace. The backdrop: Figurines depicting homeless people, surrounded by trash. Tiffany's management seemed to think trivializing human misery might amuse its clientele.

Last fall, the Holiday Inn threw a party for its executives in Chicago. The corporation hired an actress to ramble around the reception posed as a "bag lady." Amusing? I am sure most of you recall the Fort Lauderdale official who proposed spraying garbage with poison to prevent the poor from scrounging for scraps.

And, perhaps most disturbing of all, over the past year certain parties have come to argue that growing numbers of the homeless are not "truly homeless"; they suggest some homeless folks simply do not deserve assistance. Alarmingly, such a position cannot be dismissed as the ravings of a few cranks or eccentrics. Ideologically extreme they may be, but their arguments find an audience. New York City's mayor, for one, is a self-proclaimed disciple of this doctrine.

It is this brand of callousness, which has permitted our Government—the Congress, the President, States and cities, too— to preside over the spectacle of two million Americans homeless and to do next to nothing. What do we think, what do we hope our children and grandchildren will say of our complicity in watching the slow suffering—and, in due time, death—of the weakest and frailest of our fellow citizens.

What can we do? What must we do? To begin with, I continue to believe that the only way the homeless will find relief is through (1) their own actions, and (2) the good will and fundamental decency of the American people. I do not expect any longer to find that decency within the higher leadership of this Government. I do believe that once America looks at the face of the homeless, into the eyes of a homeless person, it will not turn away. Once educated as to the reality of homelessness, the vast majority of people of good will will recognize that homelessness is unacceptable, and will demand that it be ended. It will accept the homelessness for what it is and demand that it end. Then, and I fear only then, will Government act.

This committee, I submit, could help ignite this spirit of decency in America. A year ago we came to Capitol Hill to tell you of home- lessness. Homeless people, too, came to your Chambers to share with you their lives. You are to be commended for coming off the Hill and coming to an emergency shelter for today's hearing. You bring the Congress close to the problem. More of this needs to be done.

I conclude with a few modest proposals. . . . Isn't it about time for Congress to consider a national right to shelter? Let it be debated. Let the administration tell Congress how much it will cost. And then let us tell you how much homelessness costs, in dollars, in human lives and in a degraded sense of our own humanity. In 1977 Parliament enacted a Homeless Persons Act in the United Kingdom, guaranteeing a right to shelter for at least some of the British homeless. Seven years later can we not do as much?

I invite the committee to work with us to draft the legislation. I ask this committee . . . to introduce it. I would welcome the opportunity to press the opponents of the legislation on what they would offer the homeless instead.

I am sometimes shamed by how little we ask for: Is it too much to expect a right to shelter at least for homeless children, probably the fastest growing group among the homeless? Can we not, immediately, shelter them? It would not, I submit, be so difficult to amend the Social Security Act to make mandatory the provision of emergency shelter under the assistance to families with dependent children program.

Second, how long will the Congress ignore the plight of the homeless mentally ill? Again, the answer is not to reopen the asylum gates and force these frail people into lives of relentless incarceration. We know how to care for the mentally ill in the community. . . .

It is not so expensive, once a residence is established, for there are ongoing income support programs—such as, with all its current problems, the SSI program. Even if public housing is going the way of the dinosaur under this administration, can we not prevail upon the Government to support housing for the most helpless and neediest of the poor and homeless? I would urge the committee to push for a special capital program to create permanent supportive housing for the homeless mentally disabled.

Lastly, one cannot speak to this housing committee without reiterating the obvious. The root cause of homelessness absent which all the competing causes could be accommodated is the scarcity of low-income housing. Unless the Federal Government helps there, all our efforts to alleviate homelessness are bound to failure. This committee is to be commended for its efforts to salvage at least some housing programs from the wrecker's ball. But you know better than I how inadequate those efforts have been. You have heard something today about the effects of homelessness on those who endure it. What does it say about our moral integrity, about our values, about our priorities if we continue—as individuals and as a society—to walk past the old woman living on the corner, sleeping in a cardboard box?

There is a vicious Darwinian struggle going on in this country, a desperate competition for housing. As in any free market competition, it is the weak who are losing—the infirm, the elderly, the ill educated, the unemployed, the single parent families.

Each day we permit the weak to lose their struggle for survival resources, we are cheapened. Each day we permit homelessness to continue, we display our own moral shabbiness. Each day a fellow American succumbs to the cold on a city street, our national legitimacy as a civilized society is thrown into question.

Testimony of Yvette Diaz

Women and children represent one of the fastest growing segments of the homeless population. Inadequate housing resources and governmental funding requirements have often resulted in these families being sheltered in "welfare hotels," rented spaces in run-down buildings in dangerous areas. A special congressional hearing on the plight of homeless children heard this testimony from a child living in the notorious Hotel Martinique in New York City.

My name is Yvette Diaz. I am twelve years old. I live in the Martinique Hotel, Forty-nine West Thirty-second Street, New York City. I live in rooms 1107 to 1108. There are two rooms. I live here with my mother, two sisters, nine and seven, and my three year old brother. We have lived in the Martinique Hotel for almost two years now. I am living at the Martinique Hotel because my aunt's house burned down, and we didn't have any place to live.

We were living in my aunt's house in Brooklyn because my father was discharged from the United States Air Force in the State of Washington, and the family came back to New York where we originally came from. We couldn't find an apartment right away, so we stayed with my aunt. Then, the house burned down, and we went to the Martinique Hotel.

Since we are living in New York at the Martinique, I have been going to P.S. 64, which is on East Sixth Street in Manhattan. When I first started school here, I was absent a lot, because the bus that took us to school in the mornings was late a lot of times, and other times I didn't get up on time. We didn't have an alarm clock. Finally, my mother saved up enough to buy one. This year I have not been absent many times because the bus is on time, and we have an alarm clock.

I don't like the hotel, because there is always a lot of trouble there. Many things happen that make me afraid. I don't go down into the street to play, because there is no place to play on the streets. The streets are dangerous, with all kinds of sick people who are on drugs or crazy. My mother is afraid to let me go downstairs. Only this Saturday, my friend, the security guard at the hotel, Mr. Santiago, was killed on my floor. He was shot by another man and killed. The blood is still on the walls and on the floor. Anyway, people are afraid to open the door to even look out. There are a lot of people on drugs in the hotel. Sometimes you can find needles and other things that drugs come in, all over the hallways.

Our apartment was broken into when we were out. They stole the radio and our telephone alarm clock [sic]. We have a TV but they didn't get that, because we hide it in the closet under other things every time we leave the room.

We can't cook in the apartment. My mother sneaked a hot plate in, because we don't have enough money to eat out every night. They, the hotel, warned us that if we are caught cooking in the rooms, we could be sent to a shelter.

I play in the hallways with my friends from other rooms on my floor. Sometimes, even that isn't safe. A boy, about fifteen or sixteen, came over to me and wanted to take me up to the sixteenth floor. I got frightened and ran into my room and told my mother. She went to the police and she was told this same boy was showing his private parts to girls before, and that it was reported to them. If he bothered me again, I was to tell the police.

The five of us live in two rooms at this hotel. There is only one bathroom. We don't have mice or rats like some of the other people who live in the hotel, because we have a cat.

I go to the extended day program at my school, P.S. 64. We go from 3:00 to 6:00 every weekday except Friday. I get help with my homework for 45 minutes every day and then we have computer, arts and crafts, dancing, gym, and game room. I like it and we also get a hot dinner every night before we go home on the bus. I finish all my homework here as the teacher helps me and it is quiet so I can really understand what I am doing.

If I could have anything that I want, I wish that we had our own apartment in a nice, clean building and a place that I could go outside to play in that is safe. I want that most of all for me and my family.

Thank you.

Source: *The Crisis in Homelessness: Effects on Children and Families.* Select Committee on Children, Youth, and Families, U.S. House of Representatives, 100th Cong., 1st sess., 1987, pp. 9–10.

Sources of Food for Homeless People

The Select Committee on Hunger of the U.S. Congress conducted a research survey of shelter providers to discover what they knew about how homeless people were being fed. Following is a summary of findings from the survey.

I. Major Findings from a Shelter Provider Survey

Eighty-one percent of shelter providers state that the private-sector meals at shelters are a primary source of food for homeless persons; yet 52 percent of shelters do not provide two main meals daily. . . . For the purpose of this report "two main meals" are defined as lunch and dinner, which generally provide at least one-half an individual's daily nutrient requirements. Typically, homeless people must seek out food in soup kitchens when they are accessible, from dumpsters, and other free food sites.

Dumpsters are cited as a primary source of food by 9 percent of shelter providers.

II. Large Percentage of Homeless Not Receiving Food Stamps

Forty-five percent of the total number of homeless persons identified as eligible for food stamps (1,678 out of 3,751) were reported not to be receiving benefits.

Among those in family shelters, 49 percent of those identified as eligible (1,028 out of 2,112) were reported not to be receiving food stamps.

In shelters with no one available to assist in the food stamp application process, 58 percent of homeless people identified as eligible were reported not to be receiving food stamps (225 out of 440).

III. Administrative Barriers to Food Stamp Participation

Twenty-one percent of shelter providers reported their homeless residents are denied eligibility for food stamps because they do not have a permanent address or are sleeping outside.

Sixty-seven percent of responding shelter providers (60 out of 90) reported their homeless residents experience lengthy delays between applying for food stamps and receipt of benefits.

Documentation problems were the greatest single reported barrier to participation in the Food Stamp Program for eligible homeless people. Twenty-five percent of shelters reporting lengthy delays (13 out of 53) cited inadequate documentation as the cause. For 14 percent of all shelters, inadequate documentation was not only a barrier or a cause of lengthy delay, but was reported to result in denial of food stamps for eligible homeless persons.

The need for increased assistance in applying for food stamps and the use of more shelter providers as collateral contacts in the application process are supported by the survey findings of administrative barriers to food stamp participation.

IV. Shelter Providers Approve Use of Food Stamps for Prepared Meals at Soup Kitchens and/or Shelters

Sixty-five percent of all responding shelter providers would like to see the utility of food stamps improved by allowing homeless people to purchase or contribute to the cost of prepared meals at shelters and/or soup kitchens with food stamps—as authorized in Public Law 99-570, the Omnibus Drug Enforcement, Education and Control Act (enacted October 27, 1986). The providers support this change in law primarily because they believe it would greatly improve the quality and quantity of food assistance available to homeless people.

Moreover, many providers state that this change in statute can remove another barrier to food stamp participation in some areas. By allowing shelters to be certified as institutions eligible to accept food stamps, the food stamp rule denying eligibility to institutional residents will be lifted for homeless persons in certified shelters.

V. Hunger-Related Health Problems Reported among Shelter Residents

Hunger-related health problems reported include anemia, infectious diseases, low birth weight, chronic diseases requiring special diets (hypertension and diabetes), lack of infant formula, and children appearing physically underdeveloped for their age. (These reports of health problems by nonmedical shelter providers parallel the findings of many published medical reports on the health problems of homeless people.)

Source: *Hunger among the Homeless: A Survey of 140 Shelters, Food Stamp Participation and Recommendations.* Select Committee on Hunger, U.S. House of Representatives, 100th Cong., 1st sess., 1987, pp. 4–5.

Services in Alcohol Recovery Programs

Alcohol and drug problems are frequently cited as a source of difficulty in ending an individual's homelessness. The following excerpts from a report on recovery programs specifically for homeless people describe some of the services and issues as viewed by program providers.

Common Themes and Issues among Service Programs

Generally speaking, providers of comprehensive programs consider their services to consist of three major components. These components cover the intake, primary recovery, and sustained recovery aspects of the process of recovering from alcohol problems mainly through achieving and maintaining sobriety. Recovery program operators are the first to admit that theirs is an imperfect system that too often fails to attract or hold clients to the point that the individual is able to establish long-term sobriety and continuing recovery. Hope, continued effort to make services available, and encouragement of the client's motivation and desire to help one's self, are mainstays of the programs' operations.

1. *Intake services.* Special efforts are taken to make services available to homeless people with alcohol problems who are seen to need them, but resist accepting them. Special emphasis is placed on outreach and intake services. Three types of outreach were observed—active outreach (e.g., seeking out clients by positioning staff in shelters, or through mobile patrols), passive outreach (e.g., day-time drop-in centers located in skid row), and protective custody (e.g., transport (possibly involuntary) of public inebriates to sobering stations or detoxification centers.

Intake services occur through shelters, sobering stations, detoxification facilities, hospitals, jails, and residential recovery settings. Traditional "revolving door" problems of public inebriates who repeatedly utilize police, hospital, missions, emergency rooms, and alcohol recovery programs are still present, although markedly reduced from past levels by the funneling of such utilization through sobering stations and detoxification facilities.

2. *Primary recovery programs.* Recovery programs' emphasis is chiefly upon establishing sobriety and working for the individual's personal recovery from alcohol problems. Following intake/detoxification, primary recovery occurs through didactic, social, and spiritual approaches carried out in a residential setting where the client is encouraged to make a personal commitment to sobriety and to a lifetime of recovery through an alcohol-free lifestyle. Alcoholics Anonymous is almost always a critical element in these programs.

Programs for chronic public inebriates tend to be longer in duration (three to six months or longer), to put more emphasis upon restoration of physical and mental functioning, and to provide more vocational and domestic supports, than is customary for residential recovery programs serving the general population of people with alcohol problems. The goals for the individual remain fixed on achieving sobriety and self-sufficiency to the fullest extent possible. Relapses almost always require re-entry into the program from the beginning.

The basic recovery process is generally considered the same for homeless people with drinking problems as for all other problem drinkers. Although some programs put more emphasis on home-lessness than others (and these were the ones sought out for this study), nearly all publicly-funded alcohol programs serve clients who experience homelessness, or incipient homelessness. Homelessness comes in all shades and varieties in association with alcohol problems, from the person habituated to living on the streets to the recently-fired executive just evicted by a spouse. Accordingly, and wisely, alcohol service program providers are generally less concerned with the type or degree of homelessness than they are with the client's willingness to enter the recovery process.

3. *Sustained recovery.* Support and follow-up services are necessary to assure that the individual's full range of needs is met, and that all is done that can be to help the individual maintain sobriety. Support services include health, mental health, vocational, educational, legal, veterans', and housing and welfare services.

Programs vary in degree of emphasis on this, but all expect the client to be active in seeking out these services for him or herself. If the client is too debilitated to do so, efforts will probably be made to transfer the client to that service (e.g., to transfer a psychotic client to a mental health program). Unfortunately, if the transfer cannot be made, the client may be discharged in any case to "independent living." Achieving such transfers for a homeless person without insurance, especially for someone who's [*sic*] drinking has not been stopped or stabilized, is often extremely difficult.

Within this general progression of care, several themes and issues emerged from the study:

1. Public policy is lacking for service to homeless people with alcohol problems. Coherent local policies are usually lacking, and national policies have not been formally articulated by any national-level organizations, for prevention and treatment of alcohol problems among the homeless. With the exception of recommendations from two NIAAA-sponsored conferences in 1985 and 1987, formal statements on the subject have not been issued. People with alcohol problems are often subsumed in general statements of concern about the homeless, but are not thereby assured of alcohol-problem recovery services. The absence of national leadership on alcohol and homelessness requires entrepreneurship and initiative by local alcohol programs to establish their own visibility and entree into local planning activity for the homeless (see Point 8 below).

2. Homeless people with alcohol problems in the 1980s are a far more diverse group than the traditional "older white male skid row alcoholic." More younger people, more minorities, and more women, more poly-drug use, and more mental illness, and people with less education and fewer vocational skills, now comprise the population of homeless people with alcohol problems. Alcohol service programs report increasing contacts with these new groups. Some programs are feeling their way on their own initiatives to establish new programs for them (e.g., special programs for homeless women). Developing new services for the homeless has been slow in the absence of service utilization studies, lack of epidemiological and demographic data, and without any special mandates or funding from public or private sources of support.

3. Formal, critical evaluation of program activities is rarely done, and is not generally required by funding agencies. Most alcohol service

programs keep records on service utilization by clients. However, the records seem to be used more for certifying contract performance to funding sources than for critical study to further development of services. No formal mechanisms exist to encourage service providers to trade notes and learn from one another's experiences, although programs do know about each other. How much contact they have and how much they learn from each other is difficult to determine.

4. Programs generally develop on their own initiative based on local conditions and upon the orientations and backgrounds of the program's leadership. Program directors often have been associated with their program for ten years or more. Several directors were also founders of the program, or have been with the program from the beginning. Individuals' strengths and abilities are major sources for program innovations and competence. This leadership can lead to new programs which often spin off from older, well-established programs. . . .

5. Controversy exists over the proper use of protective services for public drinkers who might be a danger to self or others. Decriminalization of public drunkenness and the advent of "non-medical" or "social-model" detoxification services have raised questions about when the police and health authorities may intervene to remove a person involuntary [sic] in episodes of public drinking and public drunkenness. Police are generally cordial to relaxed handling of public inebriates, working under arrangements in which police are far more likely to transport inebriates to the alcohol program (notably the sobering station/detoxification center) than to jail. The cordiality can mask civil liberties issues that flare up when an inebriate does not want to be moved. The issues may come more to the fore if more local jurisdictions deputize alcohol-program workers . . . to take public inebriates into custody for transportation to an alcohol program.

6. Coordination of mental health and alcohol services for homeless people is often lacking. People with alcohol problems who also have mental health problems are not likely to be served, even though the psychiatric problems may be readily treatable, if trained mental health staff are not available. The recent advent of specialized "dual diagnosis" programs is a response to gaps in care between mental health and alcohol recovery programs. The problems are philosophical as well as technical. Some deep differences exist between the two fields regarding use of drugs during treatment and regarding staff training and qualifications. Some alcohol programs emphasize completely drug-free environments in contrast to mental health programs that rely on medication to stabilize their clients. Some alcohol programs with a strong self-help orientation are reluctant to accept mental health services with strong clinical and professional orientations, and vice versa.

7. Integrated city-wide planning and delivery of alcohol recovery services in conjunction with shelters and other public programs is rare. . . . More often, it appears that individual alcohol programs develop a network of ad-hoc referral relationships with other helping agencies on an as-needed basis. This informal approach may achieve many of the benefits of integrated planning without some of the costs involved in large-scale coordination. But the informal approach also may be wasteful and may fail to make important connections between services. To our knowledge, little study has been devoted to the development of linkages between alcohol programs to coordinate and integrate service delivery.

8. Initiative by the alcohol program agency is required to secure linkages to adjunct services. With one exception, non-alcohol agencies do not accept responsibility to assure linkage between alcohol recovery services and other human services that are important for recovery. These services include health care; mental health care; vocational/ education assistance; qualifications for benefits and entitlements; advocacy; legal services; protection and security; physically disabled; multiple problems. The exception is the Pew/Johnson "Health Care for the Homeless" program. In several cities, HCH medical teams have been vigorous in providing mobile outreach and clinic services in conjunction with alcohol-problem recovery services. Further study is recommended of models and strategies for effective use of other human services during the recovery process.

9. Staffing and manpower issues revolve around the integration of "clinical" approaches relying on trained people from the helping professions and "experiential" approaches to service that rely on self-help. . . . Program environments that expected the client to act vigorously on his or her own behalf usually provide both kinds of support.

10. Program organization and leadership. Creation of an environment conducive to recovery is a major theme of program organization. Recovery environments simultaneously emphasize the dignity and importance of the individual, and provide a milieu in which sobriety and principles of community living serve to establish norms for the program participants. The program's director is usually as concerned about the quality of the environment as he or she is about the quality of treatment services and counseling at the individual level.

11. Program leadership comes from diverse backgrounds. Program leaders' backgrounds are diverse professionally and in terms of life history, including both recovering individuals and professionally trained individuals from many different disciplinary backgrounds. Personal qualities are important, and flexibility and approachability are important characteristics.

12. Sound community relations are critical to successful program operations. Alcohol programs serving the homeless must answer to their neighbors as well as to their funding sources (who often are community organizations to begin with). Strategies for maintaining solid relationships include: creation of strong local boards; cultivation of local political and institutional leadership; careful attention to review procedures and community involvement in securing sites for program facilities; and positive, active participation in community events.

13. Alcohol programs serving the homeless recognize the need to eliminate conditions that create homelessness. Most of the programs studied recognize the importance of socio-economic factors in homelessness, and several are working to deal with local conditions while they are providing services to individuals. Denial of access to housing for low-income people and to jobs that pay a liveable wage are recognized as structural problems that inhibit recovery. Some programs . . . have taken initiative to increase access to housing and jobs as part of their program activities.

14. Alcohol programs are working to provide safety and support services for homeless people who continue to drink. Alcohol programs participate in the struggle of all who work to eradicate homelessness and who try to make communities safer and more tolerable for homeless people. Alcohol programs with strong community-service mandates . . . are working to increase housing, protection and street-oriented services.

A number of program directors and other observers believe that creation of places to accommodate the "homeless inebriate" in the community would relieve pressure on the existing alcohol service system. Such accommodation would decrease demand on basic shelter and protection services that could be provided more expeditiously in other settings. For example, supervised wet hotels and sobering stations, day-use occupancy of night shelters, and other walk-in day-use facilities might relieve the use of detoxification and emergency services. More facilities that can accept mail, provide spot jobs, telephones, clothes, lockers, showers and laundry, would make it easier for people to look after themselves. Community outreach work with liquor store operators, bartenders, hotels owners, store-owners, police, case managers, and others who come in contact with public inebriates can help protect inebriates and link them up with services.

Source: *Alcohol Recovery Programs for Homeless People: A Survey of Current Programs in the U.S.* National Institute on Alcohol Abuse and Alcoholism (NIAAA), 1988, pp. 2–6.

Homelessness and Mental Illness

As homelessness grew in the 1980s, some of the most visible homeless people were those with mental illness. This excerpt is from
testimony by a psychiatrist known for his work with homeless
people; it provides an overview of the problems faced by this
group.

First, in our country the number of seriously and chronically mentally
ill among the homeless is staggering (from 20 to 80 percent of the
estimated 750,000 to 3 million homeless, depending on where the
study was done, live in the streets or in shelters). . . . [U]ntil recently
the homeless were largely regarded as shiftless, poor, alcohol-abusing
vagabonds. In recent years, however, their numbers have included an
increasing number and percentage of persons suffering from serious
and chronic (long-term) mental illnesses: primarily schizophrenia,
unresponsive psychotic depression and organic mental illness. Even
taking a conservative figure of 20 percent, we are talking about a great
number, and the number and percent who have been in state mental
hospitals is even higher.

When you look at the homeless mentally ill, realize that you are
dealing with two problems with multiple causes and subgroups:
homelessness and chronic mental illnesses. Each, in and of itself, is a
formidable challenge to resolve, but combined, they present a problem
of unprecedented magnitude and complexity. The population bears
the cross of a dual disenfranchisement from society and its agents of
service delivery: the mentally ill are often excluded from programs
designed to serve the homeless, and those who are homeless are
typically screened out from receiving services designed for the chronically mentally ill. The homeless mentally ill have become our society's
"untouchables," unable to advocate for themselves, unable to protect
themselves from harm, unable to acquire the bare necessities of living.

Recently, as reported on the front page of the May 22, 1989 *New
York Times,* alcohol and drug addiction have emerged as another major
reason for the homelessness of men, women, and families. Many of
the chronically mentally ill are also addicted to either drugs or alcohol.
The crack cocaine epidemic has certainly increased the numbers of the
homeless above our earlier estimates at the time of the APA's Task
Force Report. As reported in the *Times,* experts who are finding a
substantial drug problem among the homeless found that close to
50 percent of the homeless men living in downtown Los Angeles were
addicts and 75 percent of men arriving at the Franklin Street shelter
in the South Bronx were addicts. However, tragically, treatment

programs are virtually nonexistent. While there are between 50,000 and 100,000 homeless people in Los Angeles County, there are only 20 to 25 beds available for them in residential treatment programs.

Second, for this population, a simple, single housing facility is insufficient. Instead, these disabled citizens require a range of graded, step-wise housing opportunities from large halfway houses to smaller group homes, to individual apartments or homes. As opposed to those out of work, burned out of their homes, etc., the severely and chronically mentally ill cannot resume their full personal, familial, social, vocational and community lives following treatment of their acute phase of illness. They must also slowly recuperate from their illnesses—often progressing from acute inpatient units to chronic state hospitals to rehabilitation programs to day hospitals or half-way houses to group or foster home to independent living—in a slow but progressive manner. Thus, they need a range of housing opportunities, that includes more "restrictive" and larger sized facilities, smaller groups and family homes, and eventually, individual homes or apartments.

... [I]n 1955 there were 559,000 patients in state hospitals; today, at any given time, there are approximately 123,000. Conceptually, deinstitutionalization was not flawed; its implementation was. The importance of psychoactive medication and a stable source of financial support was perceived, but the importance of developing such fundamental resources as supportive living arrangements was not clearly seen nor implemented. Nor was it foreseen how reluctant many states would be to allocate funds for community-based services. Almost immediately after deinstitutionalization occurred, society reacted vehemently to the presence of the homeless on our cities' streets.

An adequate number and ample range of graded, stepwise, supervised community housing settings must be established. While many of the homeless may benefit from temporary housing such as shelters, and while some portion of the severely chronically mentally ill are able to graduate to independent living, for the vast majority, neither shelters nor mainstream low-cost housing (such as Section 8 or Section 202 housing) are in and of themselves appropriate. Instead, there must be settings offering different levels of supervision, both more and less intensive, including quarterway and halfway houses, lodges and camps, board and care homes, satellite housing, family or foster care, and crisis housing or temporary hotels. Organized and supervised living arrangements can help stabilize the lives of such individuals to a marked extent. Supervision would help ensure that medications are taken, that an address is available for the delivery of SSI, SSDI, Medicare and Medicaid payments, and that there is an address available for case workers and health and supportive care workers.

Third, while affordable, accessible housing is necessary for this population, it is insufficient, absent supervision (ranging from full-time, on-site staff in intensive settings to potentially-frequent visits from visiting nurses, social workers, case managers and the like) when disabled persons are living more independently. They require different levels of supervision and services depending on their degree of residual mental impairment and progressive ability to resume activities of everyday living (shopping, cooking, banking, job-hunting, etc.) They thus require more intensive medical-psychiatric care as they are in the early phase of recuperation, greater full-time staff involvement as they re-enter the community, then continuing follow-up by visiting nurses, social workers and case managers (depending on their individual needs), until they are fully re-established in the "mainstream."

To summarize, *adequate, comprehensive, and accessible psychiatric and rehabilitative services must be available and must be assertively provided through outreach services when needed.*

First, there must be an adequate number of *direct psychiatric services,* both in the streets and in the housing provided, when appropriate, that provide (a) outreach contact with the mentally ill in the community, (b) psychiatric assessment and evaluation, (c) crisis intervention, (d) individualized treatment plans, (e) psychotropic medication and other somatic therapies, and (f) psychosocial treatment. A clear model for this sort of service system was established in the 1980 Mental Health Systems Act (PL 98-398) though, regrettably, that law was later repealed during the first months of the Reagan Administration.

There must be an adequate number of rehabilitative services providing socialization experiences, training in the skills of everyday living, and social rehabilitation. Programs providing such services could be patterned after day treatment programs, or some of the more social support-related services provided by senior centers. These treatment and rehabilitative services must by provided assertively, for instance, by going out to patients' living settings if they do not or cannot come to a centralized program.

General medical assessment and care must be available. Since we know that the chronically mentally ill have three times the morbidity and mortality of their counterparts of the same age in the general population, and the homeless even higher rates, the ready availability of general medical care is essential and critical. Again, this could occur within the housing sites or within the rehabilitation programs.

Crisis services must be available and accessible to both the chronically mentally ill homeless and the chronically mentally ill in general. Too often, the homeless mentally ill who are in crisis are ignored because they are presumed to reject all conventional forms of help. Even more inappropriately, they may be put into inpatient hospital units when rapid, specific interventions such as medication or crisis housing would be more effective and less costly. Others may be incarcerated in corrections facilities, even more inappropriate and more costly than other settings. Others in need of acute hospitalization are denied it because of restrictive admission criteria or commitment laws. In any case, it will be difficult to provide adequate crisis services to the homeless mentally ill until they are conceptualized and treated separately from the large numbers of other homeless persons.

A system of responsibility for the chronically mentally ill living in the community must be established, with the goal of ensuring that ultimately each patient has one person responsible for his or her care. The shift of psychiatric care from the institutional to community setting does not in any way eliminate the need to continue the provision of comprehensive services to the mentally ill. Indeed, the need for asylum for such persons may be even greater when confronted by the larger community setting. As a result, society must declare a policy of responsibility for the mentally ill who are unable to meet their own needs; governments must designate programs in each region or locality as core agencies responsible and accountable for the care of the chronically mentally ill living there; and the staff of these agencies must be assigned individual patients for whom they are responsible. The ultimate goal must be to ensure that each chronically mentally ill person in this country has one person—a case manager, if you will, who is responsible for his or her treatment and care. The entire burden must not be allowed to fall upon families as if this illness—as compared to physical illness—were their fault and they should be punished.

Source: Edited from a statement of the American Psychiatric Association on S565, "The National Affordable Housing Act," presented by John A. Talbot, M.D., Professor and Chairman, Department of Psychiatry, University of Maryland School of Medicine, before the Senate Banking and Urban Affairs Committee Subcommittee on Housing and Urban Affairs, 1 June 1989.

Education of Homeless Children

Keeping homeless children in school is a special problem. The McKinney Act provisions to address education are summarized below.

The Stewart B. McKinney Homeless Assistance Act, signed into law on July 22, 1987, provides comprehensive federal emergency assistance for homeless persons. It specifically addresses the barriers to education of homeless children. The Act establishes for the first time a national, uniform policy for the education of homeless children. In addition, the McKinney Act makes funds available for the development of programs to facilitate enrollment and attendance of homeless children in school. These funds, though limited, help to provide urgently needed relief.

The Act states that, as a matter of federal policy, homeless children are entitled to a free, appropriate public school education. It states that residency requirements may not be used to deny access to such education to homeless children. It specifically directs states to review their residency laws to ensure that those laws do not create barriers to homeless children.

The Act also creates a specific program to fund the implementation of these requirements. Under this program, states establish a "Coordinator of Education of Homeless Children and Youth" and write plans specifying how the educational needs of homeless children will be addressed. The Act requires the plans to address specific barriers faced by homeless children as follows:

1. Residency requirements

The Act states that children will be educated in one of two districts. The Act states that the local education agency of each homeless child or youth shall either a) continue the child's or youth's education in the school district of origin for the remainder of the school year; or b) enroll the child or youth in the school district where the child or youth is actually living; whichever is in the child's best interest or the youth's best interest.[1]

By law the student must be placed in either one school district or the other. In the event that school districts should disagree on the child's "best interest," the state will "provide procedures for the resolution of disputes regarding the educational placement. . . ."[2]

2. Records

The Act calls for efficient handling of records:

> The school records of each homeless child or youth shall be maintained: (A) so that records are available, in a timely manner, when a child or youth enters a new school district. . . .[3]

3. Special Education

Under the Act, homeless children are entitled to special education programs:

> Each homeless child shall be provided services comparable to services offered to other students in the school . . . including educational

services for which the child meets the eligibility criteria, such as compensatory educational programs for the disadvantaged, and educational programs for the handicapped and for students with limited English proficiency. . . .[4]

4. Guardianship

The Act facilitates placement of homeless children and youth who do not reside with their parents when it stipulates:

> The choice regarding [educational] placement shall be made regardless of whether the child or youth is living with the homeless parents or has been temporarily placed elsewhere by the parents.[5]

In addition to creating a uniform policy to guarantee access to education for homeless children, the McKinney Act also provides funds for states to develop exemplary programs to serve the special needs of homeless children. States may use such funds to formalize coordination, outreach and awareness in their service agencies. All states are encouraged to apply for these funds.[6]

Notes

1. McKinney Act, Sec. 722 (e) (3).

2. Ibid., Sec. 722 (e) (4).

3. Ibid., Sec. 722 (e) (6).

4. Ibid., Sec. 722 (e) (5).

5. Ibid., Sec. 722 (e) (4).

6. Even small grants can be put to good use. For example, the state of Washington is planning to use its grant to set up a computer system to keep track of health and birth certificates. With this system in place, homeless children will have to produce these records only once per school year.

Source: From *Broken Lives: Denial of Education to Homeless Children,* a report by the National Coalition for the Homeless, New York, December 1987, pp. 17–19.

Homeless People and the HIV/AIDS Epidemic

Homeless Women and HIV/AIDS Issues

HIV/AIDS is increasingly a problem of poor people and thus of homeless people. The National Conference on AIDS and HIV Infection in Ethnic and Racial Minorities was held in Washington, D.C., in August 1989. Phyllis Sharpe, a New York City mother and former drug user, testified at the conference about some of the unique problems facing minority women. In May 1990, Ms. Sharpe also spoke at a demonstration at the National Institutes of Health in Bethesda, Maryland, about the lack of access to drug trials for women in her situation. The following excerpts are from these two statements.

My name is Phyllis Sharpe of Brooklyn, New York. I am a victim of years of drug abuse. I have six children and two grandchildren. I am single, Black, and have very little means of finance. In February 1988, I discovered I was HIV-positive. At that time, I was still a user. The Bureau of Child Welfare was called by a family member and my youngest daughter was taken from me. This happened ten months ago. She is now two years old and is HIV-positive also. . . . I have been drug-free since November 1988. . . . I joined a women's support group to accept both my daughter's and my own illnesses. This group helped me put things in motion to get funds, medical care, and housing. . . . Without an apartment, the Bureau of Child Welfare wouldn't even think of returning my daughter to me. . . .

Being a PWA [person with AIDS] and living on a fixed income, I've been forced to experience non-treatment and poor treatment. Seeing a different doctor each appointment who asks the same questions as the one before. Never being asked or told of a drug trial for women or children. I learned of trials in a support group, but it seems as though women and children aren't included. The only medications that are offered are AZT and Bactrim. . . . Why are these the only drugs offered? . . .

I have a home now, but just 10 months ago, I was still homeless. Many people who are here today are homeless right now. One thing I can tell you about the NIH—they don't have any homeless people in their trials. And they don't have trials for people who use drugs either.

Source: From "Ending the Silence: Voices of Homeless People Living with AIDS," published by the National Coalition for the Homeless, New York City, June 1990, pp. 43–44, 51.

Homeless Men and HIV/AIDS Issues

On 21 March 1990, the House Subcommittee on Housing and Community Development held hearings in Washington, D.C., on a bill, introduced by Representative Jim McDermott (a physician from Seattle) to provide housing relief for homeless people with AIDS. Irving Porter of New York City testified at that hearing and provided a dramatic statement of the problems facing the drug user seeking treatment; he explained to the committee how he intentionally made himself homeless in order to get what little treatment was available.

. . . Approximately twelve years ago my life began to fall out of control. I found myself addicted to cocaine and alcohol. . . .

In 1985, I decided to do something about my drug problems. I knew I needed residential treatment if I was going to kick my addiction, but all the drug treatment slots were full. In October of that year, I learned that a few designated drug treatment slots were available for people who were homeless. I know it sounds crazy, but the only way I knew to get the treatment I needed was to become homeless myself.

So I gave up my job as a bookkeeper and gave up my apartment as well. I then entered the New York City shelter system. Little did I know I was only compounding my problems. I was entering a system that was easy to get into but almost impossible to ever get out of. . . .

All I wanted at this time was to be interviewed and placed in a drug program. The sooner I got the hell out of the shelter, the happier I would be. After a few days, I was sent to Daytop Village . . . one of the oldest drug treatment programs in the country. . . .

While I was in drug treatment, I revealed that I was bisexual. They then tested me for HIV without my knowledge. I was told by the nurse that my immune system was shot, but I was never told that I was HIV-positive. . . . After 21 months . . . I decided to leave the program. . . . I wound up in Greenpoint Men's Shelter in Brooklyn, New York. . . .

As time moved on, I started losing weight. I became very weak. I would lose my breath just from walking. I went to Beth Israel Hospital. I was diagnosed as having pneumonia. . . . I signed myself out of that hospital and immediately went to Beekman Hospital, where I was diagnosed as having active tuberculosis. I was advised by the doctor to be tested for AIDS. I was tested and the results were positive. When I was given the news, I just wanted to DIE. I was put into isolation and treated for TB. . . .

Again I found myself living on the streets. . . . I collapsed while standing in line for a meal and was taken to New York Hospital. . . .

The City put me in a "welfare hotel." My hotel room is certainly better than a shelter or the streets, but it is still not the proper living situation for a person with AIDS. I have been in that same room for almost a year. I am still waiting for proper housing. I presently have to share my bathroom with about 20 people. I have to be very careful not to pick up any infections. Also there are drugs throughout the hotel, so I have to deal with a lot of temptation. . . .

If you take a look at the statistics on homeless people who are now HIV-infected, you will see that my experience as a homeless Black male has been and will be the NEW TREND OF AIDS. . . . Even now the city, state and federal governments would like to pretend that we don't exist.

When I first gave up my home to enter the shelter system, I didn't realize I had gotten on a merry-go-round that I couldn't stop. The people I saw trying to get into drug treatment back then are the same ones I later saw in the shelter system. The ones I saw who finally got drug treatment are the same people I see today in the hospital and in my infectious disease clinic.

When I die, my death certificate will probably say I died of AIDS. But I want the world to know the real cause: a government that saw AIDS and left it unchecked. . . . You think AIDS will stop with us. But HIV doesn't see skin color and it can't tell a person's sexual orientation. Because you didn't care, AIDS will continue to spread. . . .

Source: From "Ending the Silence: Voices of Homeless People Living with AIDS," published by the National Coalition for the Homeless, New York City, June 1990, pp. 36–42.

Policy Recommendations on Homelessness and HIV/AIDS

The following excerpts from a report of the National Commission on AIDS make recommendations on meeting the needs of homeless people.

Introduction

The lack of affordable and appropriate housing is an acute crisis for people living with Human Immunodeficiency Virus (HIV) within the larger crisis of HIV/AIDS. Health and medical aspects of the epidemic have overshadowed the frequently desperate need for safe shelter that provides not only protection and comfort, but also a base in which and from which to receive services, care, and support.

Housing problems for people with HIV disease arise in a variety of ways. Many individuals are evicted when their HIV status becomes known; most of them are not even aware that this type of discrimination violates federal fair housing law and many state laws. For others, loss of income as a result of illness and inability to work creates an inability to pay the rent or mortgage. Some who are hospitalized find that when they are able to leave the hospital their already unstable living arrangements have fallen apart. Some had no homes before becoming HIV-infected and lived on the street; then, too ill to fend for themselves, they shuttle back and forth between shelters and acute-care hospitals. Some children with HIV have spent their entire lives in hospitals because of the lack of adequate housing for them and their parents. Women with children are often excluded from the few residential programs that do exist. The scope of these problems is vast and solutions are difficult, but there is increasing awareness that the homeless of tomorrow are being created by the failure to provide housing options for thousands of people living with HIV disease today.

This report will highlight problems and achievements associated with efforts being made to address the housing crisis that exists within the larger crisis of HIV/AIDS.

Background

Although no one knows the precise number, it has been estimated that in the United States between one and three million people are homeless.

It has been estimated that 15 percent of the homeless are infected with HIV, and the number of HIV-infected individuals who are homeless is growing rapidly (Lambert 1989). In fact, the Centers for Disease Control (CDC) reports site-specific HIV seroprevalence ranging from 0 to 21.4 percent in selected homeless populations in the United States (Allen, et al., 1991).

It is estimated that from one-third to one-half of all people with AIDS are either homeless or in imminent danger of becoming so, because of their illness, lack of income or other resources, and weak support networks (Arno, 1991; E. N. Lindblom, Department of Veterans Affairs, personal communication, Washington, D.C., June 1992).

Studies indicate that at any given time approximately 30 percent of all people with HIV diseases in acute-care hospitals are there because no community-based residential program is available to them (Hunter-Young, et al., 1990; Massachusetts Rate Setting Commission, 1992). As a result, it often costs over $1,000 per day to house a person with HIV in an acute-care hospital, when providing both housing and services in a residential setting could cost less than one-tenth of that amount.

The crisis in housing for people living with HIV disease is in part a result of our society's failure to provide adequate, affordable housing for all of its citizens. In the 1980s the number of poor households increased dramatically while the number of low-cost housing units provided by the public and private sectors dropped considerably. The federal, state, and local governments have neither made up the loss nor kept up with the growing demand. Many federal programs are essentially unavailable to the increasing number of individuals in need of them. In the context of HIV, this has meant that as the epidemic has grown, fewer and fewer resources have been available. In most of our large cities, where the epidemic has hit the hardest, the overwhelming demand for public housing and rent subsidy programs has made them essentially unavailable. In San Francisco, the Section 8 waiting list has been closed since 1986. In other cities, waiting lists are so long that they all but preclude access to people living with HIV disease.

The shortage of resources has not been the only problem that has resulted in increased homelessness among people living with HIV. In addition to a serious lack of resources for housing for all poor Americans, the federal government has been resistant to specific attempts to target federal funds for housing people with HIV. While resources are limited in most contexts, they have been all but nonexistent to those working to house people with HIV disease.

The federal Department of Housing and Urban Development (HUD) has virtually ignored the AIDS housing crisis. HUD, in effect the nation's largest landlord, housing provider, and housing developer, has resisted almost all efforts by community-based organizations, cities, and states, and Congress to meet the housing needs of people living with HIV disease.

What Is Being Done

Despite the best efforts of AIDS housing providers, there is an acute shortage of resources available for the development of housing for people with HIV disease. Community-based AIDS service organizations have attempted to meet growing housing needs by providing small-scale community-based group homes and rental assistance programs patched together with the few available local resources. Across the country, communities have sponsored projects ranging from bake sales to "Walks for Life" to raise money to supplement the few government programs that have been available to create AIDS housing. In the meantime, efforts to increase federal participation have met with limited success.

While the lack of affordable and appropriate housing continues to be one of the major problems of the HIV/AIDS epidemic, some important steps to remedy the problem have been taken. A number of AIDS housing providers throughout the United States have moved to meet the challenge of both increasing access to already existing housing programs and developing a broad range of new housing options to meet the diverse housing needs of people with HIV disease. . . . On the federal level, Congress has taken some important steps to support such efforts.

In 1990, Congress passed the National Affordable Housing Act, which includes Housing Opportunities for People with AIDS (HOPWA).

Also included in the 1990 act are 500 units of Section 811 housing nationwide specifically for people with HIV/AIDS. The funding of these 500 units helped offset HUD's failure to allow people with HIV disease access to traditional Section 811 units. The Section 811 program was designed to create supportive housing for persons who are disabled. Congress appropriated funds for these units in 1991. In addition, Congress at the time of the passage of the act made clear its intent that people with AIDS are eligible for traditional Section 811 funding.

Congress also appropriated $50 million nationally for Housing Opportunities for People with AIDS (HOPWA) under the National Affordable Housing Act. HOPWA created housing resources for those cities hardest hit by the HIV/AIDS epidemic, enabling them to fund a range of programs for people living with HIV disease, including AIDS housing information and coordination services; short-term supported housing and services; rental assistance; single-room occupancy housing; and community residences and services.

In summary, on the local, state, and national levels, some progress has been made.

Recommendations

Therefore, the Commission recommends:

1. That HUD make HIV/AIDS a top priority. The federal government must help support AIDS housing. The failure to do so contributes significantly to unnecessary human suffering and is costing the nation millions of dollars.

2. That Congress mandate that HUD recognize HIV/AIDS as a disability and not continue to deny people with HIV/AIDS access to housing funds targeted toward the disabled.

3. That people with HIV/AIDS be granted access to traditional housing programs. By the same token, Congress and HUD must adapt program requirements to meet the specific housing needs of people with HIV/AIDS.

4. That Congress make clear that HIV/AIDS-specific housing, under Shelter Plus Care and other federal programs, is both permitted and essential.

5. That Congress continue to play a leadership role in developing new funds to address the HIV/AIDS housing crisis.

6. That, as previously recommended by the Commission, the President of the United States name a lead official or agency to be responsible for a national plan to combat HIV/AIDS with cabinet level, interagency coordination.

7. And finally, that at the local level, a continuum of housing options be made available for people living with HIV disease that includes a range of alternatives from hospice care, and intermediate or supportive housing, to rental subsidies which could allow people to reside independently until such time as they need additional care.

Source: From "Housing and the HIV/AIDS Epidemic: Recommendations for Action," National Commission on AIDS, 1992.

Federal Priorities for Homeless Persons with HIV/AIDS

The Presidential Commission on AIDS reviewed federal housing and medical programs for the homeless. It found the following obstacles to progress and also made some recommendations:

An accurate estimate of the size of the homeless population of persons with HIV infection is lacking.

Seroprevalence studies have not been done on this difficult-to-track population. An adequate assessment of the size and scope of the problem of homelessness of persons with HIV infection is necessary to target future resources.

Individuals with HIV infection may receive low priority ratings for housing subsidies due to local regulations.

Construction of shelters or group residences for persons with symptomatic HIV infection has not kept pace with demand in many cities.

Municipal shelters are unable to diagnose HIV infection or target medical resources to HIV-infected persons in shelters.

Hospitals are often unable to discharge medically stable homeless patients because they have no permanent street address.

Service needs of special populations, such as adolescents and women with children, have not been defined or estimated.

Recommendations

Federal anti-discrimination protection for persons with disabilities, including persons with HIV infection, should be expanded to cover housing that does not receive federal funds. . . .

The Department of Housing and Urban Development funding for homeless assistance programs should be increased, and funds should be made more easily available to cities and private sector organizations to build both temporary shelters and permanent residences for homeless persons with HIV infection.

Operators of all homeless shelters and residences must treat those clients who are HIV-infected in an anti-discriminatory manner, protect them from abuse, and help them seek medical assistance as needed.

The Centers for Disease Control should fund and coordinate targeted seroprevalence studies (e.g., on adolescents, women, and adult men) to be conducted by city agencies in high prevalence cities to establish the size of the homeless population of persons with symptomatic HIV infection and to help cities determine the need for services. In addition to HIV antibody status, these studies should gather information on concurrent medical problems, such as tuberculosis and drug addiction, to both collect co-factor information, and determine the need for greater medical intervention in municipal shelters. Study results including geographic breakdowns should be made available to national mayors' associations, to the Association of State and Territorial Health Officials, and to state and local officials, as appropriate.

The joint project between the National Institute of Mental Health and the Health Resources and Services Administration on adolescent homeless youth and HIV infection should be expanded and funding increased. More programs on homeless youth should be funded.

The Department of Housing and Urban Development should provide renovation grants to public hospitals to convert underutilized acute care beds into long-term care beds for HIV-infected individuals requiring hospice or other long-term care.

The use of the Department of Housing and Urban Development funds to help finance construction and improvement of nursing homeless and related facilities should be encouraged to make additional long-term care and hospice care beds available.

The Veterans' Administration should conduct a short-term study to determine the extent of homelessness among veterans, and HIV infection in this population. . . .

Source: From *Report of the Presidential Commission on the Human Immunodeficiency Virus Epidemic*, 1988, pp. 104–107.

Homelessness and the Resurgent Tuberculosis Epidemic

While tuberculosis was long thought to be a disease of the past, it never really went away for very poor people. According to the Centers for Disease Control (CDC) Advisory Council for the Elimination of Tuberculosis:

Since the early 1900s, tuberculosis has been recognized as an important health problem among homeless persons and among residents of inexpensive lodging houses, night shelters, single-room occupancy hotels, and common hostels. . . . .With the increase in homelessness in the United States during the 1980s, TB among homeless persons became a subject of heightened interest and concern. . . .

Case Management

Homeless patients with newly diagnosed infectious TB should be appropriately housed to allow initial therapy to be fully supervised and to preclude continuing transmission of TB in the community. Ideally, homeless persons with active TB should be housed in a special shelter, halfway house, or other long-term treatment facility until therapy is complete or more permanent housing is identified. It is also important that ancillary services, such as substance abuse treatment and evaluation and treatment of HIV disease, be offered in these facilities.

A health department staff member should visit a homeless person with suspected or confirmed TB, in the hospital or elsewhere, as soon as possible after the diagnosis is suspected or made. The health department worker should make an assessment of the likelihood of adherence to therapy if treatment is to be given on an outpatient basis. During the initial visit, the treatment plan should be discussed and the patient's cooperation elicited. . . .

The homeless person with TB may not view TB as the highest priority concern. Other concerns—e.g., shelter, food, and safety—are likely to be of greater priority. Thus, the involvement of social workers on the treatment team to assist in solving these other problems is important for achieving successful treatment of TB.

Treatment must be carefully monitored. . . . Carrying medications may be dangerous for homeless persons; if others believe the medications are addictive or valuable, homeless persons may be robbed or assaulted. . . .

Whenever possible, TB clinics should be located close to shelters or other places (e.g., soup kitchens) where homeless people receive services. If this is not possible, transportation to the clinics should be provided. The clinic schedule should include hours that facilitate patient attendance. Incentives and enablers to encourage adherence should be used. These might include items such as food or food vouchers, cash, special lodging, transportation vouchers or tokens, articles of clothing, priority in food lines, and assistance in filing for benefits. . . .

Source: From "Prevention and Control of Tuberculosis among Homeless Persons," Centers for Disease Control, *Morbidity and Mortality Weekly Report,* vol. 41, no. RR-5 (17 April 1992): 13, 16–17.

Homelessness and Veterans

A group that has received more attention in the last several years is homeless veterans. The National Commission on AIDS, formed by the U.S. Congress in 1989, heard testimony in Washington, D.C., on 2 November 1989. One of the witnesses was Ralph Hernandez, a New York City veteran and intravenous drug user. The following is excerpted from his testimony before the commission.

My name is Ralph Hernandez. I am a Viet Nam vet. I am homeless, and I am living with AIDS. When I went to Nam, the government told me I was putting my life at risk for my country. . . . I became disabled and finally I got AIDS. . . .

I was honorably discharged from the United States Army in 1974 with a service-connected disability. But I had another illness too. In Nam, I had become addicted to drugs. Even with my handicaps I went to school, I got a job with the phone company, and I supported my wife and children. The whole time I was still using drugs.

In 1987, I started getting sores on my skin and my physical appearance started deteriorating. I left my wife and started shooting up more and more. I felt too weak to go to work. Soon I lost my apartment and then my job. I tried to get into the VA hospital but they wouldn't see me because I was homeless. They wouldn't even let me into the detox program. They told me to just stop shooting. . . .

I went to the Washington Heights Shelter. When I took my clothes off in the shower, the other homeless people kicked . . . me. Then they called the guards and the guards threw me out. I went to another shelter but I was afraid to stay there. So I started living in the tunnels under Grand Central Station. Even there I had to hide so no one would see the condition I was in. . . .

The VA had lost all my papers. I had been tested there for AIDS three times, but because I am homeless, they have lost my records each time. . . .

For six months I have been in a methadone program and I try not to use drugs any more. But the VA is still not giving me any medical treatment. I still do not have a place to live.

I wish you knew how I feel when I go on the subway and see people move away from me. . . . I served my country in time of crisis. Now that I'm in crisis, where is my country?

I am not the only one who has experienced this. There are thousands of homeless men and women with AIDS struggling to survive. . . . Like me, they have no place to turn to. . . .

Source: From "Ending the Silence: Voices of Homeless People Living with AIDS," published by the National Coalition for the Homeless, New York City, June 1990, pp. 11–13.

Homeless Youth

One of the groups of homeless people that is growing rapidly and receives little consideration or attention is homeless youth. Few studies have been done to understand their needs; few services are available for them. The following excerpt from a 1993 survey of youth in Chicago reveals similarities to young people interviewed elsewhere:

It is well-known that American families are in trouble. The failure of our schools, the epidemic of drug use, and a myriad of other social ills have been catalogued in many places. Yet the impact on young lives ... can still shock us. Approximately two hundred young people described their lives for this study, revealing cases of sexual abuse, drug and alcohol abuse, and many other problems in their families and their communities. The fact that they are so young and living alone on the street is stark evidence of the pain they are fleeing. ...

While more than half stated that "nothing could have been done" to prevent their homelessness, many reported that they should have tried harder to get along, followed the rules, done better in school, changed their attitudes and stayed out of trouble. Although it is likely that many of these young people have been troublesome adolescents, it is sad that they shoulder the burden of their homelessness as if it were their fault.

Their stories disclose backgrounds of poverty, deprivation, and instability. Many come from loosely structured or separated families, and virtually all come from low income households. Combined stresses of poverty and family conflict are exacerbated by high levels of alcohol and drug abuse, and physical and sexual abuse.

Lack of affordable housing, high unemployment, and increasing levels of abuse and violence in communities combine to break up families and spill their members onto the street. Traditional community supports such as schools, churches and community organizations do not provide the level of support and involvement with families that they did just a generation ago.

Source: From "Alone after Dark," Chicago Coalition for the Homeless, 1993, pp. 2–3.

A Federal Policy on Homelessness

In January 1993, newly inaugurated president Bill Clinton named former San Antonio, Texas, mayor Henry Cisneros as secretary of the U.S. Department of Housing and Urban Development, the federal agency with responsibility for the homeless housing assistance programs. Secretary Cisneros went out and walked the streets of downtown Washington, D.C., and talked with homeless people. Following are President Clinton's Executive Order on Homelessness, signed in May 1993, an excerpt from Cisneros's statement at his confirmation hearing, and the major recommendations of the government report released in response to Clinton's excecutive order.

Executive Order on Homelessness

Executive Order 12848 of May 19, 1993:

By the authority vested in me as President by the Constitution and the laws of the United States of America, including Title II of the Stewart B. McKinney Homeless Assistance Act, as amended (42 U.S.C. 11311-11320) and Section 301 of Title 3, United States Code, and in order to provide for the strengthening and streamlining of the Nation's efforts to break the cycle of homelessness, it is hereby ordered as follows:

Sec. 1. Federal member agencies acting through the Interagency Council on the Homeless, established under Title II of the Stewart B. McKinney Homeless Assistance Act, shall develop a single coordinated Federal plan for breaking the cycle of existing homelessness and for preventing future homelessness.

Sec. 2. The plan shall recommend Federal administrative and legislative initiatives necessary to carry out the plan and shall include a proposed schedule for implementing administrative initiatives and transmitting any necessary legislative proposals to the Congress. These initiatives and legislative proposals shall identify ways to streamline and consolidate, when appropriate, existing programs designed to assist homeless individuals and families.

Sec. 3. The plan shall make recommendations on how current funding programs can be redirected, if necessary, to provide links between housing, support, and education services and to promote coordination and cooperation among grantees, local housing and support service providers, school districts, and advocates for homeless individuals and families. The plan shall also provide recommendations on ways to encourage and support creative approaches and cost-effective, local efforts to break the cycle of existing homelessness and prevent future homelessness, including tying current homeless assistance programs to permanent housing assistance, local housing affordability strategies, or employment opportunities.

Sec. 4. To the extent practicable, the Council shall consult with representatives of State and local governments (including education agencies), nonprofit providers of services and housing for homeless individuals and families, advocates for homeless individuals and families, currently and formerly homeless individuals and families, and other interested parties.

Sec. 5. The Council shall submit the plan to the President no later than 9 months after the date of this order.

Signed, William J. Clinton
May 19, 1993

Goals of the Housing Department

... I am here because I believe we can make a difference. I am here because I believe my Department can help to create jobs and hope, can help restore opportunity and economic revitalization, can help bring about an urban renaissance in America. ... We have seen the most defenseless and hopeless of our people sleeping on grates and huddled in the doorways of buildings vacated after the workday— people whose lives are as empty as the buildings they use for shelter. This is not our vision of America, and we must work together to restore care and dignity to those bereft of hope. We need long-term solutions—a comprehensive, integrated approach to reducing home-lessness in America. At the same time, we must meet their immediate needs, and I am advocating the use of closed military bases and other military property for transitional housing. ... I believe there are solutions to every problem confronting our country and our people— and I want to find those solutions and make them work.

Source: Statement of the Committee on Banking, Finance and Urban Affairs, Subcommittee on Housing and Community Development, 17 February 1993 by Secretary Henry G. Cisneros.

The Federal Plan To Break the Cycle of Homelessness

The following is excerpted from "Priority Home: The Federal Plan To End Homelessness," a May 1994 report that offered rec-ommendations for meeting the mandate of President Clinton's Executive Order on Homelessness.

The crisis of homelessness is the culmination of policies which have either ignored or misdiagnosed the adverse impact of economic shifts, the lack of affordable housing, increased drug abuse, and other physical health and mental health problems of those who are the most vulnerable in American society. Adding to the impact of these causes were changing family structures and a breakdown in social institutions.

Two broad classes of problems are identified: the first, "crisis poverty," refers to homelessness that may be traced chiefly to the stubborn demands of ongoing poverty, made untenable by some unforeseen development; the second, "chronic disability," refers to homelessness accompanied by one or more chronic, disabling conditions, and presents a more complicated picture.

The picture assembled suggests that a prudent policy must be two-fold. Government must address the needs of homeless and at-risk families, including the specific needs of children, and individuals vulnerable to "crisis poverty," many of whom move in and out of an assortment of makeshift housing. At the same time, it must attend to the more complex situation of those who also suffer from disabling conditions, the chronically disabled, for whom stable living will be an artful marriage of rehousing and rehabilitation.

The ultimate objective of this report is to achieve the goal of "a decent home and a suitable living environment for every American." It cannot escape notice that this was also the as yet unmet aim of the Housing Act of 1949. Just as we continue to hold this aspiration dear, so too must we learn from the lessons of unsuccessful attempts to achieve it. We must remember that government's role is to help people help themselves; that the government is most effective when it relies solely neither on the invisible hand of the marketplace nor the heavy hand of policies which reward inertia and punish initiative; that government is at its best when it offers instead a helping hand to those willing to climb on the first rungs of the ladder of economic opportunity; and that ultimately, government action cannot substitute for the individual's will or responsibility. . . .

The recommendations propose a two-pronged strategy: 1) implement and expand emergency measures to bring those who are currently homeless back into our communities, workforce and families; and 2) address structural needs to provide the necessary housing, and social infrastructure for the very poor in our society to prevent the occurrence of homelessness. We recommend a full-scale attack on homelessness, focusing public and private sector energies to make a real difference during the next four years. Immediate steps with a potential for dramatic effects are recommended. These include:

"Reinvent" the Approach. The current approach is plainly not working and must be changed. We recommend an overhaul of the government programs and policies designed to address homelessness and a restructuring of the relationship between the federal, state and local governments and the not-for-profit provider community. The federal government should get out of

the business of contracting for homeless services on the local level. Local government should be responsible for marshalling resources and assessing needs. Government at all levels should move towards an approach whereby not-for-profits actually deliver services. To accomplish this "reinvention," we recommend that the majority of McKinney Act programs to aid the homeless be reorganized and consolidated to provide a streamlined application process, enabling localities and providers to focus their energies on helping homeless people rather than filling out forms and grant applications. We also recommend that mainstream programs be more responsive to homeless persons and those most at risk of becoming homeless, with some McKinney programs linking more closely with their mainstream counterparts. The systems put in place should provide and coordinate emergency, transitional, and permanent housing in a "continuum of care."

A continuum of care system provides necessary emergency housing and a continuum of housing and supportive services for homeless individuals and families to gain independent living or supportive living. This system recognizes that some homeless people need supportive services and permanent housing and others are just in need of safe, decent, and affordable permanent housing.

Increase Homeless Assistance. With the reorganized, more effective approach outlined above, an increase in funding is a worthwhile investment. We have recommended an immediate doubling of the HUD homeless budget . . . and an increase in overall homeless assistance funding . . . We believe it is justified and necessary to address the needs of the current emergency as well as the immediate implementation of prevention programs.

Make Mental Health, Physical Health, and Substance Abuse Services Work for the Poor. We must address through health care reform and enhanced coordination between services and housing the specific needs of those who comprise the second category of homeless people in this country—homeless men and women with chronic disabilities. The most visible portion of the homeless population, and the most needy, are men and women with severe and persistent mental illnesses, substance dependency, or chronic health problems (i.e., tuberculosis, AIDS). These problems can be exacerbated by a lack of decent and affordable housing. When left untreated, conditions such as diabetes, hypertension and chronic respiratory problems render this population especially vulnerable. Although people with chronic disabilities comprise a minority of the homeless and at-risk population, they are often the most visible because they tend to congregate in parks, transportation thoroughfares and other public spaces.

This proposal anticipates the use of established public and private mental health, medical, and substance abuse providers to initiate street outreach efforts, the utilization of safe havens, and the implementation of a continuum of care for homeless persons to help them move from transitional housing, with supportive services, when needed, to stable housing and adequate aftercare and continuing services for those who require them while in permanent housing. . . .

This report recommends further steps to increase the supply of affordable housing and improve linkages between economic and human development:

Increase Housing Subsidies and Fight Discrimination: We must begin to repair the damage caused by the misguided and harmful housing budget cuts of the 1980s . . . The ultimate goal of these increases is to provide those who are homeless or precariously housed with the necessary resources to obtain housing . . . And, to ensure that permanent housing—both housing providing supportive services and traditional low-income housing—can be openly sited, we must aggressively enforce federal fair housing laws.

Low Income Housing Tax Incentives: We must act to take pressure off the homeless emergency system by undertaking efforts to stem the flow of families experiencing crisis poverty. Lower income households pay disproportionately higher shares of income for the cost of housing. We should explore use of tax incentives to assist lower income households with rental and housing costs. Special attention should be given to initiatives that would work together with existing tax incentives to insure that those who work are not left to the streets because of the discrepancy between their income and affordable rents.

Economic and Human Development/Social Contract: We must place increased emphasis on the linkages between job training, employment, education and economic development and implementation of a new social contract that recognizes both individual and family rights and responsibilities. While government should help people help themselves, it is not a substitute for individual will. It makes little sense to create jobs for people who have not received the training needed to fill them. At the same time, the public has the right to expect that needy individuals take advantage of the training and other services available to them. Similarly, as individuals with chronic disabilities receive access to necessary services, they should be encouraged to move from the streets to appropriate facilities. The goal is to help individuals and families help themselves and provide them with the opportunity to better themselves. This new social contract is mutual.

. . . While the road to a total solution for homelessness is a long one, the direction is clear. These recommendations, if enacted, represent a positive step forward.

6

Federal Legislation
on Homelessness

THIS CHAPTER SUMMARIZES IMPORTANT federal legislation on
homelessness, from scattered early attempts to earmark funds for
relief, to the first passage of the Stewart B. McKinney Homeless
Assistance Act in 1987, and finally to the most current policy directions of the Clinton administration, including a proposed reorganization of the McKinney Act. The McKinney Act has become
the vehicle best identified as homelessness legislation; most of its
component programs are for emergency or temporary assistance.

Pre–McKinney Act Legislation

Emergency Jobs Appropriations Act of 1983 (PL 98-8)

Shortly after the first congressional hearings on homelessness since the
Great Depression, Congress appropriated $100 million in emergency
food and shelter funds, to be spent through the Federal Emergency
Management Agency (FEMA). This agency was ordinarily responsible
for disaster planning, and homeless advocates did not anticipate that
its record would be very good in disbursing funds for homeless
people.

A national board of voluntary organizations dispensed half the
funds, and the remaining monies were disbursed as formula grants to

the states. Under this act, the U.S. Department of Agriculture also received $125 million for a surplus food commodities effort, the Temporary Emergency Food Assistance Program (TEFAP). Some $75 million was to be used to purchase surplus foods and $50 million to distribute commodities.

Department of Defense Authorization Act of 1984 (PL 98-94)

Military installations could be used as shelters under this legislation.

Additional FEMA Appropriations (PLs 98-151, 98-181, 98-396)

Several 1984 appropriations measures provided an extra $110 million for distribution by FEMA. Although PL 98-181 also provided $60 million for distribution by the U.S. Department of Housing and Urban Development (HUD) for emergency shelter, the money was not disbursed. HUD claimed that existing funds under the Community Development Block Grants program were being used for this purpose.

Domestic Volunteer Service Act Amendments of 1983 (PL 98-288)

Volunteers in Service to America (VISTA), the federal volunteer program, was authorized to provide its workers to homeless-related projects.

Additional FEMA Appropriations (PLs 99-98, 99-160)

FEMA was allocated $90 million for emergency food and shelter in two appropriations.

Health Professions Training and Assistance Act of 1985 (PL 99-129)

By the direction of the secretary of Health and Human Services (HHS), the National Academy of Sciences was to undertake an Institute of Medicine study of the delivery of health care services to homeless people. This study, released in late 1988 as *Homelessness, Health, and Human Need,* was controversial because 11 of the 13 experts who wrote the report issued a dissent from the final version.

Military Construction Authorization Act of 1986 (PL 99-167)

Using this law, military installations could make surplus bedding available to shelters for homeless people.

Food Security Act of 1985 (PL 99-198)

The TEFAP was reauthorized by this law, with $50 million authorized per year through fiscal year 1987. However, a cost-sharing requirement was also attached, making state-level distribution efforts liable for part of the expense of the program. The law also required state welfare offices to find ways to provide food stamps to people who did not have permanent addresses.

Anti-Drug Abuse Act of 1986 (PL 99-570)

The Homeless Eligibility Clarification Act was attached to this statute. This law removed barriers faced by homeless people trying to obtain food stamps and allowed them to use food stamps to purchase prepared meals from soup kitchens and shelters. The law also required other federal agencies administering such programs as AFDC, Medicaid, and SSI to examine eligibility barriers faced by homeless people seeking to use those programs. Further, it banned the denial of veterans' benefits in cases where the applicant lacked a mailing address.

The Social Security Administration (SSA) was required to make site visits to take applications at homeless facilities for SSI and food stamps. SSA and USDA were also required to take applications for their programs from persons about to be discharged from hospitals, prisons, and other institutions.

Finally, homeless people were made eligible for job training programs at the state and local level, if those programs were authorized by the Job Corps Partnership Act.

Additional FEMA Appropriations (PL 99-591)

FEMA received an additional $70 million for emergency food and shelter programs. HUD received $15 million for the Homeless Housing Act demonstration program.

Omnibus Health Care Act (PL 99-660)

The National Institute of Mental Health (NIMH) was authorized to make grants for demonstration projects for the homeless mentally ill.

Additional Appropriations (PL 100-6)

Almost simultaneously with the introduction of "Urgent Relief for the Homeless" (HR 558), which became the McKinney Act, Congress made available additional funds for the rapidly approaching winter. H.J.Res. 102 was a supplemental appropriations measure that put an additional $45 million into shelter spending and $5 million into services for homeless mentally ill veterans. This $50 million was reallocated from traditional disaster-relief funds to homeless programs.

Stewart B. McKinney Homeless Assistance Act (PL 100-77)

This chapter devotes proportionately more attention to the McKinney Act because it has been the major federal legislative involvement in the problem of homelessness. Originally the act was introduced as HR 558, "The Urgent Relief for the Homeless Act," and was subsequently named for the late congressman Stewart B. McKinney (R-CT), one of its chief proponents. Passed by overwhelming bipartisan majorities, the McKinney Act authorized just over $1 billion to be spent in 1987 and 1988. On 22 July 1987, President Reagan reluctantly signed the bill into law. According to the White House, the president put his signature on the McKinney Act in the evening in order to demonstrate his "lack of enthusiasm" for the measure (Robert Pear, "President Signs $1 Billion Bill in Homeless Aid," *New York Times*, 24 July 1987, A1).

The original McKinney Act contained several emergency provisions as well as a smattering of "preventive" and "transitional" programs (some were later superseded by "supportive housing" programs). McKinney preventive measures, for instance, help to stave off eviction or utility cutoffs, but actually they prevent an acute event within a chronic circumstance of poverty for many people. True preventive measures would ensure that housing was decent and permanently affordable, and that wages and/or benefits were sufficient to keep an individual or household from perpetually living on the edge.

Provisions of the McKinney Act in 1987

The 1987 programs included (1) health care; (2) community-based mental health services for homeless individuals who are chronically mentally ill; (3) emergency shelter; (4) transitional housing, especially for the elderly and homeless families with children; (5) community services to provide follow-up and long-term services; (6) job and literacy training; (7) permanent housing for handicapped homeless persons; and (8) grants for groups to renovate, convert, purchase, lease, or construct facilities. In response to concerns that the overall responsibility for homelessness programs was spread among several agencies, the Congress created the Interagency Council on the Homeless, an independent body to coordinate federal homeless assistance programs.

The McKinney Act authorized 17 homeless assistance programs for fiscal years 1987 and 1988. In addition, the act authorized the property disposition programs, the Interagency Council on the Homeless, and a requirement for state and local governments to prepare a comprehensive planning document.

Further, the McKinney legislation extended the Temporary Emergency Food Assistance Program (TEFAP) until 30 September 1988, and expanded the commodities available for distribution under this program. TEFAP provided surplus agricultural commodities such as cheese, flour, and cornmeal to nonprofit food banks, soup kitchens, and other emergency feeding organizations. The legislation also amended the Food Stamp Act of 1977, allowing federal funding for state outreach efforts to provide information to homeless persons about applying for food stamps.

Table 6-1 shows the programs of the McKinney Act and appropriations and budget requests for the fiscal years 1987–1995.

Table 6-1
Appropriations for Federal Homeless Programs,
Fiscal Years 1987–95 (in Millions of Dollars)

Department of Housing and Urban Development Programs

Program	FY87–93 total	FY94 budget	FY95 request
Emergency Shelter Grants	384.1	115.0	**
Supportive Housing Demonstration	811.8	334.0	**
SAFAH	47.9	*	*
Section 8 SRO	468.2	150.0	**
Shelter + Care	377.1	123.7	**
Safe Havens	—	—	—
Housing Opportunities for People with AIDS (HOPWA)	150.0	156.0	156.0
Family Unification Program	125.0	77.4	-0-
New Voucher Program	—	—	514.0
Homeless Assistance Grants (consolidated McKinney programs)	—	—	1,120.0

* Consolidated with Supportive Housing Program.

** Proposed for consolidation in FY95 in Homeless Assistance Grants (Emergency Shelter Grants; Supportive Housing Program, including Safe Havens and Rural Homelessness Program; Shelter + Care; Section 8 SRO; Homeless Innovation Program).

Department of Health and Human Services Programs

Program	FY87–93 total	FY94 budget	FY95 request
Alcohol & Drug Treatment Demonstration Project	84.0	*	*
Chronically Mentally Ill Demonstration/ACCESS	52.7**	21.4	47.0***
Health Care for the Homeless	275.6	63.01	63.01
Mental Health Services/PATH	178.2****	29.4	30.0
Emergency Community Services	182.5	19.8	-0-
Family Support Centers	13.4	7.4	7.4
AFDC Demonstration	20.0	—	—
Health Care/Children	3.0*****		
Community Services Block Grant	19.8	19.8	-0-
Runaway & Homeless Youth	35.1	63.0	69.0******

*Consolidated with ACCESS.

Table 6-1 *continued*

**No new projects after 1990.

***Consolidated with ACCESS and other programs.

****Consolidated with PATH in 1990.

*****Administered with Health Care for the Homeless.

******Consolidation of Runaway and Homeless Youth program, Transitional Living for Homeless Youth, and Drug Education and Prevention for Homeless Youth Program.

Independent Agencies

Program	FY87–93	FY94 budget	FY95 request
FEMA Emergency Food and Shelter Program	892.9	130.0	*
Interagency Council on the Homeless	6.3	-0-	-0-**

* Proposed to be moved to HUD in FY95.
** Defunded in FY94 and made part of the White House Domestic Policy Council; to be funded from HUD operations budget in FY95.

Department of Education Programs

Program	FY87–93	FY94 budget	FY95 request
Adult Education	58.0	9.58	9.6
Education of Homeless Children and Youth	75.9	25.47	30.0

Department of Labor Programs

Program	FY 87–93	FY94 budget	FY95 request
Job Training for the Homeless Demonstration	57.1*	12.5	5.1 **
Homeless Veterans Reintegration Project	7.8*	*	*

*Consolidated with Veterans Project in FY92; JTHD figure reflects both programs after FY92.

**FY95 request is for Veterans Project only.

Table 6-1 *continued*

Department of Veterans Affairs Programs

Program	FY87–93	FY94 budget	FY95 request
Health Care for Homeless Veterans	130.25	61.8	61.8
Domiciliary Care for Homeless Veterans	66.55*	*	*

*Consolidated with HCHV in FY92; consolidated appropriations reflected in HCHV figures.

McKinney Act Reauthorization, 1988 (PL 100-628)

During the second session of the 100th Congress, the McKinney Act was reauthorized for fiscal years 1989 and 1990. The reauthorization included funding authority for a total of 18 homeless assistance programs. This legislation added a demonstration project to evaluate the cost-effectiveness of transitional housing as opposed to the shelters commonly known as "welfare hotels." In addition, the reauthorization extended the property disposition programs and the Interagency Council on the Homeless, and kept the Department of Housing and Urban Development's (HUD) homeless assistance planning document requirement. The TEFAP and Food Stamp Outreach Program were removed from the act and reauthorized under the Hunger Prevention Act (PL 100-435).

The McKinney Act Amendments also authorized several existing McKinney Act programs to use funds for activities aimed at preventing homelessness. For the first time, persons at risk of becoming homeless could receive emergency funds under several programs to pay back-rent or utilities and other costs. Finally, the amendments significantly changed the Job Training Partnership Act and several housing laws that provide housing and community services to people with lower incomes.

Second McKinney Act Reauthorization, 1990 (PLs 101-625 and 101-645)

The 101st Congress enacted two laws that reauthorized parts of the McKinney Act: (1) title VIII of the National Affordable Housing Act of 1990 (PL 101-625, approved 28 November 1990) and

(2) the McKinney Homeless Assistance Amendments Act of 1990 (PL 101-645, approved 29 November 1990). Housing provisions were contained in both laws.

Since Public Law 101-625 was signed first, it became the statutory authority for HUD's McKinney Act programs. Title VIII of PL 101-625 requires HUD to study the feasibility of converting its McKinney Act programs into a block grant. The statutory authority for all the non-HUD McKinney Act programs is contained in PL 101-645. The amendments also placed confidentiality requirements on domestic-violence shelters and made major additions to the Child Abuse Prevention Act to provide preventive services to children of homeless families.*

Homeless Assistance Programs of the Department of Housing and Urban Development

This section provides information on the Comprehensive Housing Affordability Strategy (CHAS) and McKinney Act homeless assistance programs administered by HUD: Emergency Shelter Grant (ESG), Supportive Housing Demonstration Program (SHDP), Supplemental Assistance for Facilities To Assist the Homeless (SAFAH), Section 8 Moderate Rehabilitation Program for Single-Room Occupancy (SRO) Dwellings for Homeless Individuals, and the Shelter Plus Care Program. HUD's Office of Special Needs Assistance Programs (SNAPS) manages all of these programs. General information is also provided on the Housing Opportunities for Persons with AIDS (HOPWA), a non–McKinney Act program begun in fiscal year 1992.

Comprehensive Housing Affordability Strategy (CHAS)

Title I of the National Affordable Housing Act of 1990 requires that state and local governments have an approved CHAS in order to apply for certain HUD programs, including all of the McKinney Act programs. The CHAS was designed to be used by states and local governments to identify affordable housing and supportive housing needs, including those of homeless persons and others with special or supportive service needs, and the resources and programs that can be

---

*Information on the reauthorized McKinney Act programs and related homelessness assistance is taken from *Homelessness: McKinney Act Programs and Funding through Fiscal Year 1991* (Washington, DC: U.S. General Accounting Office, 1992).

used to address these needs. HUD's 1994 legislative proposals would make the CHAS part of a new consolidated planning document.

The Emergency Shelter Grant Program (ESG)

ESG allocates funds to help improve the quality of emergency shelters, makes available additional emergency shelters, and meets the costs of operating emergency shelters and providing essential social services to homeless individuals, including activities to prevent homelessness. Projects funded under this program may be used to (1) renovate, rehabilitate, or convert buildings into emergency shelters and (2) pay for shelter maintenance, certain operating expenses, insurance, utilities, and furnishings. Up to 30 percent of ESG's funds may be used to provide essential social services including employment assistance, health care, and drug-abuse treatment or education.

The Supportive Housing Demonstration Program (SHDP)

SHDP makes funds available to state and local governments and non-profit organizations for projects providing housing and supportive services to homeless persons, including those with special needs, such as individuals with disabilities. The program has two separate components: (1) transitional housing to facilitate the movement of homeless individuals to independent living and (2) permanent housing for handicapped homeless persons. The program serves homeless individuals, including those who are handicapped, deinstitutionalized, and/or have mental disabilities; homeless families with children; and homeless families in which one parent or guardian is mentally ill.

Transitional Housing Demonstration Program

The Transitional Housing Demonstration Program (THDP) is designed to develop innovative approaches to help homeless persons make the transition into independent living by providing them with housing and supportive services. The McKinney Act requires THDP to target specific categories of homeless people—families with children, the deinstitutionalized, the mentally disabled. Residents of transitional housing are typically expected to be able to find permanent housing within 24 months. The support services provided range from employment assistance, job training, and job placement to mental health care, child care, and case management. In addition, some projects provide transportation to and from work sites.

The program provides assistance for acquisition, rehabilitation, and new construction; operating and supportive-services costs, including those for employment assistance and child care services; and technical assistance in establishing and operating transitional housing and providing supportive services to the residents.

Permanent Housing Program for Handicapped Homeless Persons

The Permanent Housing Program for Handicapped Homeless Persons, which provides the same types of assistance as THDP, funds projects that provide community-based, long-term housing and supportive services for handicapped homeless persons. The program serves mentally and physically disabled individuals, deinstitutionalized individuals, and families in which at least one parent or guardian is handicapped.

Housing projects may include such models as group homes designed solely for housing handicapped homeless persons or rental units in a multifamily housing, condominium, or cooperative project. These housing projects are required to be integrated into their neighborhoods, and generally may not serve more than eight persons.

SHDP Program Changes

HUD proposed several significant changes to the SHDP in 1992. The changes allowed housing and services to be provided in various ways: at the provider's facility, at the client's own residence, and at the provider's facility, followed by services at the client's own housing. Further, for the first time, eligibility was defined for the program; according to the new definition, homeless persons are those sleeping in shelters, or places not meant for human habitation such as cars, parks, sidewalks, and abandoned buildings. Persons are also considered to be homeless if they are about to be evicted from private dwelling units or if they have a disability and are being discharged from institutions, have no subsequent residence identified, and lack the resources and support networks needed to obtain access to housing.

Supplemental Assistance for Facilities To Assist the Homeless (SAFAH)

SAFAH, which was merged with Supportive Housing in fiscal year 1993, was designed to provide two types of homeless assistance: (1) comprehensive assistance for particularly innovative programs meeting the immediate and long-term needs of homeless individuals and families and (2) additional assistance to ESG- or SHDP-funded projects. Comprehensive assistance funds can be used to purchase, lease, renovate, or convert facilities as well as to provide support services. These services include food, child care, assistance in obtaining permanent housing, outpatient health services, employment counseling, nutritional counseling, security arrangements necessary for the protection of residents, and other services deemed essential for maintaining independent living.

Section 8 Moderate Rehabilitation Program for Single-Room Occupancy (SRO) Dwellings for Homeless Individuals

The SRO program is designed to provide funds for moderate rehabilitation through rental assistance for homeless persons to owners of SRO housing. An SRO is a one-room unit, either an efficiency apartment or with shared bath and kitchen, in a multiunit structure occupied by a single, eligible individual capable of independent living. Under the McKinney Act, homeless individuals have the highest priority for occupancy in SRO units, although other individuals are eligible as well. Under this program, a building owner who rehabilitates a substandard property for SRO units receives 10 years of guaranteed Section 8 rental assistance for the tenants. PHAs must also engage in an active outreach effort in order to make known the availability of the program to homeless persons and ensure that needed supportive services are provided.

Shelter Plus Care Program

The National Affordable Housing Act of 1990 authorized $123.2 million in fiscal year 1991 for the Shelter Plus Care Program. The program has three major components: (1) Section 8 tenant-based rental assistance, (2) moderate rehabilitation of SROs, and (3) Section 202 elderly and handicapped housing sponsor-based rental assistance (SRA). Although Congress did not fund the program in fiscal year 1991, it funded the SRO and SRA components for fiscal year 1992.

The program is designed to link supportive services to rental assistance for homeless persons with disabilities—primarily those who are seriously mentally ill, have chronic drug and/or alcohol problems, or have Acquired Immune Deficiency Syndrome (AIDS). To the maximum extent practicable, at least 50 percent of the funding must be reserved for the seriously mentally ill, persons with chronic drug or alcohol problems, and their families.

Congress authorized $258.6 million for the program, but in fiscal year 1992 funded only the SRO and SRA portions, which totaled $110.5 million. The first awards were announced on 10 June 1992. These grants totaled about $77 million and included 30 communities involved with 34 projects.

Housing Opportunities for Persons with AIDS (HOPWA)

The National Affordable Housing Act of 1990 authorized one new program administered by HUD as a non–McKinney Act program. Section 854(c) of the act provides that 90 percent of the funds be allocated by a specified formula and that the remaining amount be awarded on a competitive basis. The program will provide states and localities with the resources and incentives to devise long-term comprehensive strategies for meeting the housing needs of homeless and low-income persons with HIV/AIDS.

Eligible activities include (1) housing information services encompassing, but not limited to, counseling, information, and referral services to assist eligible individuals to locate, acquire, finance, and maintain housing; (2) resource identification to establish, coordinate, and develop housing assistance; (3) the acquisition, rehabilitation, conversion, lease, and repair of facilities to provide housing and services, (4) new construction (for SRO dwellings and community residences only); (5) project- or tenant-based rental assistance; (6) short-term rent, mortgage, and utility payments to prevent the homelessness of the tenant or mortgagor of a dwelling; (7) supportive services including, but not limited to, health, mental health, assessment, permanent housing placement, drug- and alcohol-abuse treatment and counseling, day care, nutritional services, intensive care when required, and assistance in gaining access to local, state, and federal government benefits and services; (8) operating costs for housing, including maintenance, security, operation, insurance, utilities, furnishings, equipment, supplies, staff training and recruitment, and other incidental costs; (9) technical assistance in establishing and operating a community residence, including planning and other predevelopment or preconstruction expenses; (10) for community residences only, administrative expenses including, but not limited to, costs relating to community outreach and education activities regarding AIDS and related diseases; and (11) any other activity proposed by the applicant and approved by HUD. In fiscal year 1992, $4.7 million was awarded on a competitive basis for: (1) special projects of national significance and (2) projects submitted by states that did not otherwise qualify.

Homeless Assistance Program of the Federal Emergency Management Agency (FEMA)

This section describes FEMA's homeless assistance program—the Emergency Food and Shelter Program (EFS); in 1994, this program is proposed to become a HUD program.

Emergency Food and Shelter Programs (EFS)

EFS is designed to get funds quickly into the hands of food and shelter providers to alleviate the most pressing needs of homeless persons. The program is not intended to address long-standing issues of poverty but rather to supplement the current pool of resources available to provide emergency food and shelter assistance. The program funds the purchase of food, consumable supplies essential to the operation of shelters and mass-feeding facilities, per diem sheltering costs, small equipment, the limited leasing of capital equipment, utility and rent/mortgage assistance for people on the verge of becoming homeless, first month's rent to help families and individuals move out of shelters or other precarious circumstances and into a stable environment, emergency lodging, and minor rehabilitation of shelter facilities.

Providers receiving EFS funds vary in size and types of services. The smaller scale providers (those with average annual operating budgets of between $4,600 and $26,000) mostly supply emergency food assistance such as groceries, food vouchers, or prepared meals, but in several cases they also assist with rent, mortgage, and utilities, and some provide on-site shelter. Medium-to-large-scale providers (those with average annual operating budgets of between $91,000 and $1.5 million) more routinely supply shelter, rent or mortgage, and utility assistance in addition to food assistance.

How Funds Are Distributed

The EFS National Board, which FEMA chairs, determines the local jurisdictions (and territories) eligible to receive funding through a formula that takes into consideration the most current 12-month national unemployment rate, the total number of unemployed persons within the area, the total number of individuals below the poverty level, and the total population.

The national board consists of representatives from six national charitable organizations: the American Red Cross; Catholic Charities, USA; Council of Jewish Federations, Inc.; National Council of Churches of Christ in the U.S.A.; Salvation Army; and United Way of America, which serves as the national board's secretariat and fiscal agent.

However, before eligible communities are actually awarded money, they must convene a Local EFS Program Board. The local board advertises the availability of funds, determines the programs and local providers that will receive the funds, promotes cooperation between agencies, monitors performance, and reports back to the national board on the identity of the recipients and their planned use of the money. Representatives on the local board are, for the most part, affiliates of the voluntary organizations represented on the national board. Local boards are also encouraged to expand participation by inviting or notifying other private nonprofit organizations to serve on the board. In addition to funds going directly to eligible local jurisdictions, some funds are reserved for state set-aside committees.

For fiscal year 1991, the national board allocated $134 million to over 10,000 local providers in 2,500 jurisdictions. FEMA estimated that about 61 percent of this money was allocated for emergency shelters and food assistance; about 37 percent paid for homelessness prevention services such as emergency rent, mortgage, and utility payments; and the remaining 2 percent covered administrative costs.

Homeless Assistance Programs of the Department of Health and Human Services

This section describes the Department of Health and Human Services' (HHS) homeless assistance programs.

Research Demonstration Projects for Alcohol and Drug Abuse Treatment of Homeless Persons

This research demonstration program is administered by the National Institute on Alcohol Abuse and Alcoholism (NIAAA) in consultation with the National Institute on Drug Abuse (NIDA). The purpose of the program is to implement, document, and evaluate successful and replicable approaches to community-based treatment and rehabilitation services for homeless individuals who abuse alcohol and drugs.

Projects funded in this program focus on three primary objectives: (1) a reduction of the consumption of alcohol and drugs, (2) an increase in the levels of shelter and residential stability, and (3) the enhancement of the economic and/or employment status of the target population. Applicants applying for funds under this program are strongly encouraged by NIAAA to give extra attention to minorities and other homeless subpopulations such as women with children and adolescents. The program consists of two rounds of research demonstration grants: the Community Demonstration Grant Projects for Alcohol and Drug Abuse Treatment of Homeless Individuals, and cooperative agreement grant projects. Many of the projects are testing a variety of types of alcohol- and drug-free housing. Funds were awarded by NIAAA through a process that began with a review of applications by a panel of nongovernment experts in the fields of alcohol and drug research and homelessness research.

Community Mental Health Services Demonstration Projects for Homeless Individuals Who Are Chronically Mentally Ill

Individuals Who Are Chronically Mentally Ill is a competitive grant program that supports the development of comprehensive service systems for homeless mentally ill adults. The demonstration projects are administered by the National Institute of Mental Health (NIMH). The goals of these projects are to respond comprehensively to the needs of the homeless mentally ill by demonstrating a coordinated system of mental health outreach, case management, treatment rehabilitation, and a range of housing alternatives and other supportive services; stimulating cooperation and formal linkages among health, mental health, housing, education, rehabilitation, and social welfare agencies in addressing the multiple needs of homeless mentally ill persons; and documenting and evaluating successful and replicable approaches to the provision of coordinated housing, treatment, and supportive services for homeless mentally ill persons.

One of the prime design features of this research demonstration program is to promote and improve the coordination of mental health treatment, housing, and other support services. In January 1990, a memorandum of understanding was signed between the secretary of HUD and the secretary of HHS, in part to encourage better coordination of housing and services for homeless mentally ill individuals. Applications were submitted by public and private nonprofit organizations, including universities and units of state or local governments.

Project Funding

Applications for the three-year grants are reviewed by a panel composed primarily of nonfederal scientific experts. Since 1 October 1992, these projects have been administered by the Center for Mental Health Services. Since 1990, NIMH has not made any new awards for research demonstration grants under this program; current fiscal year funding is allocated for the continuation of these projects.

Projects for Assistance in Transition from Homelessness (PATH)

The McKinney Homeless Assistance Amendments Act of 1990 somewhat restructured and redesignated the Community Mental Health Services for the Homeless Block Grant Program; the program's new name is Projects for Assistance in Transition from Homelessness. PATH is still administered by the Alcohol, Drug Abuse, and Mental Health Administration (ADAMHA). On 1 October 1992, ADAMHA became the Substance Abuse and Mental Health Services Administration.

Up to 20 percent of the funds can be used for housing-related expenses, and up to 4 percent can be used for administrative costs. Services that qualify for the grants are basically the same as those under the block grant program and include outreach; community mental health services such as crisis intervention; referrals for hospital, primary health care, and substance abuse; case management; supportive and supervisory services in specific residential settings; and training for outreach workers and other individuals who provide these services to homeless people. Under this new program, a limited set of housing services can be funded, and substance-abuse treatment is an eligible activity. Although states must offer all these services, a program does not have to make all services available at each site.

ADAMHA awards grants to the states according to a statutory formula based on the state's urban population relative to the urban population of the United States. The McKinney Act requires that each state receive no less than $300,000. Funding is not automatic.

The Emergency Community Services Homeless Grant Program (EHP)

EHP, which is operated by the Office of Community Services, provides grants to states and territories using the Community Services Block Grant (CSBG) allocation formula. State agencies distribute the funds to eligible entities, such as community action agencies, to provide critically urgent assistance to the homeless.

The McKinney Act states that EHP funds may be used only to (1) expand comprehensive services for homeless individuals by providing follow-up and long-term services to help them make the transition out of poverty; (2) provide assistance in obtaining social and maintenance services and income-support services for homeless individuals; (3) promote private-sector and other assistance to homeless individuals; and (4) provide assistance under certain conditions to an individual who has received a notice of foreclosure, eviction, or termination of utility services in order to prevent him or her from becoming homeless.

The Homeless Families Support Services Demonstration Program

The McKinney Homeless Assistance Act Amendments of 1990 created a new demonstration program to provide physical, educational, and social support services to homeless families. Congress authorized $50 million for the demonstration program, but no funds were appropriated specifically for the program in fiscal year 1991. In HHS's fiscal year 1992 appropriations funding, Congress authorized a demonstration program to be modeled after the family support centers, including the Gateway Program, described in title VII of the McKinney Homeless Assistance Act. The agency calls the program the Homeless Families Support Services Demonstration Program.

The program makes grants to state and local agencies and other organizations that develop and implement comprehensive, integrated systems of support services for homeless and at-risk families. For the community, the program should tie together support-service providers, organize a means to reduce duplication of these efforts, create a centralized locus for clients' access to mainstream service providers, and reduce the administrative and programmatic burden eventually placed upon the client.

For homeless people, the program seeks to prevent further homelessness; enhance the living conditions in low-income housing; improve the physical, social, and educational development of low-income families and children at risk; increase the potential for independence and self-sufficiency; and increase literacy levels and basic employment skills.

Health Care for the Homeless Program

This program, administered by the Bureau of Primary Health in the Health Resources and Services Administration (HRSA) of the Public Health Service, makes grants available to provide for the delivery of health services to homeless individuals. Eligible grantees are local private, nonprofit, public health organizations and organizations that provide services without charge or reimbursement from Medicaid or other insurance for primary health care, substance abuse, and mental health services for the homeless. Projects are generally administered by local public health departments, community and migrant health centers, inner-city hospitals, and local community coalitions.

The program was modeled after a national demonstration program to provide health care for the homeless funded by the Robert Wood Johnson/PEW Foundation. The RWJ/PEW Foundation program funded demonstration projects in 19 large cities in 1985 to show that homeless persons needed and would accept primary health care services if they were delivered in a dignified manner in outreach settings where homeless persons are located.

The services provided by these projects include aggressive outreach efforts to bring health care services to the homeless, as well as interdisciplinary, comprehensive health service projects. An interdisciplinary approach brings together primary health, mental

health, substance abuse, and social services, which are generally
operated by independent agencies in local communities with limited
coordination, and builds a more coordinated network. The secretary
of HHS is required to conduct a comprehensive evaluation of the
Health Care for the Homeless Program to identify successful,
replicable service-delivery models and underserved areas.

Project Funding

Grants are awarded under this program on a competitive basis;
applications are reviewed by an independent expert panel. In
addition, recipients have to explain how their project would

- provide health services at locations accessible to homeless
  persons

- provide round-the-clock access to emergency health services

- refer homeless persons for necessary hospital services

- refer homeless persons for needed mental health services
  unless the services are directly provided

- provide outreach services to inform homeless individuals of the
  availability of health services

- aid homeless individuals in establishing eligibility for assistance
  and obtaining services under entitlement programs.

Health Care for the Homeless Children Demonstration Program

The McKinney Homeless Assistance Amendments Act of 1990
authorized $5 million for a demonstration program to provide
primary health care services for homeless children and those at risk
of becoming homeless, but Congress did not fund this program for
fiscal year 1991. Services are to be available in both urban and rural
settings, and may be provided through mobile medical units. In
addition to health care, grantees will provide referrals to other health,
educational, and social services, including child-abuse prevention and
treatment. Outreach to children and their parents is another facet of
the demonstration program.

Grants are awarded under this program on a competitive basis,
with applications reviewed by an expert panel. Review panels
consisting of HRSA management and outside experts vote and
recommend funding levels on the basis of the project's adherence to
mandated requirements, such as the (1) provision of all legislatively
required services, (2) adoption of the goals and objectives of the

program, (3) establishment of collaborative arrangements and linkages with service providers, and (4) justification for the proposed funding level. In fiscal year 1992, $5 million was authorized and $3 million appropriated, to be administered in conjunction with the Health Care for the Homeless Program.

Homeless Assistance Programs of the Department of Veterans Affairs (VA)

Health Care for Homeless Veterans Program

VA redefined its specialized mental health programs for homeless veterans and titled these programs the Health Care for Homeless Veterans (HCHV) Program to (1) reflect the broader nature of services being provided to homeless mentally ill veterans and (2) eliminate the stigma associated with seeking services from a program labeled for homeless veterans with mental illness.

The HCHV Program, initially authorized by PL 100-6, was designed to meet the specific needs of homeless veterans with chronic mental health problems. The program continues on a pilot basis, and its authority has been extended through a series of public laws. Current authority for the program is provided by PL 101-237. With a funding authorization from the McKinney Homeless Assistance Amendments Act of 1988 (PL 100-628), VA has provided funds to 45 VA medical care facilities in 26 states (and the District of Columbia) to establish and maintain these programs for homeless, chronically mentally ill veterans.

These programs provide outreach staff and case managers who work closely with community coalitions to locate homeless, chronically mentally ill veterans on the streets, in soup kitchens, and in temporary shelters, and to identify others eligible for care. Once located, veterans are brought to a Veterans Administration Medical Center (VAMC), where they receive direct clinical care that can include medical and psychiatric assessment and treatment, substance-abuse treatment, job counseling, and crisis intervention. Following assessment, some veterans are placed in community-based residential treatment programs such as halfway houses or psychiatric residential centers for psychiatric care, alcohol- and drug-abuse treatment, and rehabilitation. The VA case managers monitor and supervise care provided to these veterans in the various residential treatment programs. In the Compensated Work Therapy component of the program, contracts with private industry provide therapeutic work for patients in a supportive and supervised employment program, which allows them to regain work skills and habits. While working in the CWT component of the program, patients live in supervised long-term transitional housing.

In fiscal year 1991, VA and the Social Security Administration (SSA) began a pilot initiative to reach out to homeless veterans and expedite the application process for Social Security benefits.

Project Funding

VAMCs are the only eligible recipients of HCHV funds. VA originally funded 43 VAMCs in fiscal year 1987. Fiscal year 1990 funds were used to continue operations at the 43 VAMCs and to start the HCHV pilot projects at 2 other VAMCs. Fiscal year 1991 funds were used to continue operations at the 45 VAMCs and to start VA/SSA pilot projects at 3 of the 45 HCHV sites.

When assessing the proposals, particular consideration was given to (1) the number of homeless veterans to be served by the project, (2) the degree of interest expressed by the medical center leadership and the participating community coalition, (3) the creative innovations that would enhance the value and effectiveness of the project, (4) the extent to which integration with other programs would improve the project's quality, and (5) the development of statistical data and a tracking system for monitoring purposes.

Domiciliary Care for Homeless Veterans (DCHV) Program

The DCHV Program was established as a specialized treatment component within the existing Domiciliary Care Program administered by the VA. The DCHV Program is a clinical care program that provides less intensive care than a hospital or nursing home, but a higher level than community residential care settings. The program's purpose is to use VA medical facilities to provide primary health, mental health, and social services to homeless veterans or veterans at serious risk of becoming homeless. According to the VA, the veterans admitted into the program are generally socially isolated, unemployed, impoverished, and troubled by a broad spectrum of medical and psychiatric problems, with substance abuse being most prominent among them. The program's ultimate goal is to help homeless veterans suffering from medical or psychiatric disabilities to function at their highest level of independence in the community.

The VA has established domiciliary care programs for homeless veterans at 27 sites located in 21 different states. Since November 1987, the VA has converted beds for domiciliary care in 14 VA facilities in urban areas with significant numbers of homeless veterans. In addition, the VA also established specialized homeless veterans treatment programs at 13 existing VA domiciliaries. As of January

1992, 1,145 of these domiciliary care beds had been identified as being devoted to homeless veterans.

Existing domiciliaries provide two distinct types of care. Active biopsychosocial rehabilitation targets the physical, mental health, and social impairments that inhibit the patient from reaching an optimal level of functional independence and health. Long-term health maintenance care prevents or delays degradations in health that would, if unchecked, be expected to result from the progression of chronic disease. Small (40- to 100-bed) domiciliaries focus their resources and efforts primarily on providing active biopsychosocial rehabilitation services. Patients found to require long-term health maintenance care would ordinarily be referred to the larger (100-or-more-bed) domiciliaries or to clinically appropriate alternative sources of care.

Services include medical and psychiatric assessments, psychotherapy, substance-abuse treatment, skills training, and rehabilitation services. Assistance is also available in finding housing and employment and providing ongoing support once veterans leave the domiciliaries.

Project Funding

The DCHV Program provided funds to 20 VAMCs during the first year of the program in fiscal year 1987 and maintained these 20 centers during fiscal years 1988 and 1989. Fiscal year 1990 funds were used to renew funding to the 20 VAMCs and to establish 6 additional centers. In fiscal year 1991, 1 additional site became operational.

To participate in the DCHV Program, VAMCs are required to submit applications that describe:

- how the program would be integrated with and operate in support of existing VAMC services and treatment programs

- existing medical center programs/activities related to providing care to homeless veterans

- existing underutilized space that could be redesignated to domiciliary use, and specifically discuss renovations that may be necessary to support domiciliary-care program operating requirements

- staffing enhancements that would be required to supplement staff currently assigned to areas proposed for redesignation

- actions that would facilitate the activation of domiciliary care beds within 90 to 120 days.

Homeless Assistance Programs of the Department of Education

This section describes the Department of Education's homeless assistance programs. These are the Adult Education for the Homeless Program and Education for Homeless Children and Youth Program, the latter of which contains the Local Educational Agency (LEA) Grants for the Education of Homeless Children and Youth Program, which was authorized to start in fiscal year 1991.

Adult Education for the Homeless Program

The Adult Education for the Homeless Program, a grant program for statewide literacy initiatives created by the McKinney Act, provides funds to state education agencies, enabling them to develop a plan and implement literacy training and basic skills remediation programs for homeless adults. Programs are (1) tailored to the literacy and basic skills needs of the specific homeless population being served by each state and (2) directed toward building cooperative relationships with other service agencies to provide an integrated package of support services. To accomplish this, programs are to include outreach activities, especially interpersonal contacts at locations where homeless persons are known to gather, and outreach efforts through cooperative relations with local agencies that provide services to the homeless such as community-based organizations, the Adult Basic Education Program, and nonprofit literacy-action organizations.

Project Funding

This program is conducted under the Adult Education Act, which provides for discretionary grants to state educational agencies in the 50 states, the District of Columbia, the Commonwealth of Puerto Rico, and U.S. territories. A panel of federal and outside experts reviews applications and recommends the approval of grants to the Department of Education on the basis of the degree to which the applicants meet six specific selection criteria. The criteria are (1) program factors, such as meeting the literacy and basic skills needs of the homeless, establishing a cooperative relationship with other service agencies, and providing outreach services; (2) the extent of need for the project, including an estimate of the homeless population expected to be served; (3) a plan of operation, to include written measurable goals and objectives; (4) the quality of key personnel; (5) budget and cost-effectiveness; and (6) an evaluation plan to determine the program's success. In addition, the department may also consider whether funding a particular applicant would improve the geographical distribution of the projects.

Education for Homeless Children and Youth Program

The Education for Homeless Children and Youth Program provides formula grants to state educational agencies (SEAs) and territories to enable them to prepare and carry out a state plan providing for the education of homeless children and youth; establish an Office of Coordinator of Education for Homeless Children and Youth; and carry out policies that will ensure a free and appropriate public education for homeless children. Initially, this program did not provide direct services for homeless school-age children; instead, the funds were used to establish a coordinator's office and support state efforts in reviewing and revising policies that would otherwise keep homeless children from attending public schools.

The McKinney Homeless Assistance Amendments Act of 1990 authorized additional activities for these grants. Newly authorized items include the funding of activities and services that (1) help homeless children and youth enroll, attend, and achieve success in school and (2) train school personnel to handle specific problems related to homeless children's education.

The state coordinator is required to gather data every two years on the number and location of homeless children and youth throughout the state, and on the progress made by SEAs and LEAs in addressing the problems and difficulties of providing homeless children with access to schools. The McKinney Act Amendments also give the state coordinator responsibility for coordinating with other entities (shelters, transitional housing, domestic-violence counselors, etc.) providing services to homeless children and youth, with the aim of making the services comprehensive. State plan requirements were also revised to address some new items, including before-and-after-school care for homeless children, food programs, and barriers to enrollment or retention of homeless children.

States receive funding on the basis of the basic grant formula under the Chapter 1 Program of the Elementary and Secondary Education Act of 1965, as amended by Public Law 100-197. To receive funding, states must submit to the Department of Education an application that includes assurances that states will use the funds in accordance with the requirements of the act and all applicable regulations.

Homeless Assistance Programs of the Department of Labor

This section describes the Department of Labor's homeless assistance programs. These programs are the Homeless Veterans Reintegration Project (HVRP) and the Job Training for the Homeless Demonstration Program (JTHDP).

Homeless Veterans Reintegration Project (HVRP)

HVRP is designed to expedite the reintegration of homeless veterans into the labor force; the program was consolidated with the Job Training for the Homeless Program in fiscal year 1993. The purposes of the program are to (1) contact and open communication channels with homeless veterans, (2) help homeless veterans take advantage of the other social service benefits for which they are eligible, and (3) assist homeless veterans in reentering the job market.

This program grew out of a one-year demonstration pilot program called Jobs for Homeless Veterans, funded under the Job Training Partnership Act. The pilot program demonstrated that using outreach workers to interact with homeless veterans and the bureaucracy that could provide them with needed services was an effective method of serving this population. In fiscal year 1991, the Department of Labor, through its Office of the Assistant Secretary for Veterans' Employment and Training, provided grants to 17 projects in 14 states demonstrating innovative methods of employing and assisting homeless veterans in this way. The major focus of the current projects is to provide employment and training services such as job counseling, résumé preparation, job search assistance, remedial and vocational education, on-the-job training, and job placement. In addition, supportive services deemed necessary to assist a veteran to enter the work force and to regain self-sufficiency may be provided directly by the project or by referral to other resources. Such assistance may be for transportation, clothes, or tools needed for employment, or alcohol- and drug-treatment referrals and psychiatric counseling. The projects also assess permanent and temporary housing through a variety of resources to assist the veteran returning to work in need of transitional housing.

The Department of Labor awards grants to states, counties, and municipalities, although grantees may use other public agencies or private nonprofit organizations to carry out the demonstration projects.

Job Training for the Homeless Demonstration Program (JTHDP)

JTHDP, administered by the Labor Department's Employment and Training Administration (ETA), grants funds for job-training demonstration projects that serve homeless individuals and families. These projects can provide remedial education activities; job counseling, search services, and training; basic skills instruction; supportive services; outreach; and coordination with related community programs. The purpose of this demonstration program is to provide information and direction for the future of job training programs for homeless Americans. One goal is to collect information on the most effective ways to provide employment and training services to homeless persons. Another goal is to learn how states, local public agencies, businesses, and private nonprofit organizations can develop effective systems of coordination to address the causes of homelessness and meet the needs of homeless persons. To measure the progress toward these goals, each grantee must conduct individual project evaluations and participate in a national evaluation conducted by the Department of Labor.

Of the projects supported by the program, most providers offer a variety of services, focusing on job employment skills (e.g., vocational training) as well as job services (e.g., counseling and job search techniques) to help homeless persons. In addition, basic skills courses such as remedial math and reading are provided by many programs. Typically, projects incorporate a support-services component into their programs, either by providing some services or by referring the homeless to other programs with whom they coordinate; some provide housing to their participants. While many programs serve all homeless individuals who apply, several target their programs to certain subgroups, such as families, the mentally ill, and youths.

Project Funding

The project was proposed for defunding in the fiscal year 1995 budget. Previous program grants were awarded by a competitive process to eligible grant recipients, which include state and local public agencies, private nonprofit organizations, private industry councils, private businesses, and American Indian tribes. Applicants' proposals are evaluated according to (1) the need for the project (the problems of the homeless in the applicant's state/locality to which the project will address itself), (2) the project's methodology (the project's plan for conducting outreach and coordination, as well as a timetable for such activities), (3) the evaluation's methodology (indicators to measure the success of the project), (4) expected outcomes (the project's accomplishments in concrete and measurable terms), (5) the level of effort (resources needed to conduct the project), and (6) organizational capability (the organizational structure of the entity responsible for the project). Because of the multiple problems and needs of many homeless individuals, ETA gives special consideration to proposals specializing in adult job training that provide a continuity of service to individuals from application through the end of the retention-in-employment period. In addition, proposals are to provide matching funds from nonfederal sources for 10 to 50 percent of the cost of the project. Matching funds may be in cash or in-kind contributions. Though the funds are distributed on a competitive basis, no single state may receive more than 15 percent of the appropriated amount for a fiscal year.

Because of the knowledge-building and demonstrative nature of the program, fiscal year 1991 funding was restricted to the 44 grantees who were operating JTHDP projects at the time of the solicitation. The fiscal year 1991 JTHDP reflected an increased emphasis on improving job retention and the attainment of permanent housing for the homeless. The fiscal year 1992 program continued the stronger focus initiated in fiscal year 1991 on closer coordination between the Labor Department and HUD in using various HUD housing subsidy programs to better provide permanent job and housing opportunities for homeless people.

New Administration Brings New Policy Directions

After taking office in the Clinton Administration in 1993, HUD Secretary Henry Cisneros repeatedly stated that homelessness would be the top priority of his agency. With all federal agencies mandated to "reinvent" themselves for increased administrative and program efficiency and effectiveness, Cisneros said that he believed that no other group has more claim on the resources of HUD than the nation's homeless people. A few weeks later came the highly publicized death of Yetta Adams, a chronically ill homeless woman who succumbed to diabetes while sleeping in a bus shelter across from HUD headquarters. While Secretary Cisneros had already sought and received from Congress the authorization to undertake new homeless programs, Yetta Adams's death hastened his agenda. Cisneros moved to distribute some funds rapidly in order to have quicker results from what he believes are new and more effective approaches to solving homelessness. These approaches and their new and proposed legislative measures are described below. These new programs are distinct from the McKinney Act programs, which are discussed in the final section of this chapter.

HUD Demonstration Act of 1993 (PL 103-120)

In late 1993 the 103d Congress passed legislation that established the "Innovative Homeless Initiatives Demonstration Program." This authorizing legislation created the framework for two new HUD homeless programs: the "Comprehensive Homeless Initiative" (community partnerships to undertake comprehensive strategies against homelessness) and "Innovative Projects." For fiscal year 1994, the legislation authorized $200 million, and $100 million was subsequently appropriated (HUD Appropriations Act of 1994, PL 103-124). The Clinton Administration's general housing reauthorization bill (HR 3838) for fiscal year 1995 and fiscal year 1996 was introduced in February 1994 and seeks $206 million for fiscal year 1995 and $212 million for fiscal year 1996 for these programs. Of the amount, $75 million will support the demonstration projects, including $20 million to be spent in Washington, D.C., and another $20 million in Los Angeles, the second initiative site. The other $25 million was distributed almost immediately for other new projects.

The Continuum of Care Concept

The foundation of HUD's new homeless programs is the concept of the "continuum of care," an idea brought to HUD by Assistant Secretary for Community Planning and Development Andrew Cuomo. Assistant Secretary Cuomo came to his job with a background as a nonprofit transitional housing and service provider to homeless families in New York City, and a record as chair of the New York City Commission on the Homeless (the "Cuomo Commission"), which also proposed this idea. The continuum relies on a three-part model: (1) outreach and assessment, (2) transitional housing combined with rehabilitative services, and (3) placement into permanent housing. The shift in emphasis reflects a rejection of emergency shelter as a solution to homelessness on the grounds that it does not provide the services and resources necessary for resolving homelessness. It also rejects the idea that homeless people who refuse shelter—because they perceive it to be dangerous, unsafe, unhealthy, coercive, or inappropriate—can then choose to live in public spaces as an alternative.

The philosophy of the continuum asserts that, once necessary services and resources are being offered, there is a subsequent obligation for homeless people to maximize their use of the system. Calling this "a new social contract" that requires the government to provide needed resources, the D.C. initiative planning document states: "This approach necessitates that homeless families and single individuals do all they can to help themselves live independently where they are able."[1]

Comprehensive Homeless Initiative

The first of the homeless initiative projects was designated for Washington, D.C., which Secretary Cisneros selected in June 1993 for its national significance and its serious homelessness problem. Los Angeles was chosen next, and future sites will be chosen based on the size of their homelessness problem; the extent to which existing public and private efforts (including homelessness prevention, outreach, assessment, shelter services, transitional services, and transitional and permanent housing) would benefit from additional funds for comprehensive programs; the demonstrated willingness and capacity of local jurisdictions and providers to establish a partnership; local government commitment to policy and procedural change that would provide necessary and flexible resources to sustain the initiative; and geographic diversity.

Participants in local demonstration sites must develop a comprehensive strategic plan in order to carry out the program and include a strategy for implementation and delivery, evidence of the cooperative partnership that will support the plan, details of the projects and activities to be funded, a cost estimate for implementation, and estimates of financial contributions from the partners. In mid-September 1993, Secretary Cisneros and D.C. officials and homeless service providers unveiled the D.C. planning document.

Innovative Projects

The second part of the new HUD program is its "Innovative Projects" effort, a competitive grant program for "continuum of care" activities. The $25 million funding will go to fill gaps in existing local service systems. The announcement that was quickly issued in December 1993 stated that monies "will not be used to fund activities isolated from a systematic approach."[2] Funding decisions started almost immediately, with rapid turnaround of money going to applicants on a first-come, first-served basis, and generally to applicants seeking amounts of $250,000 to $1 million. Both local government jurisdictions and nonprofit organizations were eligible for funds, although HUD had clearly expressed a preference for local government/nonprofit partnerships in this effort. The grantees are authorized to serve homeless individuals or families (as defined by the McKinney Act) as well as very-low-income persons (under the Housing Act definition) or those at risk of homelessness.

Selection Criteria

Grantees for innovative programs were required to demonstrate that their projects could serve as models for replication by others, as well as provide evidence that their projects could begin operation quickly and achieve the program's purposes. The extent of local need for homeless assistance would be considered, as well as geographic and community diversity. Applicants must demonstrate that the proposed project fits within the continuum and that other partners will contribute additional resources to the effort.

Awards

In early February 1994, Secretary Cisneros announced 48 grants to applicants in 26 states, with the largest total—$2.13 million—going to five programs in Boston. New York City and Chicago each received about $1.75 million and New Orleans $1.05 million. Several cities received approximately $1 million: Atlanta, Baltimore, Buffalo, Burlington (Vermont), Detroit, Greensboro (North Carolina), Houston, Newark, San Antonio, and San Diego.

Programs funded ranged from health care (Phoenix) to transitional living for youth (Los Angeles) to services and housing for rural homeless people (Canyon County, Idaho). A number of projects that were funded focus on the needs of single homeless adults.

Administration Proposes McKinney Reorganization

The 1994 housing bill includes proposals to consolidate most of the HUD McKinney programs into one "Homeless Assistance

Grant Program." Since the original passage of the Stewart B. McKinney Homeless Assistance Act in 1987, the HUD homeless programs have functioned as the core of the federal government's efforts to address the problem of homelessness, now acknowledged to be substantially larger in size and scope than previously supported either by officials or social science research.[3] The six HUD programs represent 60 percent of the total federal expenditure in this area: Supportive Housing Programs (SHP); Shelter + Care; Section 8 Moderate Rehabilitation for Single Room Occupancy (SRO) Dwellings; Emergency Shelter Grants (ESG); Safe Havens; and the Rural Homelessness Assistance Program. The FEMA shelter program, proposed to be moved to HUD, and the HOPWA program will not be part of the consolidation.

The Existing System

Under the existing system, which is viewed as burdensome by both applicants and HUD officials, applicants are required to compete for funding in each of the discrete programs aimed at particular needs or populations. Each categorical program has its own appropriation, regulations, funding criteria, and reporting requirements. Not only do several times the number of potential projects seek funding in each round for each program,[4] but providers view the overlapping process as wasteful of time and money. Further, because funding round decisions are made on individual applications, there is no mechanism or motivation—on the part of either HUD or the applicant—for the proposed project to fit into a comprehensive analysis of need by the provider or by the local community.

Basis of the New Approach

In proposing consolidation, HUD relies in large part on its new "continuum of care" philosophy, which seeks a comprehensive, coordinated response to homelessness. Since the existing programs are viewed as lacking in the flexibility needed to design comprehensive approaches, the proposal is seen as a route to eliminate problem areas while encouraging programs that move homeless people along a path to independent living.

Proposed Reorganization

The proposed new single grant to states and localities is composed of several elements, as outlined below. If passed by Congress and implemented by HUD, the reorganized programs would be in effect in the coming year.

A. Comprehensive approach based on need. States, local government, and urban counties will be eligible for a formula grant based on need. Seventy-five percent of funds would go to these jurisdictions. Twenty-five percent of funds will be awarded to nonformula cities via the states in a manner similar to the CDBG program. The new program will be governed by a consolidate rule.

B. Coordinated application process. HUD seeks to ensure community development and maintenance of the continuum of care in local communities, via a homelessness plan that describes the development of a comprehensive system, including systems for outreach and assessment, emergency shelter, transitional housing, permanent housing, and necessary services.

Local government will convene the local application process, although a local government or state will be permitted to designate a public agency, nonprofit organization, or consortium of organizations to be the applicant. If the applicant did not submit an acceptable application or any application at all, HUD will step in to operate the process for funds going to a specific community.

C. Community participation. Both formula and nonformula participants would be required to involve various sectors of the local community in the creation of the community's plan and the strategy for and implementation of the program. Government officials, homeless persons, nonprofit organizations, foundations, and community organizations would be part of a planning panel to participate in this process.

Eligible activities. All activities presently funded under the HUD McKinney programs will be eligible activities for the new grant. HUD will require that the application process make maximum use of existing providers and other organizations.

Distribution of funds. At least 51 percent of the funds will be required to go to eligible not-for-profit providers. States would also be required to establish systems to distribute funds to small communities, groups of communities, and rural communities.

Match and maintenance of effort. Present match requirements differ from program to program; under the new
grant a uniform match of 25 percent of the grant amount
will be required in cash or in-kind contributions. Recipients
will also be required to certify that federal dollars will not
be substituted for current local and state spending for
homelessness. HUD views this provision as a way to progress beyond mere maintenance of the present system and
toward the development of the continuum of care.

Notes

1. U.S. Department of Housing and Community Development, "The D.C. Initiative: Working Together To Solve Homelessness" (September 1993): 8.

2. *Federal Register* 67,616, vol. 58, no. 243.

3. Celia W. Dugger, "Study Finds Vast Undercount of New York City Homeless,"
New York Times, 16 November 1993, A-1.

4. Only 42 grants were made in the 1993 Supportive Housing Program,
although there were 1,400 applications.

7

A Summary of Significant Litigation on Homelessness

LITIGATION ON BEHALF OF HOMELESS PEOPLE has grown along with the problem, and more issues are introduced as federal and state programs come into being and local communities respond to the possibility of specialized housing and services within their borders. Cases on the rights of homeless people in homeless housing assistance programs under federal law, for instance, have only been brought as the programs have matured and problems have arisen for individuals trying to use them. Since cases ordinarily take some time to find their way through the court system, specific topics come to the courts' attention as the legal process moves to different stages.

Listed in this chapter are some important cases that give an overview of the litigation that has occurred; many more can be researched using tools described in "Additional Resources" at the end of this chapter or elsewhere in this book. Material presented here is drawn largely from the litigation docket described after the case material.

Right to Shelter

Callahan v. Carey, No. 425821 79, N.Y.L.J., Dec. 11, 1979; (N.Y. Sup. Ct. Dec. 5, 1979)

This suit was filed in 1979 on behalf of homeless men in New York City; it was the first case of its kind and resulted in an initial ruling by the state supreme court that the New York constitution requires the state and city to provide shelter to homeless men. In August 1981, following complex litigation and after the city and state lost the initial legal ruling, a settlement was reached requiring the city to provide safe and decent shelter to homeless men. The *Callahan* case was brought with a focus on homeless men because of the significant difference in shelters for the two sexes in the late 1970s.

Since the consent decree was entered, a number of proceedings have been brought by both the plaintiffs and the city. Typically, the plaintiffs have challenged the city's noncompliance with the decree. Orders have been secured requiring the city to open additional beds, increase some kinds of facilities in certain shelters, and reduce the population in others. Violations of the decree are charged on an ongoing basis.

Eldredge v. Koch, 118 Misc. 2d 163, 489 N.Y.S. 2d 960 (N.Y. Sup. Ct. 1983)

The *Callahan* decree was to apply equally to homeless men and women, according to the city, but it soon became apparent that shelters for women did not meet the *Callahan* standards. This case affirmed that the *Callahan* decree applied to women's shelters as well.

Hodge v. Ginsberg, 303 S.E. 2d 245 (W. Va. 1983)

The West Virginia Supreme Court of Appeals ruled that, under protective services laws, the state must provide shelter, food, and medical care for homeless people in that state.

Jedlicka v. Baltimore County, No. 90-CSP-1298 (Md. Cir. Ct., Baltimore Cty.) (1992)

Brought on behalf of homeless men, this case sought to keep open a public shelter; it relied on a number of claims, including the Universal

Declaration of Human Rights. The county was prohibited from closing the shelter without providing the men with a written notice and an opportunity for an individual hearing.

Klosterman v. Cuomo, 61 N.Y. 2d 525, 463 N.E. 2d 588, 475 N.Y.S. 2d 247, *on remand,* 126 Misc. 2d 247, 481 N.Y.S. 2d 580 (Sup. Ct. N.Y. Co. 1984)

Supportive community housing for some 6,000 former state psychiatric patients who had become homeless after release was the goal of this case. The state's highest court held that state officials should enforce the rights of homeless mentally ill people and that lack of funds was not a defense for failing to provide those rights.

Committee for Dignity and Fairness for the Homeless v. Pernsley, No. 886 (Pa. Ct. of Common Pleas, settled April 1985)

A right to shelter was successfully forced through local law in this case brought by homeless people in Philadelphia.

Graham et al. v. Schoemehl, No. 854-00035 (St. Louis Cir. Ct., Nov. 15, 1985)

This suit on behalf of homeless people asserted that an 1815 state statute providing for the poor required St. Louis to aid its homeless. A subsequent consent decree in the case provided for shelter and services as well as additional permanent housing.

McCain v. Koch, 70 N.Y. 2d 109, *rev'g in part* 117 A.D. 2d 198, 502 N.Y.S. 2d 720 (1st Dep't 1986), *rev'd and remanded on other grounds,* 70 N.Y. 2d 109, 510 N.E. 2d 62, 517 N.Y.S. 918 (1987)

Homeless families in New York were guaranteed a right to emergency shelter by this suit. When the city exhausted its supply of shelter and hotel beds for homeless families in late 1984, mothers and their children were relegated to sleeping in welfare offices when city officials refused to procure other accommodations. Under the continuing case, officials are compelled to provide adequate and safe shelter placements, and referrals to permanent housing or placements to alternative housing.

Palmer v. Cuomo, Index No. 2307/85 (Sup. Ct. N.Y. Co. 1985, aff'd, 121 A.D. 2d 194, 503 N.Y.S. 2d 20 (1st Dep't 1986))

A group of homeless young people under the age of 21 were the plaintiffs in this suit, which successfully sought relief for young persons who were discharged from the foster-care system onto the streets. The plaintiffs sought care until age 21, as well as education and training necessary for independent living. The state subsequently issued new regulations defining this responsibility.

Emergency Assistance to Families (EAF)

Coker v. Sullivan, 902 F. 2d 84 (D.C. Cir. 1990)

The National Coalition for the Homeless sought to force the U.S. Department of Health and Human Services to require that the 25 states participating in the Emergency Assistance to Families program of AFDC provide emergency shelter to homeless families. The Court of Appeals decided that the appropriate remedies for alleged violations of state EA plans are fair hearings and direct suits against the states.

Franklin v. New Jersey Department of Human Services, 225 N.J.Super. 504 (App. Div. 1988) aff'd on other grounds, 111 N.J. 1 (1988)

The court upheld the state limit of five months on provision of emergency-shelter assistance to families and general assistance recipients threatened by homelessness. The court did not reject a right-to-shelter claim, but found that the time limit could be enforced if there were other programs to prevent homelessness.

Koster v. Webb, 598 F. Supp. 1134 (1983)

A group of homeless families in Nassau County, New York, brought this case in late 1982, charging that the county failed to provide them with decent emergency shelter. For the first time, the court recognized a federal claim in a case of this type, citing the families' right to shelter under the federal Social Security Act, which governs the AFDC program and its optional Emergency Assistance to Families program.

This suit was settled in 1987, with the jurisdictions agreeing to provide shelters that meet specific standards for all homeless families.

Maticka v. Atlantic City, 216 N.J. Super. 434 (App. Div. 1987)

The court held that state protective services law guarantees a right to shelter for emergency-assistance applicants who are homeless.

Shelter Standards

Atchison v. District of Columbia 585 A. 2d 150 (D.C. App. 1991)

This agreement settled an enforcement case of the now-repealed District of Columbia right-to-overnight-shelter law, passed in 1984. The agreement set operating and quality standards for men's and women's shelters, as well as terms for opening additional shelters. The city was repeatedly found in contempt of the law, and fines totaling $4 million were imposed and subsequently transferred to a trust fund for the development of housing for homeless people. The consent decree was vacated in 1990 on the grounds that it no longer had a basis in law, after the repeal of the right-to-shelter law in November 1990.

Intake Requirements

Lubetkin v. City Manager of Hartford, No. CV-83-0280505S (Conn. Super. Ct. filed Feb. 4, 1983)

This class-action case alleged that the City of Hartford's practice of requiring verification of residence before accepting or processing applications for general assistance (including shelter) violated state law.

Eisenheim v. Los Angeles Board of Supervisors, No. C-479453 (Cal. Supr. Ct. 1983)

Homeless people in Los Angeles challenged the county's refusal to offer shelter vouchers to persons who lacked extensive identification papers. Officials agreed to stop requiring identification and to process homeless people on the same day they applied for shelter.

Tucker v. Battistoni, No. 6297/86 (Dutchess County)

This action challenged a practice in about 50 percent of New York's upstate counties where persons were deemed ineligible for emergency shelter if they missed a single appointment with a welfare officer. These so-called sanctions were used to deny persons shelter for up to 90 days, even when the person appeared for an appointment the following day.

Due Process

Williams v. Barry, 490 F. Supp. 941 (D.D.C. 1980), 708 F. 2d 789 (D.C. Cir. 1983)

The District of Columbia sought to close its only publicly sponsored shelters for homeless men on 48 hours' notice. This suit on behalf of some shelter residents asserted that the men had a constitutionally protected property interest based on the fact that the facilities had been open more than two years and their residents had an expectation of continued services, but the court found that due process required only notice and an opportunity for the homeless men to submit written comments before the closing took place. Plaintiffs' belief that oral hearings were more appropriate for those at risk was rejected. A court order kept the shelters open for more than two years while the case was pending.

Weiser v. Koch, 632 F. Supp. 1369 (S.D.N.Y. 1986)

Homeless men and women challenged the city's practice of evicting people from municipal shelters without set guidelines or procedures. An agreement was reached strictly limiting the circumstances under which a person could be ejected.

Policing of Public Spaces

City of Seattle v. Webster, No. 88-1-02856-3 (King County Super. Ct. 1988) *rev'd* 802 P. 2d 1333 (Wash. Super. Ct. 1990), *cert. denied* 111 S. Ct. 1690 (1991)

This case challenged unsuccessfully Seattle's "Pedestrian Interference Ordinance," which prohibits begging and obstruction of traffic.

Clark v. Community for Creative Non-Violence (CCNV),
468 U.S. 288, 104 S. Ct. 3065, 82 L.E.D. 2d 21 (1984)

An unusual First Amendment case involving CCNV's challenge to federal regulations prohibiting homeless people from sleeping in Lafayette Park, across from the White House, as part of a demonstration protesting federal policies that cause homelessness. In June 1984, the Court upheld the regulations.

Davenport v. People of the State of California,
176 Cal. App. 3d Supp. 10, 222 Cal. Rptr. 736 (1985)

Homelessness was effectively being criminalized by the enforcement of a county statute in Santa Barbara, California, which banned sleeping in public places at night. The lower court found the ordinance unconstitutional, but the decision was later reversed. The National Coalition for the Homeless sought to have the U.S. Supreme Court review the convictions of homeless people prosecuted under the ban. The Court refused.

Kreimer v. Bureau of Police of Morristown, N.J.,
No. 91-5501 60 U.S.L.W. 2607 (3d Cir. Mar. 1992)

In this well-publicized case, the court held that the public library's attempt to bar a homeless man from the library violated the First Amendment.

Loper v. New York City Police Dep't.,
802 F. Supp. 1029 (S.D.N.Y. 1992)

This case certified a class action by beggars who sued the police department for enforcing loitering laws against them.

Pottinger v. City of Miami, 810 F. Supp. 1551 (S.D. Fla. 1992)

This challenge to the city's right—absent any public shelters—to prevent homeless people from living on public property was decided in 1992, with the court ruling that "safe zones" should be created for homeless people near freeway overpasses.

Young v. New York City Authority, 903 F. 2d 146 (2nd Cir. 1990), *cert. denied,* 498 U.S. 983, 111 S. Ct. 516 (1990)

The court upheld a ban on begging in the subways on the grounds that it did not violate the First Amendment.

Right to Housing

Baby Jennifer v. Koch, 86 Civ. 9676 (S.D.N.Y.)

This class action was brought against New York State and New York City officials on behalf of several hundred healthy infants, known as "boarder babies." Living in hospital wards simply because officials had not found homes for them, most of them had been abandoned by drug-addicted mothers. A final consent judgment was entered mandating that the city develop sufficient foster-care placements with families so that it could cease to leave infants in hospitals.

Hanson v. McMahon, 238 Cal. Rptr. 232 (Cal. App. 2d 1987)

In this case, a California intermediate appellate court determined that the California child welfare and AFDC/EA laws, when read together, require the state Department of Social Services to prevent the separation of families through homelessness by providing emergency shelter to keep families intact. The court invalidated a state EA regulation that authorized shelter services only for children who had been removed from their parents; the court held that the regulation impermissibly required parents to choose between keeping the family together and securing shelter for the children.

In response to the problems raised by the litigation, the California legislature enacted an AFDC Special Needs Program, the Homeless Assistance Program (HAP), which provided for up to four weeks of temporary assistance, as well as financial assistance for obtaining permanent housing. The temporary assistance component provided cash that had to be paid to qualifying families on the day of application. Permanent housing assistance consisted of such move-in costs as the last month's rent and security and utility deposits; these had to be paid by the next working day to qualified families.

Heard v. Cuomo No. 44429 (N.Y. Sup. Ct., App. Div., Jan. 14, 1992, *aff'g* No. M-3009 (N.Y. App. Div. July 2, 1991)

In this case, the court found that the city has an obligation not to discharge patients from psychiatric hospitals unless the patient has appropriate housing.

In the Matter of P. et al. No. 12823 (D.C. Super. Ct. filed April 12, 1988)

After a family was homeless for six months because of a fire in their public housing unit, the children were placed in foster care. The city would not rehouse the family because of a debt dispute. One year later, the family was still separated. A consent decree placed the family in housing while the city searched for a subsidized unit; the family was reunited.

Love v. Koch, No. 4514/88 (N.Y. Supreme Court, N.Y. Co.)

This class-action suit for mentally disabled people alleges that a place to live is a component of appropriate mental health care. Either community care, acute hospitalization, or residential treatment must be provided; outpatient treatment with a referral to a shelter is inappropriate.

Mixon v. Grinker, 595 N.Y.S. 2d 876, 157 Misc. 2d 68 (Sup. Ct. N.Y. Co. 1993)

This class-action suit sought medically appropriate housing— including a private sleeping accommodation and private sanitary facilities—for those homeless persons who are HIV-seropositive. Conditions in the city shelters and on the streets endanger people with HIV/AIDS, according to the suit, and placement in a shelter, with its exposure to infection, inadequate nutrition and health care, and lack of private sanitary facilities, is inadequate. The court found that placing up to 12 persons with weakened immune systems in the same room lacked a rational basis, but that up to 4 persons could be so sheltered, with the option of additional separate eating and bathroom facilities. The plaintiffs appealed in 1994.

Right To Vote

Pitts v. Black, 608 F. Supp. 696 (S.D.N.Y. 1984)

Homeless people sued the state and city boards of election to challenge their disenfranchisement, which was based on their homelessness. Since they were living in hotels, in shelters, or on the street, they were not permitted to register to vote, officials claiming that "a place of temporary shelter cannot be deemed a residence." A consent decree was signed before trial, permitting homeless people in shelters to vote, and in October 1984, the federal court ordered election officials to allow those homeless people living on the street to register and also included a provision extending their registration period by two weeks.

In the Matter of: The Applications for Voter Registration of Willie R. Jenkins, et al. before the District of Columbia Board of Elections and Ethics (June 7, 1984)

While not a court case, this District of Columbia proceeding interpreted the residency requirement for voting in favor of home-less persons by allowing designation of a location as home, with an accompanying effective local mailing address. This challenge occurred when homeless advocates sought to register homeless voters so that they would be eligible to sign and circulate petitions to put a right-to-shelter initiative on the ballot.

Preservation and Displacement

Lacko v. City of Chicago No. 82-C-5031 (E.D. Ill, June 12, 1984)

A federally funded urban-renewal project displaced 300 men from two residential hotels in Chicago; homeless, they were subsequently denied relocation benefits and services by the city. The city paid each man $10 if he could show that he had rented another unit. A consent decree required additional significant payments to the men, as well as a study of low-income housing opportunities in the city, including units recently demolished or converted.

Seawall Associates v. City of New York, 74 N.Y. 2d 92, 542 N.E. 2d 1059 (Ct. App. 1989)

A group of New York real estate developers sued to enjoin enforcement of a city statute barring the demolition or conversion of single-room occupancy (SRO) hotels and requiring that habitable units in SROs be made available for rent, a so-called antiwarehousing provision to prohibit hoarding of units in order to empty a building. A lower court held the law unconstitutional, but the New York City Coalition for the Homeless and several residents of SRO hotels intervened, and the law was upheld on appeal.

Federal Programs

Community for Creative Non-Violence v. Pierce, 786 F. 2d 1199 (D.C. Cir. 1986), No. 84-5632

The controversial 1984 HUD study of homelessness arrived at a relatively low figure for the size of the population: 250,000–300,000. The CCNV suit alleged that the inaccuracy of the report would have severe consequences for future federal spending. The case was dismissed in September 1984, with the judge saying that CCNV lacked standing for failing to show that the study would adversely affect either public or private spending for homeless people.

Bruce v. Department of Defense (DOD), Civ. Action No. 87-0425 (D.D.C. filed June 16, 1987)

In this suit, a homeless man, an emergency shelter, and the National Coalition for the Homeless sued DOD under a federal program to make unused military facilities available as emergency shelter. Congress enacted such a statute in 1983, and plaintiffs stated that DOD had ignored the mandate to implement the program. In June 1987, the court ordered DOD to issue regulations to implement the program by mid-November.

National Coalition for the Homeless v. Pierce, Civ. Action No. 87-2640 (D.D.C. filed September 25, 1987)

This case was the first of several filed after the 1987 passage of the Stewart B. McKinney Homeless Assistance Act in order to implement some portion of the legislation. The suit alleged that the U.S. Department of Housing and Urban Development (HUD) had failed to enforce the Supplemental Assistance to the Homeless program by failing to make funds available by a specified date, which was intended to ensure operation by the next winter. HUD secretary Samuel Pierce issued necessary guidelines for the release of the funds on the morning of the scheduled court hearing.

National Coalition for the Homeless v. Department of Education, Civ. Action No. 87-3512 (D.D.C. filed January 21, 1988) (settlement)

This McKinney-related suit, brought by the National Coalition for the Homeless, five homeless children, and two shelters, charged that the Department of Education had failed to comply with the legislative requirement to implement a program ensuring access to education for homeless children. The law required such measures by the fall of 1987, to conform to the upcoming school year, but the department guidelines challenged in the case resulted in a delay to the following spring.

National Law Center on Homelessness and Poverty et al. v. Veterans Administration et al., 695 F.Supp. 1226 (D.D.C. 1988), aff'd No. 91-5208 (D.C. Cir. May 29, 1992)

This suit was filed against five major federal landholding agencies, alleging that they violated the Title V McKinney requirements to make underutilized federal government property available to states, local governments, and private nonprofit organizations for use as facilities to assist homeless people. The court issued a strongly worded opinion, and ordered the federal agencies to comply with the law on a strict schedule, with properties to be available exclusively for use by homeless people during the first 30 days of their listing; HUD was further required to list such properties weekly in the *Federal Register*.

Welfare-Related Cases

Boehm v. County of Mercer, 178 Cal. App. 3d 494 (1988)

The county reduced general assistance grants without making a determination of the costs of minimum subsistence. General assistance statutes mandate the provision of shelter, clothing, food, medical care, and transportation, at a level determined by an objective examination of their market costs.

Jiggetts v. Grinker, 75 N.Y. 2d 411, 553 N.E. 2d 570 (1990), rev'g 148 A.D. 2d 1 (1st Dept. 1989)

This case challenged the level of shelter allowances in AFDC payments as clearly inadequate to meet the cost of housing. A preliminary injunction ordered shelter allowances at an adequate level and rent arrearages for the plaintiffs. The state's highest court affirmed the decision.

Massachusetts Coalition for the Homeless v. Secretary of Human Services, 400 Mass. 806, 511 N.E. 2d 603 (1987)

Based on state AFDC law, this case claimed that grant amounts were insufficient to comply with the law's requirement that they support a child being brought up in the parent's home. The court agreed, but did not order higher grants; the state increased its appropriation for payments and also targeted housing subsidies to homeless families and those at risk of homelessness.

Rensch v. Board of Supervisors, LASC No. C595155, August 6, 1986

The county must identify mentally and developmentally disabled applicants for General Assistance and provide them with special assistance in complying with application requirements.

Other Claims

Robbins v. Reagan, 780 F. 2d 37 (D.C. Cir. 1985)

This was a unique case of federal government involvement in the operation of a local shelter, since the Washington, D.C.–based Community for Creative Non-Violence (CCNV) was using a previously vacant, federally owned building near the U.S. capitol as an emergency shelter. Following a number of threatened closures and several highly publicized political actions, President Reagan had publicly promised to renovate the facility into a model shelter with federal funds. When the federal government backed out of the promise, CCNV and several homeless residents sued the administration, citing the president's pledge and other grounds. Although the court upheld the government's decision to close the building, the situation was reversed through public pressure and the building was renovated.

Burton v. New Jersey Department of Institutions and Agencies, App. Div. A-2965-75 (Feb. 4, 1977)

A family of eight, which had lost all of its funds and food stamp authorization card, was denied emergency assistance because they continued to have a place to live, even though they had no resources to obtain food. The court interpreted the regulation in question to mean that homelessness and the provision of emergency assistance extend to those who require food and clothing as well as shelter.

Additional Resources

The Legal Services Homelessness Task Force publishes a regularly updated catalog of litigation and other related materials on homelessness. "An Annotated Docket of Selected Cases and Other Material Involving Homelessness" is available from the National Clearinghouse for Legal Services, 205 West Monroe, Second Floor, Chicago, IL 60606. It contains comprehensive information on more than 20 subject areas of litigation, including a right to shelter, a right to housing, welfare benefits, access to education for homeless children, voting rights, criminalization of homelessness, and more. Copies of papers in the cases described here are also generally available from the clearinghouse for the cost of copying. Papers in many additional cases not covered here are also on deposit there.

8

Directory of Organizations, Associations, and Government Agencies

National Nonprofit Organizations and Associations

ACORN
522 Eighth Street SE
Washington, DC 20003
(202) 547-9292

ACORN is a national organization of more than 75,000 grass roots low- and moderate-income people seeking to change basic conditions of poverty through local actions to turn over vacant housing to low-income residents.

American Bar Association
Commission on Homelessness and Poverty
1800 M Street NW
Washington, DC 20036
(202) 331-2291; (202) 331-2220 FAX
Patricia M. Hanrahan, Director

The commission assists local and state bar associations and other legal organizations to create pro bono programs aiding poor people.

PUBLICATIONS: "State and Local Bar Association Homeless Programs," a catalog of local programs; training videos and books on low-income housing development; reports and data.

American Institute of Architects (AIA)
Search for Shelter Program
1735 New York Avenue NW
Washington, DC 20006
(202) 626-7468; (202) 626-7421 FAX
Charles Z. Buki, Director

The Search for Shelter is an AIA program to assist local groups in meeting the needs of homeless people. The program seeks to support the development of local coalitions of providers, professionals, government officials, and others to foster education and action in the community.

PUBLICATIONS: *The Search for Shelter; Search for Shelter* program workbook; *Creation of Shelter;* as well as related resources, such as an exhibit.

American Psychiatric Association (APA)
Office of Psychiatric Services
1400 K Street NW
Washington, DC 20005
(202) 682-6091; (202) 682-6114 FAX
Claudia Hart, Associate Director

The APA is a membership organization of approximately 37,000 psychiatrists. Its Committee on Homelessness promotes national and local advocacy and the development of programs for mentally ill homeless persons.

American Red Cross
National Headquarters
Seventeenth and D Streets NW
Washington, DC 20006
(202) 639-3610
Enso V. Bighinatti, Emergency Food and Shelter National Board Member

The Red Cross has traditionally provided services to those made homeless by disasters such as fires or floods. More than 600 local chapters now provide services to homeless people through McKinney Act FEMA funding. Local Red Cross chapters can provide more information.

Judge David L. Bazelon Center for Mental Health Law
(formerly Mental Health Law Project)
1100 Fifteenth Street NW, Suite 1212
Washington, DC 20005
(202) 467-5730; (202) 223-0409 FAX
Bonnie Milstein, Director, Community Watch

The Bazelon Center is a legal advocacy organization for the rights of mentally disabled people, including those concerning fair housing issues, and it provides technical assistance and public education.

PUBLICATIONS: *The Housing Center Bulletin,* published six times a year.

Campus Outreach Opportunity League (COOL)
University of Minnesota
264 North Hall
2005 Lower Buford Circle
St. Paul, MN 55108
(612) 624-3018; (612) 624-1296 FAX
Carol Bowar, Field Support Coordinator

This national student organization promotes campus involvement in community action around hunger and homelessness. COOL offers technical assistance to campus groups and hosts local and national conferences.

PUBLICATIONS: *Building a Movement: A Resource Book for Students in Community Service; Hunger/Homelessness Action: A Resource Book.*

Catholic Charities USA
1731 King Street, Suite 200
Alexandria, VA 22314
(703) 549-1390; (703) 549-1656 FAX
Brother Joseph Berg, Emergency Food and Shelter National Board Member

This nationwide federation of organizations and individuals, including more than 600 agencies, is a traditional service provider to the hungry and homeless.

PUBLICATIONS: *Charities USA,* a magazine.

Center for Community Change
1000 Wisconsin Avenue NW
Washington, DC 20007
(202) 342-0519; (202) 342-1132 FAX
Pablo Eisenberg, President

Local low-income, community-based organizations can seek technical assistance in the areas of Community Development Block Grants

(CDBG), Community Reinvestment Act (CRA), housing trust funds, organizational development, funding, housing, and economic development.

PUBLICATIONS: *Community Change,* a quarterly newsletter; *Housing Trust Funds,* by Mary Brooks, a guide to state programs for housing funds.

Center for Law and Education
955 Massachusetts Avenue, Suite 3A
Cambridge, MA 02139
(617) 876-6611; (617) 876-0203 FAX
Kathleen Boundy, Director

This legal services national support center addresses the McKinney Act education access and continuity issues.

PUBLICATIONS: Various packets on McKinney Act education requirements, updated periodically.

Center for Law and Social Policy
1616 P Street NW
Washington, DC 20036
(202) 328-5140; (202) 328-5195 FAX
Alan W. Houseman, Executive Director

The center is a public-interest law firm that advocates and provides technical assistance on all aspects of state and federal welfare and social service programs affecting poor families.

PUBLICATIONS: *States Update* (ten times yearly); *Family Matters* (quarterly); as well as periodic reports on welfare-related topics.

Center on Budget and Policy Priorities
777 North Capitol Street NE, Suite 705
Washington, DC 20001
(202) 408-1080
Robert Greenstein, Director

The center issues regular reports analyzing data and policy issues affecting poor Americans; reports on poverty among women, minorities, and rural residents; and analysis of federal budget issues and programs for the poor.

PUBLICATIONS: *Holes in the Safety Net: Poverty Programs and Policies in the States,* a national overview, and 50 state reports; *A Place To Call Home,* a study of the housing crisis and the poor.

Center on Social Welfare Policy and Law
275 Seventh Avenue, Sixth Floor
New York, NY 10001
(212) 633-6967; (212) 633-6371 FAX
Henry Freedman, Executive Director

The center is a national legal services support project on welfare law.

PUBLICATIONS: Numerous periodic reports on AFDC, including listings of recent reports, court decisions, and developments in welfare law; general publications on program rules, reference, and statistical sources for research on programs; summaries of national trends in programs.

Child Welfare League of America (CWLA)
440 First Street NW, Suite 310
Washington, DC 20001
(202) 638-2952; (202) 638-4004 FAX
David S. Liederman, Executive Director

CWLA is a membership organization of children's advocacy agencies as well as public and voluntary organizations; it is active in the areas of research, training, and legislative advocacy on children's issues, including the needs of homeless children.

PUBLICATIONS: *Child Welfare*, a bimonthly journal; *Washington Social Legislation Bulletin*, a biweekly report; *Homeless Children and Families; The Youngest of the Homeless II*, a report on boarder babies.

Children's Defense Fund (CDF)
25 E Street NW
Washington, DC 20001
(202) 628-8787
Marian Wright Edelman, President

CDF's goal is to educate policymakers about the needs of poor and minority children. It monitors federal and state policy and legislation on health, education, child welfare, mental health, teen pregnancy, and youth employment.

PUBLICATIONS: *CDF Reports,* published monthly as an update on relevant issues; *A Children's Defense Budget,* exhaustive annual analysis of federal budget proposals and their effects on children; other specialized reports and fact books.

Coalition on Human Needs
1000 Wisconsin Avenue NW
Washington, DC 20007
(202) 342-0726
Jennifer Vasiloff, Executive Director

A wide range of groups concerned with issues affecting low-income people participate in this coalition, which seeks to reduce poverty and improve the education and welfare systems. Research assistance and legislative information are provided to affiliates.

PUBLICATIONS: *Insight/Action*, a monthly newsletter; *The National Technical Assistance Directory: A Guide for State Advocates and Service Providers*, a directory of national organizations providing technical assistance and analytical publications.

Comic Relief
2049 Century Park East, Suite 4250
Los Angeles, CA 90067
(213) 201-9317
Bob Zmuda, President

This annual marathon comedy performance benefit was first broadcast in 1986. Featuring dozens of nationally known comedians, the program raises funds for homeless health care programs around the country.

Corporation for Supportive Housing
342 Madison Avenue, Suite 505
New York, NY 10173
(212) 986-2966; (212) 986-6552 FAX
Julie Sandorf, President

This national organization promotes the expansion of supportive housing for special-needs groups through direct financing for projects. It also provides technical assistance and information about program models.

Council of Large Public Housing Authorities (CLPHA)
601 Pennsylvania Avenue NW, Suite 825
Washington, DC 20004
(202) 638-1300; (202) 638-2364 FAX
Sunia Zaterman, Executive Director

CLPHA represents the directors of more than 50 of the largest public housing authorities in the nation; it seeks increased funding for improved programs. CLPHA publishes some information on the profile of current projects.

Council of State Community Development Agencies (COSCDA)
444 North Capitol Street NE, Suite 224
Washington, DC 20001
(202) 393-6435
John M. Sidor, Executive Director

This national network of state-level community development officials monitors federal legislation and state initiatives on affordable housing and economic development and employment issues.

PUBLICATIONS: *States and Housing,* a newsletter; *Put Up or Give Way,* a book about state jobs and employment strategies.

Empty the Shelters (ETS)
1515 Fairmount Avenue
Philadelphia, PA 19130
(215) 765-4546; (215) 232-7277 FAX
Phil Wider, Community Outreach Coordinator

ETS seeks to create diverse student-community partnerships focused on ending homelessness and poverty through action and training. Students have a summer-long experience of community and campus organizing training, leadership development, group process, and more.

Enterprise Foundation
500 American City Building
Columbia, MD 21044
(410) 964-1230; (410) 964-1918 FAX
James Rouse, President

The Enterprise Foundation provides technical assistance and financial aid to community development corporations and low-income housing developers.

PUBLICATIONS: *Network News* and *Cost Cuts,* newsletters; *A Decent Place To Live Revisited: The State of Housing in America.*

Food Research and Action Center (FRAC)
1875 Connecticut Avenue NW, Suite 540
Washington, DC 20009
(202) 986-2200; (202) 986-2525 FAX
Robert Fersh, Director

FRAC is a national legal services support center on food, nutrition, and hunger issues; its primary strategy is to reduce hunger in the United States through the improvement of federal food programs, and it acts as a clearinghouse on public policy, legislation, technical assistance, education, and the formation of statewide coalitions.

PUBLICATIONS: *Foodlines,* a monthly newsletter; *FRAC's Guide to the Food Stamp Program; WIC Facts.*

Habitat for Humanity
Habitat and Church Streets
Americus, GA 31709
(912) 924-6935; (912) 924-6541 FAX
Rick Hathaway, Director of Affiliates

Habitat for Humanity is a Christian housing organization that operates in the United States and 35 other countries. It builds or renovates simple homes for persons without adequate shelter; "Habitat for Homeless Humanity" is its project for homeless housing. Volunteers and potential residents cooperate in building or renovation.

PUBLICATIONS: *Habitat World,* a newsletter.

Health Care for the Homeless Support Services
John Snow, Inc.
210 Lincoln Street
Boston, MA 02111
(617) 482-9485; (617) 482-0617 FAX
Suz Friedrich, Project Director

This contractor provides support for McKinney Act health care grantees in the Health Care for the Homeless program. The support includes regional training, an annual conference, and an information service.

PUBLICATIONS: *Opening Doors,* a newsletter; annual directory of projects.

Home Builders Institute
1090 Vermont Avenue NW, Suite 600
Washington, DC 20005
(800) 795-7955; (202) 898-7777 FAX

The institute is the educational arm of the National Association of Home Builders, and it runs Department of Labor projects for training and employment of homeless people. HEART (Homeless Employment and Related Training) offers training, social services, housing, and job placement.

PUBLICATIONS: *Heart to Heart,* a manual on operating a homeless training program.

Housing Assistance Council (HAC)
1025 Vermont Avenue NW, Suite 606
Washington, DC 20005
(202) 842-8600; (202) 347-3441 FAX
Moises Loza, Executive Director

HAC provides technical assistance, loans, research, and information on rural low-income housing development, especially Farmers Home Administration programs. It publishes regular reports on federal rural programs and trends in rural poverty and development.

PUBLICATIONS: *HAC News,* a biweekly newsletter; *State Action Memorandum,* a bimonthly newsletter; *HAC Technical Manuals,* on rural housing and community issues.

Housing Trust Fund Project
570 Shepard Street
San Pedro, CA 90731
(310) 833-4249; (310) 831-2178 FAX
Mary E. Brooks, Director

Neighborhood groups can receive technical assistance from this project of the Center for Community Change, which monitors the 41 housing trust funds in the states.

PUBLICATIONS: *News from the Housing Trust Fund Project,* a newsletter; *A Survey of Housing Trust Funds; A Guide to Developing Housing Trust Funds; A Citizen's Guide To Creating a Housing Trust Fund.* Publications are free to community-based nonprofit organizations.

Legal Services Homelessness Task Force
National Housing Law Project
122 C Street NW, Suite 740
Washington, DC 20001
(202) 783-5140; (202) 347-6765 FAX
Mary Ellen Hombs, Director

The task force is an interdisciplinary consortium of legal services attorneys and advocates from national, state, and local programs, including specialists in housing, public assistance, child welfare, and other areas. It was established in 1988 to integrate the range of issues affecting homelessness for legal service practitioners.

PUBLICATIONS: *Annotated Docket of Selected Cases and Other Materials Involving Homelessness,* a catalog of significant litigation and other agency action on homelessness issues including criminalization, voting rights, and access to shelters; substantive training materials on current topics in homelessness (criminalization, tuberculosis, HIV/AIDS, establishing a right to housing). Available from the National Clearinghouse for Legal Services.

Local Initiatives Support Corporation (LISC)
733 Third Avenue, Eighth Floor
New York, NY 10017
(212) 455-9800; (212) 682-5929 FAX
Paul Grogan, Director

This project of the Ford Foundation and six corporations offers financing and technical assistance to nonprofit organizations working on community development and low-income housing by channeling private-sector resources into community development corporations.

McAuley Institute
8300 Colesville Road
Silver Spring, MD 20910
(301) 588-8154

The Sisters of Mercy of the Union formed the McAuley Institute in 1991 with the proceeds from the sale of their suburban Washington property. Through the institute, they returned to their historic mission of providing shelter, especially for women and children, by working with community groups across the nation to provide low-income housing. The institute offers technical assistance, information and training, and loans.

National Alliance for the Mentally Ill (NAMI)
1901 North Fort Myer Drive, Suite 500
Arlington, VA 22209
(703) 524-7600

This national advocacy and research organization for the mentally ill seeks to create a coordinated system of care.

PUBLICATIONS: Bimonthly newsletter.

National Alliance To End Homelessness
1518 K Street NW, Suite 206
Washington, DC 20005
(202) 638-1526; (202) 638-4664 FAX
Thomas L. Kenyon, President

The alliance is a coalition of corporations, service providers, and individuals that sponsors conferences and uses research and public education in its efforts to address homelessness.

PUBLICATIONS: *The Alliance,* newsletter.

National Association of Community Health Centers (NACHC)
1330 New Hampshire Avenue NW, Suite 122
Washington, DC 20036
(202) 659-8008; (202) 659-8519 FAX
Freda Mitchem, Associate Director for Research and Policy Development

This membership organization represents McKinney-funded Health Care for the Homeless projects, as well as other health care providers and migrant health centers. NACHC provides technical assistance, training, and public policy information.

National Association of State Mental Health Program Directors
66 Canal Center Plaza, Suite 302
Alexandria, VA 22314
(703) 739-9333; (703) 548-9517 FAX
Grace Stuckey, PATH Specialist

The association provides technical assistance for the McKinney Act PATH programs in the states and works with advisory and consumer groups to improve mental health services.

National Center for Youth Law
114 Sansome Street, Suite 900
San Francisco, CA 94104
(415) 543-3307; (415) 956-9024 FAX
John O'Toole, Director

The center is a legal services national support project on youth issues, including homeless and runaway youth.

PUBLICATIONS: *Youth Law News,* published six times a year.

National Center on Women and Family Law
799 Broadway, Room 402
New York, NY 10003
(212) 674-8200; (212) 533-5104 FAX

This national legal services support center addresses domestic-violence issues through its National Battered Women's Law Project, which serves as a clearinghouse on domestic-violence issues, produces technical assistance and public education materials, and analyzes federal and state legislative and administrative action.

National Clearinghouse for Legal Services
205 West Monroe, Second Floor
Chicago, IL 60606
(312) 263-3830; (312) 263-3846 FAX
Rita McLennon, Executive Director

The clearinghouse banks legal and other documents on a range of poverty-related issues; it provides them free to legal services programs and to general distribution for a small charge.

PUBLICATIONS: *Clearinghouse Review,* a monthly journal of poverty law developments; legal papers on numerous homelessness-related cases are available.

National Coalition against Domestic Violence (NCADV)
P.O. Box 34103
Washington, DC 20043
(202) 638-6388

This membership organization works to help battered women and their children. Members are individuals and community-based organizations run by women.

National Coalition for the Homeless/Homelessness Information Exchange
1612 K Street NW, Suite 1004
Washington, DC 20006
(202) 775-1322; (202) 775-1316 FAX; (202) 775-1372
Legislative Hotline
Fred Karnas, Jr., Executive Director

This federation of individuals, agencies, and organizations acts as a national network for enacting and monitoring legislation related to homelessness. The coalition merged with the Homelessness Information Exchange, which maintains an on-line database and provides literature searches and case studies on specific types of programs.

PUBLICATIONS: *Safety Network,* a monthly newsletter; reports on local and national aspects of homelessness and related issues; and model legislation and programs. *Homewords* is the newsletter of the Homelessness Information Exchange. The coalition is preparing a directory of homeless self-help, artistic, and political groups.

National Community Development Association
522 Twenty-first Street NW, Suite 120
Washington, DC 20006
(202) 293-7587; (202) 887-5546 FAX
Reginald Todd, Chief Executive Officer

The association represents local-government human services programs; it monitors federal legislative and administrative action on housing and community development programs.

National Conference of State Legislatures (NCSL)
1560 Broadway, Suite 700
Denver, CO 80202
(303) 830-2054
William T. Pound, Executive Director

NCSL serves the members of the nation's 50 state legislatures through publications and other tools with current information on state and federal public policy issues.

PUBLICATIONS: *State Legislatures,* published ten times annually; *Federal Update,* a newsletter; *State Legislative Report,* a policy update; *Directory of Legislative Leaders,* a national guide.

National Council of Community Mental Health Centers
12300 Twinbrook Parkway, Suite 320
Rockville, MD 20852
(301) 984-6200
Stephen Townsend, Government Relations Associate

This trade association of mental health service providers and state organizations seeks to affect public policy and service delivery to those in need of mental health care. It monitors the following programs: PATH, ACCESS, Shelter Plus Care, Safe Havens, Supportive Housing, and Rural Homelessness.

PUBLICATIONS: *National Council News,* a newsletter.

National Council of La Raza
810 First Street NE, Suite 500
Washington, DC 20002
(202) 289-1551
Raul Yzaguirre, President

An improved quality of life for Hispanics is the purpose of this umbrella organization, which has affiliations with more than 4,000 Hispanic groups nationwide. The organization provides technical assistance, public education materials, public policy analysis, and advocacy on behalf of its constituency.

PUBLICATIONS: *The Hispanic Housing Crisis,* a newsletter.

National Council of State Housing Agencies
444 North Capitol Street NW, Suite 438
Washington, DC 20001
(202) 624-7710
Glenn Petherick, Director of Special Projects

The council provides information on housing programs in the states, including programs for homeless persons.

National Employment Law Project
475 Riverside Drive, Suite 815
New York, NY 10115
(212) 870-2121; (212) 870-2197 FAX

The project is a national legal services support center on employment issues for poor people, including the Job Training Partnership Act.

PUBLICATIONS: *Employment Law News.*

National Health Care for the Homeless Council
P.O. Box 68019
Nashville, TN 37206
(615) 386-0302; (615) 385-2157 FAX
John Lozier, Executive Director

Two dozen Health Care for the Homeless projects belong to this council. The projects provide primary health care, mental health services, and drug and alcohol services; the council coordinates their advocacy.

National Health Law Program (NHeLP)
2639 South La Cienega Boulevard
Los Angeles, CA 90034
(213) 204-6010
Laurence Lavin, Director

NHeLP is a legal services national support center on health-related issues and programs affecting poor people.

PUBLICATIONS: *The Health Advocate,* a quarterly newsletter; *An Advocate's Guide to the Medicaid Program; Access to Emergency Medical Care.*

National Housing Institute (NHI)
439 Main Street
Orange, NJ 07050
(201) 678-3110; (201) 678-0014 FAX

NHI is a public policy education and research organization focused on housing issues.

PUBLICATIONS: *Shelterforce* magazine, published six times a year; a survey of homelessness prevention programs; a catalog of housing courses; congressional report card; various working papers.

National Housing Law Project (NHLP)
2201 Broadway, Suite 825
Oakland, CA 94612
(510) 251-9400; (510) 251-0600 FAX
Manuel Romero, Director

NHLP is a national legal services support center to advise and assist local legal services lawyers working on housing and community development issues with training, litigation assistance, and research.

PUBLICATIONS: *Housing Law Bulletin,* published bimonthly; as well as numerous manuals on federal housing programs.

National Law Center on Homelessness and Poverty
918 F Street NW, Suite 412
Washington, DC 20004
(202) 638-2535; (202) 628-2737 FAX
Maria Foscarinis, Executive Director

The law center was established in 1989 and monitors federal agency action on McKinney Act programs. It provides technical assistance to local service providers and authored the "Beyond McKinney" program.

PUBLICATIONS: *In Just Times*, a newsletter.

National Low Income Housing Coalition (NLIHC)
Low Income Housing Information Service (LIHIS)
1012 Fourteenth Street NW, Suite 1200
Washington, DC 20005
(202) 662-1530; (202) 393-1973 FAX
Cushing Dolbeare, Acting Director

NLIHC is a national organization focused on education, advocacy, and organizing for low-income housing. LIHIS emphasizes federal housing programs and policies.

PUBLICATIONS: *Low Income Housing Round-Up*, published monthly; supplemented by *Special Memorandum*, on specific housing topics.

National Mental Health Association (NMHA)
1021 Prince Street
Alexandria, VA 22314
(703) 684-7722; (703) 684-5968 FAX

NMHA works to improve citizen advocacy on mental health services, prevent mental illness, and promote mental health through citizen effort. It has 600 local and state affiliated groups across the country.

PUBLICATIONS: *FOCUS*, newsletter; *Homeless in America*, video.

National Network of Runaway and Youth Services
1319 F Street NW, Suite 401
Washington, DC 20004
(202) 783-7949; (202) 783-7955 FAX
Della Hughes, Executive Director

More than 1,000 local shelter agencies and state networks are members of this national network, which sponsors training, offers information on model programs, and sponsors a national telecommunications system for youth programs.

PUBLICATIONS: *Network News,* a quarterly newsletter; *Policy Report,* published eight times yearly; *Alcohol and Drug Use among Runaway, Homeless, and Other Youth; To Whom Do They Belong?*

National Resource Center on Homelessness and Mental Illness
Policy Research Associates, Inc.
262 Delaware Avenue
Delmar, NY 12054
(800) 444-7415; (518) 439-7612 FAX
Deborah Dennis, Director

This center, under contract to the federal government, provides technical assistance and other information on housing and services needed by homeless mentally ill people; it maintains a database of published and unpublished work and offers bibliographies, custom searches, and other material.

PUBLICATIONS: *Access,* published quarterly, and a national organizational referral list of groups working in the field of homelessness.

National Student Campaign against Hunger (NSCAH)
29 Temple Place, Fifth Floor
Boston, MA 02111
(617) 292-4823; (617) 292-8057 FAX
Jennifer Coken, Executive Director

NSCAH combines the efforts of state Public Interest Research Groups (PIRGs) to aid students in fighting hunger and homelessness. Three major campus events are promoted each semester, and NSCAH provides technical assistance and acts as a clearinghouse for projects. SPLASH is the campaign's national legislative-action program.

PUBLICATIONS: *Students Making a Difference,* a newsletter.

Poverty and Race Research Action Council (PRRAC)
1711 Connecticut Avenue NW
Washington, DC 20009
(202) 387-9887; (202) 387-0764 FAX
Chester Hartman, Director

PRRAC is a grant-making organization supporting work that connects advocacy and strategic efforts (public education, litigation) on issues of race and poverty. It has funded dozens of local projects and maintains a Social Science Advisory Board to assist local groups with the efforts described.

PUBLICATIONS: *Poverty & Race,* a newsletter.

Salvation Army
615 Slaters Lane, Box 269
Alexandria, VA 22314
(703) 684-5521; (703) 684-5538 FAX
*Lt. Col. Eugene Slusher, Emergency Food and Shelter National Board
Member*

This international religious charity is one of the historic providers of shelter and alcohol and drug rehabilitation services, with more than 10,000 local chapters.

Second Harvest
343 South Dearborn, Suite 410
Chicago, IL 60604
(312) 341-1303
Steven Whitehead, Executive Director

This food-banking network is the largest nongovernmental food program in the nation, intercepting tons of surplus edible food and routing it to 38,000 charitable organizations for use in local relief efforts.

Share Our Strength (S.O.S.)
1511 K Street NW, Suite 940
Washington, DC 20005
(202) 393-2925
Bill Shore, Executive Director

This nationwide organization of over 5,000 restaurateurs, chefs, and other food-service and creative professionals conducts a "Taste of the Nation" annual national event to raise funds for local hunger relief. It also conducts national readings by prominent authors to fight hunger.

PUBLICATIONS: *Louder Than Words, Voices Louder Than Words, HOME,* anthologies of contributed stories that benefit S.O.S.; *Frontier,* a quarterly news magazine; calendars; cookbooks.

Travelers Aid International
918 Sixteenth Street, Suite 201
Washington, DC 20006
(202) 659-9468; (202) 659-2910 FAX
Mark Clark, President

Travelers Aid is a network of service providers, often located in public transportation terminals, who assist stranded travelers and the homeless with emergency financial aid, food, shelter, and clothing.

United States Conference of Mayors
1620 I Street NW
Washington, DC 20005
(202) 293-7330; (202) 293-2352 FAX
Laura DeKoven Waxman, Assistant Executive Director

The Conference of Mayors is an education and lobbying organization for mayors of cities with populations over 30,000, providing background information and position statements on vital issues. Its Task Force on Hunger and Homelessness conducts an annual survey of member cities and their services and conditions.

PUBLICATIONS: *The Continued Growth of Hunger, Homelessness, and Poverty in America's Cities,* an annual report; *Mentally Ill and Homeless; A City Assessment of the 1990 Shelter and Street County Survey.*

United Way of America
701 North Fairfax Street
Alexandria, VA 22314
(703) 836-7100

United Way helps fund and coordinate many local and national programs for the homeless and hungry.

Volunteers of America (VOA)
3813 North Causeway Boulevard
Metairie, LA 70002
(504) 837-2652; (504) 837-4200 FAX

VOA operates more than 400 local programs for the homeless, the elderly, alcoholics, and drug users. Local programs produce some publications on homelessness.

Women's Institute for Housing and Economic Development
43 Kingston Street
Boston, MA 02111
(617) 423-2296
Jean Kluver, Executive Director

This nonprofit group offers technical assistance to social service agencies and community-based women's organizations seeking to develop emergency shelter, transitional housing, and permanent housing for low-income women.

PUBLICATIONS: *A Development Primer: Starting Housing and Business Ventures by and/or for Women; A Manual on Transitional Housing; Bricks and Roses,* a newsletter.

State Homeless and Low-Income Housing Organizations

The list below demonstrates that most states have at least one organization devoted to issues of homelessness, housing for low-income people, and related issues. In addition, most large and medium-sized cities have at least one of these organizations. The state coalitions listed here can provide information on the urban organizations, as well as details on specific activities such as state legislative action or advocacy on behalf of homeless people. Also, most of the organizations and the local coalitions publish newsletters and actively seek volunteers and other resources. They can also provide referrals to organizations and services operated by homeless people for other homeless people. Some of the latter also publish their own newspapers or newsletters as a means of support.

Alabama Coalition for the Homeless
2101 West Daniel Payne Drive
Birmingham, AL 35214
(205) 791-2040; (205) 791-0902 FAX

Alabama Low Income Housing Coalition
P.O. Box 95
Epes, AL 35460
(205) 652-9676; (205) 652-9678 FAX

Alaska Coalition for the Homeless
P.O. Box 75286
Fairbanks, AK 99707
(907) 456-3876; (907) 456-7864 FAX

Arizona Coalition To End Homelessness
P.O. Box 933
Phoenix, AZ 85001
(602) 258-7201; (602) 258-7275 FAX

Arkansas Coalition for the Prevention of Homelessness
P.O. Box 164009
Little Rock, AR 72216
(501) 374-1748; (501) 375-5134 FAX

Arkansas Low Income Housing Coalition
c/o Newton County Housing Council
P.O. Box 542
Jasper, AR 72641
(501) 466-5880

California Coalition for Rural Housing
926 J Street, Suite 422
Sacramento, CA 95814
(916) 443-4448; (916) 447-0458 FAX

California Homeless and Housing Coalition
926 J Street, Suite 422
Sacramento, CA 95814
(916) 447-0390; (916) 447-0458 FAX

California Homeless and Housing Coalition
Southern California Office
1010 South Flower Street, Suite 500
Los Angeles, CA 90015
(213) 746-7690; (213) 748-2432 FAX

Housing California
926 J Street, Suite 422-B
Sacramento, CA 95814
(916) 447-0503; (916) 447-0458 FAX

Colorado Affordable Housing Partnership
1981 Blake Street
Denver, CO 80202
(303) 297-2548; (303) 297-2615 FAX

Colorado Coalition for the Homeless
2100 Broadway
Denver, CO 80205
(303) 293-2217; (303) 293-2309 FAX

Connecticut Coalition To End Homelessness
30 Jordan Lane
Wethersfield, CT 06109
(203) 721-7876

Connecticut Housing Coalition
30 Jordan Lane
Wethersfield, CT 06109
(203) 563-2943; (203) 721-8896 FAX

Delaware Housing Coalition
P.O. Box 1633
Dover, DE 19903
(302) 856-7761; (302) 856-2599 FAX

Delaware Task Force on Homelessness
20 East Division Street
P.O. Box 1653
Dover, DE 19903
(302) 674-8500; (302) 674-8145 FAX

Coalition of Housing and Homeless Organizations
c/o Community Partnership
1700 Pennsylvania Avenue NW, Suite 80
Washington, DC 20006
(202) 639-3804; (202) 737-2345 FAX

Florida Coalition for the Homeless
119 Ferndale Drive
Tallahassee, FL 32302
(904) 878-1239; (904) 576-8319 FAX

Florida Low Income Housing Coalition
P.O. Box 932
Tallahassee, FL 32302
(904) 878-4219; (904) 942-6312 FAX

Georgia Homeless Resource Network
363 Georgia Avenue SE
Atlanta, GA 30312
(404) 230-5008; (404) 589-8251 FAX

Georgia Housing Coalition
c/o Housing Assistance Council
615 Peachtree Street NW, Suite 1130
Atlanta, GA 30308
(404) 892-4824; (404) 892-1204 FAX

Affordable Housing Alliance
2331 Seaview Avenue
P.O. Box 1329
Honolulu, HI 96807
(808) 946-2244; (808) 531-7196 FAX

Hawaii Statewide Coalition for the Homeless
c/o Waikiki Health Center
277 Ohua Avenue
Honolulu, HI 96815
(808) 922-4787; (808) 922-4794 FAX

Homeless Aloha
1002 North School Street, Building H
Honolulu, HI 96817
(808) 848-8801; (808) 841-1848 FAX

Idaho Housing Coalition
P.O. Box 1805
Boise, ID 83701
(208) 338-7066; (208) 338-7076 FAX

Illinois Coalition To End Homelessness
522 East Monroe Street, Suite 304
Springfield, IL 62701
(217) 788-8060; (217) 544-0067 FAX

Illinois Coalition To End Homelessness
c/o Chicago Coalition for the Homeless
1325 South Wabash Street, Suite 205
Chicago, IL 60605
(312) 435-0225; (312) 435-0198 FAX

Statewide Housing Action Coalition
202 South State Street, Suite 1414
Chicago, IL 60604
(312) 939-6074; (312) 939-6822 FAX

Indiana Coalition for Housing and Homeless Issues
902 North Capitol Avenue
Indianapolis, IN 46204
(317) 636-8819; (317) 634-7949 FAX

Iowa Coalition for Housing and the Homeless
921 Pleasant Street, Suite 111
Des Moines, IA 50309
(515) 288-5022

Homeless and Housing Coalition of Kentucky
3407 Rowena Road, Suite 2
Louisville, KY 40218
(502) 589-6488; (502) 456-4994 FAX

Louisiana Coalition for the Homeless
c/o Orleans Parish School System
4100 Touro Street
New Orleans, LA 70122
(504) 286-2884; (504) 286-2980 FAX

Louisiana for Low Income Housing Today
P.O. Box 50100
New Orleans, LA 70150
(504) 943-0044; (504) 944-3157 FAX

Maine Coalition for the Homeless
P.O. Box 415
Augusta, ME 04332
(207) 626-3567

Action for the Homeless
1021 North Calvert Street
Baltimore, MD 21202
(410) 659-0300; (410) 659-0996 FAX

Maryland Low Income Housing Coalition
28 East Ostend
Baltimore, MD 21230
(410) 727-4200; (410) 727-7515 FAX

Massachusetts Affordable Housing Alliance
25 West Street, Third Floor
Boston, MA 02111
(617) 728-9100; (617) 426-5162 FAX

Massachusetts Coalition for the Homeless
288 A Street, Fourth Floor
Boston, MA 02210
(617) 737-3508; (617) 737-3290 FAX

Massachusetts Shelter Providers
Office Tower #4
135 Copley Place, Mailbox 129
Boston, MA 02116
(617) 536-4352; (617) 262-3736 FAX

Michigan Coalition against Homelessness
1210 West Saginaw
Lansing, MI 48915
(517) 377-0509; (517) 377-0315 FAX

Michigan Housing Coalition
1210 West Saginaw
Lansing, MI 48915
(517) 377-0509; (517) 571-7307 FAX

Minnesota Coalition for the Homeless
122 West Franklin Avenue, Suite 318
Minneapolis, MN 55404
(612) 870-7073; (612) 870-7073 FAX

Minnesota Housing Partnership
122 West Franklin Avenue, Suite 522
Minneapolis, MN 55404
(612) 874-0112; (612) 874-9685 FAX

Mississippi Housing Coalition
c/o Planning and Community Development
P.O. Box 1898
Hattiesburg, MS 39403
(601) 545-4595; (601) 545-4608 FAX

Mississippi United against Homelessness
c/o Multi-County Community Services
P.O. Box 905
Meridian, MS 39302
(601) 483-4838; (601) 482-9861 FAX

Missouri Association for Social Welfare/
Low Income Housing Task Force
308 East High Street
Jefferson City, MO 63110
(314) 634-2901; (314) 634-8499 FAX

Montana Low Income Coalition
P.O. Box 1029
Helena, MT 59624
(406) 449-8801

Montana People's Action
208 East Main Street
Missoula, MT 59802
(406) 728-5297; (406) 728-5297 FAX

Nevada State Homeless Coalition
701 East Bridger, Suite 101
Las Vegas, NV 89107
(702) 883-0404; (702) 883-7074 FAX

New Hampshire Coalition for the Homeless
1039 Auburn Street
Manchester, NH 03103
(603) 623-1209

Non-Profit Affordable Housing Network of New Jersey
P.O. Box 1746
Trenton, NJ 08607
(609) 393-3752; (609) 393-9016 FAX

Right to Housing Coalition of New Jersey
118 Division Street
Elizabeth, NJ 07201
(908) 352-2989

New Mexico Coalition To End Homelessness
c/o Albuquerque Health Care for the Homeless
P.O. Box 25141
Albuquerque, NM 87125
(505) 247-3361; (505) 247-3364 FAX

Coalition for the Homeless
500 Eighth Avenue, Ninth Floor
New York City, NY 10018
(212) 695-8700

New York State Coalition for the Homeless
235 Lark Street
Albany, NY 12210
(518) 436-5612; (518) 436-5615 FAX

New York State Rural Housing Coalition
350 Northern Boulevard, Suite 101
Albany, NY 12204
(518) 434-1314; (518) 426-1258 FAX

North Carolina Low Income Housing Coalition
P.O. Box 27863
Raleigh, NC 27611
(919) 833-6201; (919) 828-1341 FAX

North Dakota Coalition for Homeless People
401 Third Avenue North
Fargo, ND 58102
(701) 241-1360; (701) 241-8559 FAX

Ohio Coalition for the Homeless
1066 North High Street
Columbus, OH 43201
(614) 291-1984; (614) 291-2009 FAX

Ohio Housing Coalition
1066 North High Street
Columbus, OH 43201
(614) 299-0544

Ohio Rural Housing Coalition
P.O. Box 787
Athens, OH 45701
(614) 594-8499; (614) 592-5994 FAX

Oklahoma Homeless Network
c/o Community Mental Health Center
P.O. Box 400
Norman, OK 73070
(405) 360-5100; (405) 360-5171 FAX

Oregon Housing Now
4626 Northeast Nineteenth
Portland, OR 97212
(503) 288-0317

Oregon Shelter Network
2211 Eleventh Street
Tillamook, OR 97141
(503) 842-5261; (503) 842-5261 FAX

Pennsylvania Low Income Housing
c/o Action Housing
#2 Gateway Center
Pittsburgh, PA 15222
(412) 281-2102; (412) 391-4512 FAX

Coalition for the Rights of the Homeless
Montebello A-O
Garden Hills, PR 00966
(808) 724-4051

Rhode Island Coalition for the Homeless
c/o Amos House
415 Friendship Street
Providence, RI 02907
(401) 421-6458; (401) 351-6917 FAX

Rhode Island Housing Network
P.O. Box 23188
Providence, RI 02903
(401) 351-8719

Rhode Island Right to Housing Coalition
c/o Amos House
P.O. Box 2873
Providence, RI 02907
(401) 272-0220; (401) 272-2137 FAX

South Carolina Citizens for Housing
P.O. Box 86
Columbia, SC 29202
(803) 734-6122; (803) 734-6220 FAX

South Carolina Coalition for the Homeless
3425 North Main Street
Columbia, SC 29203
(803) 779-4706

South Carolina Low Income Housing Coalition
P.O. Box 1520
Columbia, SC 29202
(803) 734-6122; (803) 734-6220 FAX

South Dakota Homeless Coalition
c/o South Falls Homeless Coalition
P.O. Box 1643
Sioux Falls, SD 57101
(605) 335-4217

Tennessee Housing and Homeless Coalition
2012 Twenty-first Avenue South
Nashville, TN 37212
(615) 385-2221; (615) 385-2157 FAX

Texas Homeless Network
411 West Second Street
Austin, TX 78701
(512) 478-9971; (800) 531-0828

Texas Low Income Housing Information Service
1100 East Eighth Street
Austin, TX 78702
(512) 477-8910; (512) 469-9802 FAX

Utah Homeless Coordinating Conference
c/o Utah Issues
1385 West Indiana
Salt Lake City, UT 84104
(801) 521-2025; (801) 355-7540 FAX

Vermont Affordable Housing Coalition
P.O. Box 827
Montpelier, VT 05602
(802) 223-1448

Vermont Coalition for the Homeless
P.O. Box 1616
Burlington, VT 05402
(802) 864-7402; (802) 862-1477 FAX

Interfaith Coalition of St. Croix
P.O. Box 88
Frederiksted
St. Croix, VI 00841
(809) 772-1142; (809) 772-2909 FAX

Virginia Coalition for the Homeless
7825 Cherokee Road
Richmond, VA 23225
(804) 320-4577; (804) 323-3950 FAX

Virginia Housing Coalition
c/o Eastern Shore Area Aging/CAA
P.O. Box 8
Onancock, VA 23417
(804) 787-3532; (804) 787-4230 FAX

Housing Trust Fund Coalition
c/o Fremont Public Association
P.O. Box 31151
Seattle, WA 98103
(206) 634-2222; (206) 633-6408 FAX

Washington Low Income Housing Coalition
315 West Mission Avenue
Spokane, WA 99201
(509) 325-0755; (509) 325-5882 FAX

Washington Low Income Housing Network
107 Pine Street, Suite 103
Seattle, WA 98101
(206) 442-9455; (206) 643-4669 FAX

Washington State Coalition for the Homeless
P.O. Box 955
Tacoma, WA 98401
(206) 572-4237; (206) 572-4237 FAX

West Virginia Housing Coalition
P.O. Box 987
Elkins, WV 26241
(304) 636-5897; (304) 636-6179 FAX

Wisconsin Coalition To End Homelessness
c/o Hebron House
807 North East Avenue
Waukesha, WI 53186
(414) 549-8720; (414) 549-8730 FAX

Wyoming against Homelessness
c/o COMEA Shelter
P.O. Box 15566
Cheyenne, WY 82003
(307) 632-3174; (307) 638-8905 FAX

Federal Agencies

Bureau of the Census
Suitland, MD 20233
(301) 763-5190
John G. Keane, Director

The agency conducts a count of homeless people in conjunction with the national census count each decade. Its efforts in 1980 were criticized by shelter providers and advocates as unrealistic and ineffective.

Center for Mental Health Services
Homeless Programs Section
Substance Abuse and Mental Health Services Administration
5600 Fishers Lane, Room 11C-05
Rockville, MD 20857
(301) 443-3706; (301) 443-0541 FAX
Walter Leginski, Ph.D., Acting Chief

This federal agency is concerned with mental illness prevention and treatment. The Homeless Programs Section administers national demonstration projects researching housing and service coordination for homeless mentally ill adults. It also manages the PATH (Projects for Assistance in Transition from Homelessness) programs and ACCESS (Access to Community Care and Effective Services and Supports) for severely mentally ill homeless persons, who may also have drug and/or alcohol problems.

Department of Agriculture (USDA)
Fourteenth Street and Independence Avenue NW
Washington, DC 20250
(202) 447-3631
Michael Espy, Secretary

USDA, through the Food and Nutrition Service, administers the Food Stamp and McKinney Act regulations to aid homeless people. In addition, it manages the Temporary Emergency Food Assistance Program (TEFAP) to provide surplus food commodities to the homeless. The Farmers Home Administration (FmHA), an agency of USDA, operates two programs to make foreclosed Section 502 rural homes available to the homeless.

Department of Education (USED)
400 Maryland Avenue SW
Washington, DC 20202

Adult Education for the Homeless Program
Room 4426
(202) 205-5499; (202) 205-8973 FAX
James Parker, National Coordinator

The Adult Education for the Homeless Program is a McKinney Act program of discretionary grants to the states. Programs are often offered together with other support services.

Education for Homeless Children and Youth Program
Office of Elementary and Secondary Education
Room 2004
(202) 401-1692; (202) 401-1112 FAX
Francine Vinson, Education Program Specialist

This McKinney Act program provides formula grants to the state education agencies to ensure that homeless children have access to the same education services as other children. Support services are designed to facilitate enrollment, attendance, and transportation; some grants support demonstration projects. Each state has a state monitor to oversee local programs.

Department of Health and Human Services (HHS)
200 Independence Avenue SW
Washington, DC 20201
(202) 245-6296
Donna Shalala, Secretary

HHS oversees the McKinney Act program to provide primary health care to homeless people through public and private nonprofit organizations. Component parts of the agency also administer other portions of the legislation; these are listed separately in this section.

Department of Housing and Urban Development (HUD)
451 Seventh Street SW
Washington, DC 20410
Henry Cisneros, Secretary

HUD administers a variety of low-income housing programs, with components involving housing for homeless people. These include conventional public housing projects, as well as other forms of assisted and subsidized housing. Under the McKinney Act, HUD operates the following: Emergency Shelter, Supportive Housing, Shelter Plus Care, Section 8 SRO, Surplus Property, Single Property Disposition, and other programs.

HUD USER
P.O. Box 6091
Rockville, MD 20850
(800) 245-2691; (301) 251-5154; (301) 251-5747 FAX

HUD USER is sponsored by the HUD Office of Policy Development and Research; it is a research information service and offers on-line bibliographic databases.

PUBLICATIONS: Recent Research Results.

Department of Labor
Job Training for the Homeless Demonstration Program
Employment and Training Administration
Francis Perkins Building, Room N5637
200 Constitution Avenue NW
Washington, DC 20210
(202) 219-8660; (202) 219-5455 FAX
John Heinberg, Special Assistant, Office of Planning and Policy Development

Under the McKinney Act, the agency administers a job training demonstration program for homeless people that provides competitive grants to state and local public agencies and nonprofit organizations. Grants may be used for basic skills instruction, remedial education, literacy instruction, job search activities, job counseling, and job readiness training.

Department of Transportation (DOT)
Outreach Demonstration Program
Office of Drug Enforcement and Program Compliance
400 Seventh Street SW, Room 10200
Washington, DC 20590
(202) 366-3784; (202) 366-3897 FAX
Robert Knisely, Special Assistant to the Secretary

The agency administers a joint interagency demonstration project to provide outreach to homeless people in transportation centers and help them with housing and services.

Department of Veterans Affairs
810 Vermont Avenue NW
Washington, DC 20420
(202) 233-2300
Jesse Brown, Secretary of Veterans Affairs

Domiciliary Care for Homeless Veterans Program
(202) 535-7530; (202) 535-7006 FAX
Richard Olson, Chief

The domiciliary care program is designed to address clinical needs of homeless veterans with psychiatric illness or alcohol or drug problems. Services include outreach, assessment, treatment, and aid in securing housing and employment.

Homeless Chronically Mentally Ill Veterans Program
(202) 535-7303; (202) 535-7581 FAX
Gay Koerber, Associate Director

This McKinney Act program provides outreach, case management, and residential psychiatric treatment for veterans.

Homeless Veterans Reintegration Projects
Veterans Employment and Training Service
Francis Perkins Building, Room S1316
(202) 523-9110; (202) 523-7341 FAX
Eileen Conners, Veterans Employment Specialist

These McKinney Act programs provide grants to the states for innovative employment and training services for homeless unemployed veterans.

Emergency Food and Shelter National Board
701 North Fairfax Street, Suite 310
Alexandria, VA 22314
(703) 706-9660; (703) 706-9679 FAX
Wiley B. Cooper, Director

The board was established in 1983 as a public-private partnership of the federal government and six national nonprofit organizations; it administers emergency McKinney Act funds for nonprofit organizations serving the homeless with food, shelter, transportation, and emergency rent, mortgage assistance, or first month's rent. Membership of the national board, which makes grants to local boards, is composed of: United Way of America, American Red Cross, Catholic Charities, Council of Jewish Federations, Salvation Army, and Council of Churches.

PUBLICATIONS: A quarterly newsletter; *Checklist for Success,* a description of programs.

General Services Administration (GSA)
General Services Building
Washington, DC 20405
(202) 525-0800
Richard Austin, Acting Director

GSA is responsible for McKinney Act provisions to make underutilized federal space and buildings available to assist the homeless. The agency also administers a similar requirement affecting state surplus personal property.

Health Resources and Services Administration (HRSA)
Division of Special Populations
5600 Fishers Lane, Room 9-12
Rockville, MD 20857
(301) 443-2512; (301) 443-4786 FAX
James L. Gray, Chief, Health Care for the Homeless Branch

HRSA manages the McKinney Act Health Care for the Homeless programs, which are supported by discretionary grants for primary care, alcohol and drug treatment, and mental health services provided by public and private nonprofit organizations. HRSA also administers the Health Care Services for Homeless Children program under the McKinney Act; the program's goal is to develop innovative outreach, health services, and referral services for children.

Interagency Council on the Homeless
451 Seventh Street SW, Room 7274
Washington, DC 20410
(202) 708-1480; (202) 708-3672 FAX
Marsha A. Martin, Executive Director

The council, created by a McKinney Act requirement for federal leadership and coordination, supports a working group of all participating federal agencies to review, monitor, evaluate, and recommend improvements to the McKinney Act. The council also provides technical assistance.

PUBLICATIONS: *Council Communique,* a newsletter; annual report; list of state contacts for homeless programs.

National Clearinghouse for Alcohol and Drug Information (NCADI)
P.O. Box 2345
Rockville, MD 20847
(800) 729-6686; (301) 468-2600; (301) 468-6433 FAX; (800) 487-4889
or (301) 230-2867 TDD

NCADI is supported by the U.S. Center for Substance Abuse Prevention; it distributes publications on alcohol and drug use, as well as grant announcements, training materials, and prevention literature. Free database searches are offered, and NCADI supports a state network for information dissemination to meet community needs.

National Institute of Mental Health
5600 Fishers Lane, Room 10-105
Rockville, MD 20857
(301) 443-3648; (301) 443-4045 FAX
Cille Kennedy, Special Assistant to the Director, Division of Epidemiology and Services Research

National Institute on Alcohol Abuse and Alcoholism (NIAAA)
Homeless Demonstration and Evaluation Branch
5600 Fishers Lane, Room 13C-02
Rockville, MD 20857
(301) 443-0786; (301) 443-9334 FAX
Robert Huebner, Acting Chief

This NIAAA component supports research demonstrations on homelessness under the McKinney Act, as well as technical assistance papers on housing and services.

Social Security Administration
Office of Supplemental Security Income
3-R-1 Operations Building
6401 Security Boulevard
Baltimore, MD 21235
(410) 965-4441; (410) 966-1337 FAX
Georgina Harding, Chief, SSI Outreach Branch

The Outreach Demonstration Program of SSA supports programs to increase outreach efforts and identify persons potentially eligible for benefits, assist them with applications, and help them receive benefits for the duration of their eligibility. Some projects focus specifically on homeless people and mentally ill persons. SSA collaborates in a joint project with the Department of Veterans Affairs to handle claims for homeless veterans.

9

Print Resources

THIS CHAPTER CONTAINS FOUR LISTS OF print resources. The first covers some of the major books and other materials published on homelessness. Some are included because they have historical value, others because they are a good resource on a specific topic. Increasingly, understanding homelessness means understanding poverty, so some of the selections serve as resources on aspects of poverty or its solutions that are especially relevant. Entries that are hard to access have been kept to a minimum. This list does not include the numerous articles published in periodicals and journals, or the useful, detailed reports or monographs issued by most of the organizations listed in Chapter 8. These organizations often publish a list of materials that they currently distribute.

The second list contains bibliographies that cover some of the above sources as well as periodicals and journal articles of note. The third list covers key resources for staying current on homelessness materials, including some periodicals produced by national organizations, to keep the reader up to date on new publications of interest.

The final bibliography includes some of the major publications of the federal and state governments, as well as information on how to locate and use them. Included here are important congressional hearings, government reports on specific programs to aid homeless people, and agency reports and monographs on related topics.

General Reference Materials

Activism and Advocacy

Barak, Gregg. **Gimme Shelter: A Social History of Homelessness in America.** New York: Praeger, 1992. 212p. $14.95. ISBN 0-275-94401-8.

As a criminologist, the author analyzes homelessness as a crime against those who experience it. He also examines advocacy efforts, both in public education and litigation.

Day, Dorothy. **The Long Loneliness: An Autobiography.** New York: Harper & Row, 1981. 286p. $5.95. ISBN 0-06-061751-9.

In the decades preceding the 1980s, there were two significant sources of help for homeless people: the traditional missions and Salvation Army establishments, and the Catholic Worker Houses of Hospitality spread around the nation. The author, cofounder of the CW movement and its newspaper editor for over 30 years, tells the story of the Depression-era founding of the small shelters and soup lines that still exist today, and of her longtime leadership on issues of social justice, peace, and racial equality.

Lewis, Barbara A. **The Kids' Guide to Social Action.** Minneapolis: Free Spirit Publishing, 1991. 185p. $14.95. ISBN 0-915793-29-6.

This guide is focused on children's action on social problems and environmental concerns, but it contains helpful step-by-step information for any reader interested in communicating with Congress, putting on a fund-raising event, or getting a public-service announcement aired. It explains in clear terms the processes by which state and federal laws are passed, and gives success stories of other kids' groups.

Miller, William. **Dorothy Day: A Biography.** New York: Harper & Row, 1982. 527p. $10.95. ISBN 0-06-065752-8.

This biography of Catholic Worker cofounder Dorothy Day offers a candid portrait of her work in the social justice movement.

Rader, Victoria. **Signal through the Flames: Mitch Snyder and America's Homeless.** Kansas City, MO: Sheed & Ward, 1986. 272p. $10.95. ISBN 0-934134-24-3.

The work of Washington, D.C.'s Community for Creative Non-Violence is explored from a campaign viewpoint, with the development of the organization's various public efforts for peace and justice examined from inception to retrospective analysis. Significant insights into the workings of the community result from the availability of community members past and present, as well as the group's extensive archives on its work.

Ward, Jim. **Organizing for the Homeless.** Ottawa: Canadian Council on Social Development, 1989. 117p. $15. ISBN 0-88810-390-5.

While homeless people themselves have taken steps to organize on their own behalf, very few written works address the need for this action, or the issues involved when nonhomeless people try to foster such empowerment among homeless people. The importance and particulars of organizing are stressed, along with insights into supporting homeless-driven efforts to address larger institutions and to raise funds.

Alcohol and Drug Use and Treatment

Argerious, Milton, and Dennis McCarty. **Treating Alcoholism and Drug Abuse among Homeless Men and Women.** Binghamton, NY: Haworth Press, 1990. 164p. $24.95. ISBN 0-86656-992-8.

This collection of 11 articles includes examinations of nine community demonstration grants in alcohol and drug treatment among homeless people, funded by the National Institute on Alcohol Abuse and Alcoholism. Two chapters cover the overall thrust of the program and some initial research findings. The projects include those for dually diagnosed individuals, chronic public inebriates, and women at risk of alcoholism.

Currie, Elliott. **Reckoning: Drugs, the Cities, and the American Future.** New York: Hill and Wang, 1993. 405p. $25. ISBN 0-8090-8049-4.

The epidemic of urban drug use is already known as a symptom of larger ills, but the author dissects the documentation of when drug use occurs in poor families, especially immigrants, and how this plague has been increased by the destruction of poor communities through economic policy, loss of housing, and other social components. He suggests ways that employment and redirected spending can end or prevent the resulting problems, including homelessness.

Tidwell, Mike. **In the Shadow of the White House.** Rocklin, CA: Prima Publishing, 1992. 341p. $19.95. ISBN 1-55958-108-5.

Images of homeless single men as users of drugs and alcohol abound. For those who work to pull themselves out of addiction, the road is hard and unwelcoming: a daily struggle with recovery, no transportation, no résumé, few chances at employment that pays enough to acquire housing or reunite a family. The author tells in gritty detail the efforts—frequently unsuccessful—of the men he encountered as a drug counselor in a transitional housing program in Washington, D.C.

Wiseman, Jacqueline P. **Stations of the Lost: The Treatment of Skid Row Alcoholics.** Chicago: University of Chicago Press, 1979. 346p. $9. ISBN 0-226-90307-9.

This book examines the chronic inebriate, or skid row alcoholic, from two points of view: that of the alcoholic and that of the social service agencies whose work brings them in contact with those whose chronic drinking and homelessness is institutionalized in the term "public nuisance." The author examines the social service providers as agents of management on behalf of larger social interests.

Children and Families

Bach, Victor, and Renee Steinhagen. **Alternatives to the Welfare Hotel: Using Emergency Assistance To Provide Decent Transitional Shelter for Homeless Families.** New York: Community Service Society (105 East Twenty-second Street, New York, NY 10010), 1987. 56p. $6.50.

Family homelessness in New York City is examined, as well as alternative models for shelters operated with emergency assistance funds. This report advances the idea that short-term shelters can become permanent low-income housing.

Bassuk, Ellen L., Rebecca W. Carman, and Linda F. Weinreb. **Community Care for Homeless Families: A Program Design Manual.** Newton Centre, MA: Better Homes Foundation, 1990. 161p. $10.

This manual contains a series of articles by different authors who focus on the nature of family homelessness, community-based programs, children's and special group needs, and family empowerment.

Berck, Judith, with Robert Coles. **No Place To Be: Voices of Homeless Children.** New York: Houghton Mifflin, 1992. $14.95. ISBN 0-395-53350-3.

This book gives the point of view of homeless children through over 30 interviews with those living in welfare hotels and shelters. Poems and photos are included.

Born, Catherine E. **Our Future and Our Only Hope: A Survey of City Halls Regarding Children and Families.** Washington, DC: National League of Cities (NLC), September 1989. 118p. $15. ISBN 0-933729-52-9.

The NLC surveyed city halls around the nation to find the most pressing issues for children and families. Families ranked the shortage of affordable housing highest on the list of priorities. A wide variety of successful local programs, in areas ranging from housing to substance abuse to family support, are profiled.

Boxhill, Nancy A., ed. **Homeless Children: The Watchers and the Waiters.** Binghamton, NY: Haworth Press, 1990. 156p. $27.95. ISBN 0-86656-789-5.

This collection of articles covers a range of issues affecting children in shelters; those in Atlanta were studied here. Material on mother-and-child relations, behavior of children, and children's health is included.

Jackson, Shelley. **Materials on the Education of Homeless Children.** Cambridge, MA: Center on Law and Education, 1987.

This packet contains materials on both state and federal statutes and regulations on the education of homeless children. Also included are court decisions; materials are periodically updated.

————. **State Plans for the Education of Homeless Children and Youth.** Cambridge, MA: Center for Law and Education, 1990. 75p.

This report assesses state plans for 35 states, and finds that most have failed to meet the needs of homeless children as required under the McKinney Act.

Kozol, Jonathan. **Rachel and Her Children: Homeless Families in America.** New York: Ballantine Books, 1989. 261p. $8.95. ISBN 0-449-90339-7.

This vivid account of life in the welfare hotels of New York City demonstrates not only the financial waste of this method of serving homeless families, but also the damage done to young lives and struggling parents. Alongside the personal stories told by mothers, fathers, and children are the chilling statistics that explain how poverty works in daily life.

Kryder-Coe, Julee H., Lester M. Salamon, and Janice M. Molnar. **Homeless Children and Youth.** New Brunswick, NJ: Transaction Press, 1992. 323p. $34.95. ISBN 0-88738-386-6.

This book collects a series of papers presented at a 1991 conference; the authors covered housing, welfare, and child welfare policy, and the scope, impact, and causes of child and youth homelessness.

National Council of Juvenile and Family Court Judges, Child Welfare League of America, Youth Law Center, and National Center for Youth Law. **Making Reasonable Efforts: Steps for Keeping Families Together.** New York: Edna McConnell Clark Foundation, 1992. 120p. Free.

Poor families split up by the child welfare system frequently end up as separate but homeless households: parents in shelters or institutions, children in often multiple foster-care placements. Family reunification is not emphasized, and foster-care children without family ties or living skills often graduate to homelessness as young adults. This monograph examines the responsibilities of agencies, attorneys, and judges in making and continuing these placements.

National League of Cities. **Children, Families & Cities: Programs That Work at the Local Level.** Washington, DC: National League of Cities, 1987. 201p. $15. ISBN 0-933729-32-4.

Program profiles of more than three dozen local efforts to address child and family issues, including homelessness, make up this directory, which provides project contacts and "lessons learned."

Stanford Center for the Study of Families, Children, and Youth. **The Stanford Studies of Homeless Families, Children, and Youth.** Menlo Park, CA: Stanford University, 1991.

The ongoing studies of this research program are presented, with information on how homelessness affects the physical and mental health of children and families.

Counting Homeless People

Community for Creative Non-Violence (CCNV). **A Forced March to Nowhere—Homelessness: A National Priority.** Washington, DC: Community for Creative Non-Violence (425 Second Street NW, Washington, DC 20001), September 1980. 87p. $5.

In 1980, the U.S. House of Representatives Committee on the District of Columbia sought to compare the little-known problem of homelessness in the nation's capital to the difficulties faced in the rest of the nation. CCNV, a Washington-based service and advocacy organization, prepared this testimony after canvassing service providers and officials around the country.

Hombs, Mary Ellen, and Mitch Snyder. **Homelessness in America: A Forced March to Nowhere.** 2d ed. Washington, D.C.: Community for Creative Non-Violence (425 Second Street NW, Washington, DC 20001), 1983. 146p. $5. ISBN 0-686-39879-3.

This national survey of homelessness and its origins was first released in conjunction with the original 1982 congressional hearings of the same title. When it was subsequently updated the following year, it included the estimates of national homelessness that engendered national controversy.

Horowitz, Carl F. "Mitch Snyder's Phony Numbers: The Fiction of Three Million Homeless." **Heritage Foundation Policy Review** (Summer 1989).

This article attempts to refute the numbers used by homeless advocate Mitch Snyder, who repeatedly stated that 3 million Americans are homeless. Certain portions of other research efforts are summarized in support of the author's argument.

Kondratas, S. Anna. "Myth, Reality, and the Homeless." **Insight** (14 April 1986), 73.

The author, the chief public defender of government efforts at counting homeless people, became in 1989 the HUD official in charge of homeless programs. As a policy analyst for the Heritage Foundation, she addresses three assertions about homeless people: that there are very large numbers of them, that the Reagan Administration worsened their condition by its policies, and that the federal government is failing to help them.

————. "A Strategy for Helping America's Homeless." **Heritage Foundation Backgrounder** 431 (6 May 1985).

The author argues against expanded federal involvement as the cure for increased homelessness, asserting that voluntary, state, and local efforts are needed to assist those in need.

Tucker, William. "America's Homeless: Victims of Rent Control." **Heritage Foundation Backgrounder** 685 (12 January 1989). 12p.

The size of the problem of homelessness is studied here, from the perspective of conservative political thought that sees the tight housing markets of some cities with large homeless populations as being directly connected to the presence of rent regulation. The author relies on the data of the 1984 HUD report for his claims.

Criminalization of Homelessness

National Law Center on Homelessness and Poverty. **Go Directly to Jail.** Washington, DC: National Law Center, 1991. 88p. $12.

This report surveys the local conditions in areas where antihomeless laws have been passed in recent years. It looks for similarities in the inadequacy of welfare benefits, high housing costs, and lack of shelter and services in communities that have cracked down on homeless people.

Educational Materials and Curricula

Educators for Social Responsibility of New York. **Poverty in the United States: Myths and Realities.** New York: Educators for Social Responsibility (425 Riverside Drive, New York, NY 10115), 1987. 20p.

This teaching unit is geared toward use in U.S. history, economics, or social problems courses for high school students. It includes a teacher's manual, background materials, and a quiz for students.

Housing Now! **Housing and Homelessness: A Teaching Guide.** Washington, DC: Community for Creative Non-Violence, 1989. 71p. $10. Available from the National Low Income Housing Coalition (1012 Fourteenth Street NW, Washington, DC 20005).

This curriculum, with lesson plans for both elementary and high school students, examines the nation's background of increased homelessness and myths about poverty. Affordable housing is explored as a solution to homelessness. The teacher's guide includes a glossary of key terms, as well as a listing of other reading materials and films.

Pennsylvania Homeless Student Initiative. **Homelessness Curricula: Five Exemplary Approaches.** Available from the Pennsylvania Homeless Student Initiative Education Liaison, (215) 348-2940.

Five samples of approaches to teaching about homelessness are included; each covers causes and effects, what it is like to be homeless, myths about homelessness, and government and community responses.

Vermont Department of Education. **Unsheltered Lives: An Interdisciplinary Resource and Activity Guide for Teaching about Homelessness in Grades K–12.** 1992. Available from the Vermont Department of Education, (802) 828-2753.

The activities covered in this package have three components: examining stereotypes and feelings, doing research in the local community, and action projects.

Elderly Homeless People

Keigher, Sharon M., ed. **Housing Risks and Homelessness among the Urban Elderly.** Binghamton, NY: Haworth Press, 1991. 156p. $24.95. ISBN 1-56024-165-9.

Gentrification, demolition, and federal cuts in benefits have all contributed to homelessness in the last decade, yet the elderly appear to be underrepresented among homeless people. This collection of articles examines the unique housing problems of the older American, as well as the growing shortage of affordable housing.

Emergency Shelter

Hamberg, Jill. **Building and Zoning Regulations: A Guide for Sponsors of Shelters and Housing for the Homeless in New York City.** New York:

Community Service Society (105 East Twenty-second Street, New York, NY 10010), 1984. 49p. $4.

Local regulation is often an impediment to the creation of facilities for homeless people and other groups. Although written for a New York audience, this guide offers a basis for activity anywhere. It presents some of the basic laws covering building and zoning matters, the process of procuring permits and approvals, and issues in site selection.

Seldon, Paul, and Margot Jones. **Moving On: Making Room for the Homeless—A Practical Guide to Shelter.** New York: United Church Board for Homeland Ministries, 1982. 63p. $3. Available from the Coalition for the Homeless (500 Eighth Avenue, New York, NY 10018).

Setting up a shelter can require a church or community group to obtain zoning permits, notify city agencies, examine other programs, and address community concerns. This manual covers all the basics of "how-to" in New York City, but can easily be applied to other situations, as it also discusses operating procedures, staffing, and funding.

Employment

Schwarz, John E., and Thomas J. Volgy. **The Forgotten Americans.** New York City: W. W. Norton, 1992. 219p. $19.95. ISBN 0-393-03388-0.

Forty percent of all full-time workers with a family of four live below the poverty line. Combined with rising housing costs and lack of health care coverage, this fact places many at risk of homelessness. The authors examine the issues and needs of the working poor.

Shapiro, Isaac, and Marion Nichols. **Unprotected: Unemployment Insurance and Jobless Workers in 1988.** Washington, DC: Center on Budget and Policy Priorities (777 North Capitol Street NE, Washington, DC 20001), 1989. 20p.

Record cutbacks in unemployment insurance and a sharp increase in long-term unemployment resulted in a record-tying low of only one in three out-of-work Americans receiving benefits in 1988. This report profiles problems faced by minorities, state efforts, and reductions in training programs.

Southern Regional Council. **Hard Labor: A Report on Day Labor and Temporary Employment.** Atlanta: Southern Regional Council (60 Walton Street NW, Atlanta, GA 30303), 1988. 48p. $10.

Day labor is one of the nation's fastest growing industries, and one easily accessed by many homeless people in need of work. This year-long study looks at day labor in 37 metropolitan areas where poor people do dangerous and difficult work for less than subsistence wages. The report also finds that many agencies routinely violate federal and state anti-discrimination laws.

Food and Hunger

Brown, J. Larry, and H. F. Pizer. **Living Hungry in America.** New York: Macmillan Publishing Company, 1987. 212p. $18.95. ISBN 0-02-517290-5.

In 1985, a team of prominent physicians set out to learn firsthand about hunger in the nation. Accompanied by other health professionals, social workers, and clergy, they toured schools, day care sites, and homes in 19 states. This book details the startling extent of the hunger and malnutrition they found.

Physician Task Force on Hunger in America. **Hunger in America: The Growing Epidemic.** Middletown, CT: Wesleyan University Press, 1985. 231p. $8.95. ISBN 0-8915-6158-4.

In early 1984, the Physician Task Force, composed of physicians, health experts, and academic and religious leaders, set out to travel the country to document the nature and scope of hunger, much as had been done in New England. Their major findings painted a worsening picture of hunger for the poor.

Fund-Raising

The Foundation Center. **Grant Guides.** New York: The Foundation Center, 1992. (Available from The Foundation Center, 1001 Connecticut Avenue NW, Washington, DC 20006.) $60 each.

These specialized guides cover grants from foundations and other sources for programs in the areas of alcohol and drug abuse; children and youth; community development, housing, and employment; health programs; homelessness; mental health, addictions, and crisis services; physically and mentally disabled people; public health; public policy; and social services.

General

Baum, Alice S., and Donald W. Burnes. **A Nation in Denial: The Truth about Homelessness.** Boulder, CO: Westview Press, 1993. 247p. $16.95. ISBN 0-8133-8245-9.

The authors make a case for homelessness being tied more to problems of alcohol and drug use, as well as mental illness, than to housing costs and low incomes.

Baxter, Ellen, and Kim Hopper. **Private Lives/Public Spaces: Homeless Adults on the Streets of New York City.** New York: Community Service Society (105 East Twenty-second Street, New York, NY 10010), 1981. 129p. $6.50.

This 15-month study primarily reports on the causes of contemporary homelessness as they were first revealed in New York and other cities. It describes in detail the procedures and operations of the existing public and private shelters and the ways that homeless persons survive on the streets.

Bingham, Richard D., Roy E. Green, and Sammis B. White, eds. **The Homeless in Contemporary Society.** Beverly Hills, CA: Sage Publications, 1986. 277p. $18.95. ISBN 0-8039-2889-0.

A brief history of homelessness in the United States is presented in this anthology, with essays on veterans, women and children, and the debate over numbers. Attention is then turned to the roles of nonprofit and religious organizations and local, state, and federal government, as well as programs in other countries.

Blau, Joel. **The Visible Poor: Homelessness in the United States.** New York: Oxford University Press, 1992. 235p. $22.95. ISBN 0-19-505743-0.

This book is intended for a general audience, and, as such, the author takes pains to examine the economic, social, and political basis of homelessness in straightforward terms. Consequently, the more sophisticated reader also receives a fresh examination of some basic themes underlying homelessness and the public and public policy response to it.

Boston Foundation. **Homelessness: Critical Issues for Policy and Practice.** Boston: Boston Foundation, 1987. 64p. $4.

Eleven short essays on homelessness, health, housing, and other topics, prepared for a Boston conference of academics and activists, are presented here as a general overview of the problem.

Burt, Martha R. **Over the Edge: The Growth of Homelessness in the 1980s.** Washington, DC: Urban Institute Press and Russell Sage Foundation, 1991. 267p. $29.95. ISBN 0-87154-177-7.

Persistent homelessness is related to structural changes in the nation, according to this author, who surveyed numerous cities and interviewed homeless people seeking services. She calls for increased low-rent housing production, more subsidies, restructured employment (including education and training), and more community-based care.

Caton, Carol L. M. **Homeless in America.** New York: Oxford University Press, 1990. 236p. $29.95. ISBN 0-19-503918-1.

This collection includes essays by some of the more prominent social scientists involved in homelessness. They discuss the history and causes of homelessness, as well as the effects of housing and shelter policies.

Coates, Robert C. **A Street Is Not a Home.** Buffalo: Prometheus Books, 1990. 356p. $15.95. ISBN 0-87975-621-7.

This San Diego municipal court judge proposes solutions to homelessness based on his ideas and experiences. He suggests that different groups of homeless people (women, children, unskilled men) need specific aid, including affordable housing and empowering support.

Cohen, Carl I., and Jay Sokolovsky. **Old Men of the Bowery.** New York: Guilford Press, 1989. 248p. $29.95. ISBN 0-89862-509-2.

The history and current state of the Bowery, as seen in surveys of men who live there, are presented, along with proposals for intervention and support, as well as temporary housing.

Cuomo, Mario M. **1933/1983—Never Again. A Report to the National Governors' Association Task Force on the Homeless.** Portland, ME: NGA, 1983. 88p.

This national survey of the problems of hunger and homelessness offers portraits of the needy juxtaposed against the images of the Great Depression. It proposes a national policy for ending homelessness based on adequate emergency relief, improved income and benefits, and federal action to provide permanent housing.

Giamo, Benedict. **On the Bowery.** Iowa City: University of Iowa Press, 1989. 261p. $28.95. ISBN 0-87745-243-1.

Like skid row, the Bowery historically embodies the very notion of homelessness. The author examines the history and cultural significance of such places in relation to contemporary homelessness.

Giamo, Benedict, and Jeffrey Grunberg. **Beyond Homelessness.** Iowa City: University of Iowa Press, 1992. 210p. $25.95. ISBN 0-87745-364-0.

This book consists of conversations with several people commenting on contemporary homelessness and advocacy, including Dr. Robert Jay Lifton, expert on the psychology of victims and survivors; Dr. Robert Coles, a psychiatrist who has worked with poor children and families; and Sister Mary Rose McGeady of the youth shelter Covenant House.

Hamberg, Jill, and Kim Hopper. **The Making of America's Homeless: From Skid Row to New Poor 1945–1984.** New York: Community Service Society (105 East Twenty-second Street, New York, NY 10010), 1984. 91p. $6.50.

A definitive historical perspective on homelessness since World War II, this report offers analyses of poverty and the growing gap between rich and poor, the emergence of widespread homelessness, and the impact of deinstitutionalization, as well as postwar housing trends and the development of public programs.

Hoch, Charles, and Robert A. Slayton. **New Homeless and Old.** Philadelphia: Temple University Press, 1989. 299p. $29.95. ISBN 0-87722-600-8.

The authors use case studies from several cities to show how the old hotels of urban neighborhoods offered community, support, and security for a variety of residents, and how their demolition and loss across the country has created difficulties for those who relied on this form of housing.

Hope, Marjorie, and James Young. **The Faces of Homelessness.** New York: Lexington Books, 1986. 318p. $15.95. ISBN 0-669-14200-X.

This general view of homelessness includes a national survey of the problem, with special focus on Washington, D.C., and Cincinnati. The authors look at the role of displacement, the lack of community supports for the mentally ill, and the problem of unemployment.

Hopper, Kim, Ellen Baxter, Stuart Cox, and Lawrence Klein. **One Year Later: The Homeless Poor in New York City, 1982.** New York: Community Service Society (105 East Twenty-second Street, New York, NY 10010), 1982. 92p. $6.50.

This update on the ground-breaking *Private Lives/Public Spaces* examines the plight of homeless people in New York City one year after the original study.

Kroloff, Rabbi Charles A. **54 Ways You Can Help the Homeless.** New York: Hugh Lauter Levin Associates and Behrman House, 1993. 96p. $1.95. ISBN 0-88363-888-6.

Included are concrete ideas on how to give directly to homeless people, how to find volunteer opportunities, how children can help, and how to make a difference in policy work.

Momeni, Jamshid A., ed. **Homelessness in the United States. Vol. I: State Surveys.** Westport, CT: Greenwood Press, 1989. 250p. $49.95. ISBN 0-313-25566-0.

This survey of homelessness across the country contains 14 chapters, each authored by a different individual or group, presenting a wide variety of perspectives. There is no standard data source or analytical method, but all attempt to define and solve the problem of homelessness.

Rossi, Peter. **Down and Out in America: The Origins of Homelessness.** Chicago: University of Chicago Press, 1989. 247p. $15.95. ISBN 0-226-72828-5.

Homeless people who sleep outside, as well as those who use shelters, are studied here. The author distinguishes between homelessness and extreme poverty in concluding that the loss of affordable housing, the decline in demand for unskilled labor, and the fluctuation of public assistance account for the resurgence of homelessness.

————. **Without Shelter: Homelessness in the 1980s.** New York: Priority Press Publications, a Twentieth Century Fund paper, 1989. 79p. $8.95. ISBN 0-087078-234-7.

This volume examines the recent growth of homelessness, with a focus on research studies attempting to assess the problem.

Salerno, Dan, Kim Hopper, and Ellen Baxter. **Hardship in the Heartland: Homelessness in Eight U.S. Cities.** New York: Community Service Society (105 East Twenty-second Street, New York, NY 10010), 1984. 184p. $10.

This well-documented report looks at the growth of homelessness in Cleveland, Tulsa, Chicago, Denver, Detroit, Milwaukee, Cincinnati, and Madison, providing a summary of existing research efforts and a specific examination of the mentally ill homeless.

Schwartz, David C., and John H. Glascock. **Combating Homelessness: A Resource Book.** New Brunswick, NJ: Rutgers University Press, 1989. 178p. $19.95. ISBN 0-87722-568-0.

A wide variety of resource materials is presented, including recent basic information on homelessness, summaries of federal laws, an overview of funding sources, a listing of state prevention programs, some sample statutes, a federal agency contact list, and an extensive bibliography. The information is indexed for easier access.

Snow, David A., and Leon Anderson. **Down on Their Luck.** Berkeley: University of California Press, 1993. 391p. $15. ISBN 0-520-07989-2.

The authors tell the first-person stories of homeless people around the nation, and present the results of extensive interviews and profiles done in Austin, Texas, among homeless people. The outcome is a vivid picture of the coping mechanisms of those without shelter, from how they make money to how they get a laugh on a long day.

Sosin, Michael R., Paul Colson, and Susan Grossman. **Homelessness in Chicago: Poverty and Pathology, Social Institutions and Social Change.** Chicago: Chicago Community Trust, 1988. 397p. ISBN 0-9615118-0-X.

This survey of Chicago homelessness examines social and economic conditions surrounding poverty and finds some characteristics associated with homelessness that appear to be common to all poverty. The report also contains findings about the episodic nature of homelessness.

U.S. Conference of Mayors. **A Status Report on Hunger and Homelessness in America's Cities.** Washington, DC: U.S. Conference of Mayors (1620 I Street NW, Washington, DC, 20006), published annually. $10.

The mayors annually survey more than two dozen cities to examine the state of the problems of hunger and homelessness in their communities. They offer profiles of the growth of demand for services, waiting lists for housing, and primary causes of these problems.

Wright, James D. **Address Unknown.** New York: A. de Gruyter, 1989. 170p. $17.95. ISBN 0-202-30364-0.

This sociologist analyzes many of the prevailing ideas about homeless people and shows how diverse the problem really is. He argues against the idea of personal pathology being a root cause, and proposes social and economic factors that he believes generate homelessness.

Health and Mental Health

Bassuk, Ellen L., ed. **The Mental Health Needs of Homeless Persons.** New Directions for Mental Health Services. Paperback Sourcebook 30. San Francisco: Jossey-Bass, 1986. $14.95. ISBN 0-87589-724-X.

This anthology examines medical, service, and housing needs of homeless persons with mental illness.

Brickner, Philip, Linda Keen Scharer, Barbara Conanan, Alexander Elvy, Marianne Savarese, eds. **Health Care of Homeless People.** New York: Springer, 1985. 349p. $29.95. ISBN 0-8261-4990-1.

An overview of health issues for homeless people is presented, with special sections on medical disorders, mental health and illness, the organization of health services, and models of health care for homeless people. The offerings are by 24 authors or collaborators with expertise on subjects ranging from infestations to alcoholism to nutrition.

Brickner, Philip, et al., eds. **Under the Safety Net: The Health and Social Welfare of the Homeless in the United States.** New York: W. W. Norton, 1990. 439p. $27.95. ISBN 0-393-02885-2.

More than two dozen chapters by groups of authors engaged in the direct service of providing health care to homeless people paint a grim picture of the depth of need and the failure of primary health care systems to aid homeless people. Current information on respite care facilities, the resurgence of tuberculosis, and establishing and sustaining programs is provided.

Dear, Michael J., and Jennifer R. Wolch. **Landscapes of Despair: From Deinstitutionalization to Homelessness.** Princeton, NJ: Princeton University Press, 1987. 220p. $35. ISBN 0-691-07754-1.

Early social welfare institutions in the United States are examined here, in an analysis of the development of large-scale treatment settings for the retarded, elderly, mentally disabled, indigents, offenders, and orphans. The significant public policy turn toward community-based care resulted in massive depopulation of facilities and has been closely linked to homelessness by many writers. The book looks in depth at the case of San Jose, California, and attempts to offer some answers for the future development of institutions and land-use tools.

Lamb, H. Richard, ed. **The Homeless Mentally Ill.** Washington, DC: American Psychiatric Association (APA), 1984. 280p. $19.95. ISBN 0-89042-200-1.

Many nationally recognized researchers in homelessness and mental illness contributed to the APA's position paper addressing the needs of this group. This volume incorporates both the medical and social viewpoints of those writers in examining the plight and needs of the estimated 30 percent of homeless people who suffer from mental illness.

Levine, Adele, ed. **Housing for People with Mental Illness: A Guide for Development.** Princeton, NJ: Robert Wood Johnson Foundation, 1988. 160p. (Available from Robert Wood Johnson Foundation Program on Chronic Mental Illness, Massachusetts Mental Health Center, 74 Fenwood Road, Boston, MA 02115.) $2.40.

Practical information is offered in this volume, including site selection tips, analyzing financial feasibility, choosing a developer, and managing housing.

Rafferty, Margaret, et al., eds. **The Shelter Worker's Handbook: A Guide for Identifying and Meeting the Health Needs of Homeless People.** New York: Coalition for the Homeless (89 Chambers Street, New York, NY 10007), 1984. 150p. $5.

Life on the streets takes an enormous physical and mental toll on home-less people. Often the most common problems are unfamiliar ones to those who volunteer in shelters and soup lines: lice and scabies, tubercu-losis, and psychiatric illness. For volunteer help to make a difference, understanding the person and understanding the problem must go hand in hand. This guide offers basic information by experienced volunteers and professionals.

Report of the Presidential Commission on the Human Immuno-deficiency Virus Epidemic. Washington, DC: U.S. Government Printing Office, June 1988. 201p. $11. GPO 0-214-701: QL 3.

This report examines a number of aspects of the HIV epidemic, with a chapter devoted to the disproportionate impact of HIV on the poor. Drug abuse and treatment are discussed, with a recommendation that treatment on demand be a goal. The special needs of the homeless person who is HIV-seropositive are also examined.

Sheehan, Susan. **Is There No Place on Earth for Me?** New York: Houghton Mifflin, 1982. 320p. $14.95. ISBN 0-395-31871-8.

This carefully detailed account of the repeated hospitalization and treat-ment of Sylvia Frumkin, a chronically mentally ill woman in New York, paints a careful portrait of the deficiencies of the public mental health system and the toll of mental illness on one family.

Shilts, Randy. **And the Band Played On: Politics, People and the AIDS Epidemic.** New York: St. Martin's, 1987. 613p. $12.95. ISBN 0-14-011-369-X.

Widely heralded as the definitive documentary study of how AIDS devel-oped into a major health and social issue in the United States, this book traces the beginning of the infection from pre-1980 identification as a gay disease to the mid-1980s when it became a political and social issue as well as a health problem.

Torrey, E. Fuller. **Nowhere To Go: The Tragic Odyssey of the Home-less Mentally Ill.** New York: Harper & Row, 1988. 256p. $18.95. ISBN 0-06-015993-6.

The careless depopulation of public mental hospitals resulted in the creation of community mental health centers and a vast new federal government structure of ready financing. But the seriously mentally ill, whose plight was supposed to be bettered by these developments, instead were displaced by the "worried well" who sought treatment at these facilities, and they found themselves unable to reenter hospitals that had tightened admissions standards.

Torrey, E. Fuller, Eve Bargmann, and Sidney Wolfe. **Washington's Grate Society: Schizophrenics in the Shelters and on the Street.** Washington, DC: Public Citizen Health Research Group (2000 P Street NW, Washington, DC 20036), April 1985. 23p.

Perhaps no homeless people are as visible as those who exhibit signs of severe mental illness in public places; few shelter residents are more disruptive than those whose illness is untreated or unrecognized. This survey of public shelters in Washington, D.C., found that 39 percent of the residents suffered from schizophrenia, which was the primary reason for their homelessness. The report also contains significant findings about the prevalence of illness among those not in shelters.

Torrey, E. Fuller, and Sidney M. Wolfe. **Care of the Seriously Mentally Ill: A Rating of State Programs.** Washington, DC: Public Citizen Health Research Group (2000 P Street NW, Washington, DC 20036), 1986. 105p.

A state-by-state profile of services for the seriously mentally ill examines the quality of care provided by the state agencies that historically have been responsible for the treatment and rehabilitation of those in need.

Housing

Apgar, William C., Jr., and H. James Brown. **The State of the Nation's Housing.** Cambridge, MA: Joint Center for Housing Studies of Harvard University, 1988. 28p.

The late 1980s witnessed an avalanche of housing reports as experts of all sorts sought to analyze the role of the housing market in the growing problem of homelessness. This brief examination of a variety of housing issues looks at homelessness, home ownership, and housing costs.

Baxter, Ellen. **The Heights: A Community Housing Strategy.** New York: Community Service Society (105 East Twenty-second Street, New York, NY 10010), 1986. 69p. $6.50.

The author, who conducted some of the ground-breaking research on New York homelessness, has completed a series of supportive SRO facilities in the Washington Heights section of New York City, financed by a combination of public and private resources. This report describes in detail the necessary steps to achieve this model of housing for previously homeless people.

Bratt, Rachel G., Chester Hartman, and Ann Myerson, eds. **Critical Perspectives on Housing.** Philadelphia: Temple University Press, 1986. 686p. $19.95. ISBN 0-87722-396-3.

This anthology of articles by experts on the structure and economics of the housing market examines a wide variety of housing topics, including the federal, local, and nonprofit roles in providing housing.

Dolbeare, Cushing N. **Out of Reach: Why Everyday People Can't Find Affordable Housing.** Washington, DC: Low Income Housing Information Service (1012 Fourteenth Street NW, Washington, DC 20005), 1989. 72p. $8.

Detailed information is provided on a state-by-state basis of the gap between the cost of decent housing and what people can afford to pay. Profiles are offered of the gap faced by persons earning the minimum wage in various housing markets, as well as those renters who rely on public assistance for their income.

————. **The Widening Gap: Housing Needs of Low Income Families.** Washington, DC: Low Income Housing Information Service, 1992. 20p.

This report contains information from the 1990 American Housing Survey showing how the cost of housing for poor people continues to escalate.

Erickson, Jon, and Charles Wilhelm, eds. **Housing the Homeless.** New Brunswick, NJ: Rutgers University Center for Urban Policy Research, 1986. 430p. $19.95. ISBN 0-88285-112-8.

This anthology of articles addresses the political ramification of homelessness, examining the changing public face of the problem and its many sources. Closer study is given to three groups: the traditional homeless population, the deinstitutionalized mentally ill, and women and children.

Gilderbloom, John, and Richard Appelbaum. **Rethinking Rental Housing.** Philadelphia: Temple University Press, 1988. 280p. $16.95. ISBN 0-87722-538-9.

The authors examine the rental housing crisis as a social issue, not simply an economic one. They examine the possibilities of a national housing program similar to Sweden's with elements of nonprofit community-based housing giving strong rights to tenants.

Hartman, Chester, ed. **America's Housing Crisis: What Is To Be Done?** Boston: Routledge & Kegan Paul, 1983. 249p. $10.95. ISBN 0-7102-0041-2.

Not only has the shortage of affordable housing made it harder for many homeless people to find their way back from the streets, but more and more of this housing is lost each year. Presented here is the background of this problem, as well as legal strategies to protect low-income units, how the problem relates to the economic crisis of the 1980s, and a look at the burgeoning tenants' movement.

Institute for Policy Studies, Working Group on Housing. **The Right to Housing: A Blueprint for Housing the Nation.** Washington, DC: Institute for Policy Studies (1601 Connecticut Avenue NW, Washington, DC 20009), 1989. 72p. $5. ISBN 0-89758-046-X.

A nationwide group of housing experts produced this paper, which argues that the free market will never meet the housing needs of the low- and moderate-income person. It provides the basis for a major piece of pending federal housing legislation.

Leonard, Paul A., Cushing N. Dolbeare, and Edward B. Lazere. **A Place To Call Home: The Crisis in Housing for the Poor.** Washington, DC: Center on Budget and Policy Priorities and the Low Income Housing Information Service (777 North Capitol Street NE, Washington, DC 20001), 1989. 80p. $8.

The first new housing census data in over four years is extensively analyzed for its significant impact on poor Americans. The causes of the housing crisis are examined, as are the special needs of minorities, the elderly, and single parents.

Lieberman, Betsy, and Donald Chamberlain. **Breaking New Ground: Developing Innovative AIDS Care Residences.** Seattle: AIDS Housing Services of Washington, 1993. 284p. $39.95.

This book is partly a how-to guide about project development and partly an exploration of questions about public policy in the area of integrated housing development for people with special needs. The authors are developers of two successful AIDS housing projects in Seattle.

McRae, Jean A., and Michael U. Mbanaso. **The Right to Housing: A Final Report.** Washington, DC: Howard University Housing and Community Studies Center, Institute for Urban Affairs and Research, 1991. 139p. Free.

This monograph contains the transcript of the Spring 1991 Fannie Mae University Colloquium Series on Domestic Housing Policy, which focused on a right to housing in the United States. A series of speakers presented a range of ideas on the desirability and possibility of establishing such a right.

Ringheim, Karin. **At Risk of Homelessness.** New York: Praeger, 1990. 263p. $52. ISBN 0-275-93582-5.

Four metropolitan areas are examined for the relation of income and rent to risk of homelessness.

Roisman, Florence Wagman. **Establishing a Right to Housing: An Advocate's Guide.** Washington, DC: National Support Center for Low Income Housing, 1991. 55p. $20. (Available from the Low Income Housing Information Service, 1012 Fourteenth Street NW, Washington, DC 20005).

This discussion of housing rights based on statutes dealing with an array of programs (AFDC, child welfare, mental health) focuses on drawing out a right to housing from state and local statutory bases. The author is an experienced housing lawyer for poor people and has been involved in significant litigation for homeless people.

Schwartz, David C., Richard C. Ferlauto, and Daniel N. Hoffman. **A New Housing Policy for America: Recapturing the American Dream.** Philadelphia: Temple University Press, 1988. 332p. $19.95. ISBN 0-87722-568-0.

This book's goal is to arrive at a plan to meet America's housing needs in the 1990s; the authors examine more than 200 state, national, and international housing efforts.

SRO Housing Inc. **Single Room Occupancy Development Handbook.** Los Angeles: SRO Housing Corporation (311 South Spring Street, Los Angeles, CA 90013), 1987. 40p. $14.50.

The development of an SRO facility is examined here, with accompanying sample space layouts, income calculations, and a checklist for managers.

Stegman, Michael A., and J. David Holden. **Nonfederal Housing Programs.** Washington, DC: Urban Land Institute, 1987. 231p.

As federal resources decline, state and local programs must play an increasing role in meeting the needs of low-income people. This book explores ways that such programs can help, and over 60 programs are abstracted.

Legal Issues and Litigation

Citizens' Commission on Civil Rights, National Center for Policy Alternatives. **Barriers to Registration and Voting: An Agenda for Reform.** Washington, DC: Citizens' Commission on Civil Rights, 1987. 171p. ISBN 0-89788-095-1.

Once they become homeless, people easily lose a number of other intangibles. Among these has often been the right to vote, lost because local laws are interpreted to require a permanent roof over one's head in order to exercise the franchise. Beginning in 1984, a number of local efforts across the country were made to alleviate this problem. This report, the product of three hearings around the nation, includes information on barriers faced by homeless persons.

Mental Health Law Project. **Federal and State Rights and Entitlements of People Who Are Homeless.** Chicago: National Clearinghouse for Legal Services (407 South Dearborn, Chicago, IL 60605), 1987, 1988.

The Mental Health Law Project prepared several state-specific guides to rights and entitlements for homeless people. Those working with homeless people will find these guides useful in helping them obtain welfare rights, income assistance, housing, food and nutrition aid, health care, and veterans' services.

Practising Law Institute. **The Rights of the Homeless 1992.** Litigation and Administrative Practice Series (Litigation Course Handbook Series Number 428; cochairmen, Steven Banks and Robert M. Hayes). New York: Practising Law Institute (810 Seventh Avenue, New York, NY 10019), 1992. 840p. $50. H4-5123, PLI.

PLI has regularly presented a one-day course for attorneys and others working with homeless people on current developments in the application of their rights. This volume, from the 1992 course, covers emergency-assistance rights, the right to vote, right to treatment for the mentally ill, the prevention of homelessness, welfare rights, housing for homeless people with HIV, and other legal cases. It includes decisions and pleadings from some of the cases.

Photography

Hollyman, Stephenie. **We the Homeless: Portraits of America's Displaced People.** New York: Philosophical Library, 1988. 256p. $45. ISBN 0-8022-2542-X.

For over a year, photographer Stephenie Hollyman traveled around the United States, meeting and photographing homeless people in a 15,000-mile trek, resulting in these pictures of homeless families and their children, Vietnam veterans, the chronically mentally ill, and the many others who populate the nation's streets and shelters. Text by Victoria Irwin of the Christian Science Monitor.

Hubbard, Jim. **American Refugees.** Foreword by Jonathan Kozol. Minneapolis: University of Minnesota Press, 1991. 109p. $19.95. ISBN 0-8166-1927-1.

The author, one of the first to photograph increasing homelessness in America, documents the rise of the problems, especially among families, through the decade of the 1980s.

National Mental Health Association and Families for the Homeless. **Homeless in America.** Acropolis Books, 1988. $19.95. ISBN 0-87491-904-5.

Under the auspices of this joint public education project, some of the best-known photojournalists in the nation created images of homeless people, with the goal of raising public awareness. This resulting volume was issued in conjunction with an exhibit of the photographs.

Shooting Back Education and Media Center. **Shooting Back: A Photographic View of Life by Homeless Children.** San Francisco: Chronicle Books, 1991. 115p. $14.95. ISBN 0-8118-0019-9.

The Shooting Back project took volunteer professional photographers in Washington, D.C., into family shelters to teach youngsters how to shoot images of their daily lives. Their compelling photos and commentary, assembled here, became an international traveling exhibit, with accompanying publicity and opportunities for some of them. The project and others like it now operate around the country.

Poverty

Center on Budget and Policy Priorities. **Holes in the Safety Net: Poverty Programs and Policies in the States.** Washington, DC: Center on Budget and Policy Priorities (777 North Capitol Street NE, Washington, DC 20001), 1988. $8 (national report); $3.50 (state reports).

Federal policies and programs affecting poor people are examined in the national overview, and the individual state reports portray how residents fare with general assistance, food stamps, medical assistance, in the housing market, and more.

Harrington, Michael. **The New American Poverty.** New York: Penguin Books, 1985. 255p. $7.95. ISBN 0-14-008112-7.

From the author who wrote the eye-opening *The Other America*, credited with starting the War on Poverty, comes this volume on poverty in the 1980s. Noteworthy is the section devoted to a discussion of the use of numbers in counting the poor and assessing their poverty.

Jencks, Christopher. **Rethinking Social Policy.** New York: Harper Perennial, 1993. 280p. $12. ISBN 0-06-0974534-2.

The author explores the way Americans think about race, poverty, crime, and welfare and concludes that specific programs need more attention than traditional ideas of conservatives or liberals.

Katz, Michael B. **The Undeserving Poor.** New York: Pantheon Books, 1989. 293p. $14.95. ISBN 0-679-72561-X.

The roots of the War on Poverty and the war on welfare of the 1980s are described here, and the author analyzes how the language used to characterize poor people affects social policy.

Katz, Michael B., ed. **The Underclass Debate: Views from History.** Princeton, NJ: Princeton University Press, 1993. 507p. $16.95. ISBN 0-691-00628-8.

This anthology presents several commentaries on the historic aspects of the dialogue on the origins of contemporary poverty: Is the presence of poor people—and more of them—a new development or a rediscovery of a continuing problem in our society?

Piven, Frances Fox, and Richard A. Cloward. **Regulating the Poor: The Functions of Public Welfare.** New York: Vintage Books, 1993. 524p. $12. ISBN 0-679-74516-5.

This reissue of a classic book on social welfare presents updated material on poverty and public spending, as well as reflections on the War on Poverty.

Stone, Michael E. **Shelter Poverty.** Philadelphia: Temple University Press, 1993. 423p. $18.95. ISBN 1-56639-092-3.

Burdensome housing costs result in what is referred to as "shelter poverty." Homelessness is the most extreme example of this problem. The author explores the reasons for the crisis, as well as what can be done to overcome it.

Programs and Program Issues

National Governors' Association. **Status of Programs under the Stewart B. McKinney Homeless Assistance Act and Related Legislation.** Washington, DC: National Governors' Association (444 North Capitol Street NW, Washington, DC 20001), 1988. 34p. $5.

This summary of McKinney Act programs is part of the NGA effort to monitor the success of legislation at the state level.

Nenno, Mary, ed. **Assistance for Homeless Persons: A NAHRO Resource Book for Housing and Community Development Officials.**

Washington, DC: National Association of Housing and Redevelopment Officials (NAHRO) (1320 Eighteenth Street NW, Washington, DC 20036), 1988. 143p. $15.

Federal programs for homeless people are summarized, as are state efforts in legislation, programs linking housing and human services, and other resources. Selected state programs are presented in more depth, as are statutes and case studies of local agency work.

Nenno, Mary K., and George Colyer. **New Money and New Methods: A Catalog of State and Local Initiatives in Housing and Community Development.** Washington, DC: National Association of Housing and Redevelopment Officials (NAHRO) (1320 Eighteenth Street NW, Washington, DC 20036), 1988. 106p. $25.

This collection of articles, reports, and case studies examines public and private initiatives to assist housing.

Sprague, Joan F. **A Manual on Transitional Housing.** Boston: Women's Institute for Housing and Economic Development, 1986. 48p. $10.

Emergency shelter can solve a number of immediate needs, but many homeless people need a next step before permanent housing and any effort at independent living. Transitional housing can fill this need by providing supportive services, a training period, and concrete time for building self-sufficiency. This manual offers definitions of this type of housing, program options, a guide to development, models, and tips on operating a transitional program.

The Urban Institute. **State Activities and Programs for the Homeless: A Review of Six States.** Washington, DC: The Urban Institute, 1988. 140p. $15.

As homelessness increases around the nation and federal dollars prove inadequate to solve the problem, some states have undertaken their own initiatives to help. This survey for the Interagency Council on the Homeless covers California, Connecticut, Georgia, New Mexico, Ohio, and Wisconsin, and offers a look at efforts to implement the entire range of programs that can address homelessness.

Technical Assistance

Carter, Nicala. "Resources for Nonlawyers." **Clearinghouse Review** 19 (1985). 14p. Free from National Clearinghouse for Legal Services (205 West Monroe Street, Second Floor, Chicago, IL 60606).

This annotated bibliography is reprinted from a special issue on advocacy for the poor. It includes a useful list of resources for the nonlawyer who needs information on legal issues, seeks to help a poor person with a legal situation, or wishes to more actively engage the legal system as an advocate.

Coalition on Human Needs. **The National Technical Assistance Directory: A Guide for State Advocates and Service Providers.** Washington, DC: Coalition on Human Needs, 1989. 47p. $10.

Summaries of organizational activity, publications, and available technical assistance are provided for major groups working on poverty issues.

Welfare

Coalition on Human Needs. **The Family Support Act: An Early Implementation Guide.** Washington, DC: Coalition on Human Needs, 1989. 101p.

The Family Support Act, passed in 1988, offers the opportunity for states to assist welfare recipients out of poverty through the use of the new "JOBS" program. This manual, directed at advocates and community organizations, covers work, education, and job-training activities, as well as related child care and health care issues.

Ellwood, David T. **Poor Support: Poverty in the American Family.** New York: Basic Books, 1988. 271p. $10.95. ISBN 0-465-05995-3.

Family poverty and welfare have been perceived as nearly intractable problems subject to the winds of political policymaking. The author looks at the problems—operational and perceptional—with the present system, as well as the increasing difficulty of raising America's changing families out of poverty with minimum-wage jobs, and suggests avenues for change.

Newman, Sandra J., and Ann B. Schnare. **Subsidizing Shelter: The Relationship between Welfare and Housing Assistance. Part 1: Analysis and Findings. Part 2: Data Book.** Washington, DC: The Urban Institute Press, 1988. 193p. $8. ISBN 0-87766-414-5.

Welfare recipients receive at least $10 billion annually for housing assistance, funds that are part of their public assistance benefits. The HUD stream of funding for low-income housing is about the same, yet the relationship between the two programs is largely unexamined and their effects uncoordinated.

Women

Amott, Teresa L., and Julie A. Matthaei. **Race, Gender, and Work.** Boston: South End Press, 1991. 433p. $16. ISBN 0-89608-376-4.

The substantially greater poverty of women in the United States—whether from lower wages or from reliance on cash assistance programs—shapes their entire economic history. Homeless women who must look to low-paying jobs or welfare checks as they attempt to end their homelessness face an almost impossible struggle. This book provides vivid documentation of these realities.

Birch, Eugenie Ladner, ed. **The Unsheltered Woman: Women and Housing in the 80's.** New Brunswick, NJ: Rutgers University Center for Urban Policy Research, 1985. 313p. $14.95. ISBN 0-88285-104-7.

These 20 essays on women and their housing needs were prepared as an overview of necessary shelter and support services for a joint program of the Ford Foundation and Hunter College.

Dobash, R. Emerson, and Russell P. Dobash. **Women, Violence, and Social Change.** New York: Routledge & Kegan Paul, 1992. 366p. $17.95. ISBN 0-415-03610-0.

Significant numbers of homeless women are believed to be fleeing violence at home, yet their homelessness is often not connected to that of women who lose their housing for other reasons. One cause of this separation is that a different network of shelters and services has developed to address the needs of battered women. This book looks at the growth of this response in both the United States and Great Britain by examining the actions of the judiciary, academia, and the therapeutic community.

Golden, Stephanie. **The Women Outside: Meanings and Myths of Homelessness.** Berkeley: University of California Press, 1992. 319p. $25. ISBN 0-520-07158-1.

The history and stereotypes of homeless women are examined by an author who spent an extended period working with and listening to women in a New York City shelter. The women tell their own stories, and the author describes what life on the streets is like for them and others. She also identifies the obstacles women face in ending their homelessness.

Gordon, Linda, ed. **Women, the State, and Welfare.** Madison: University of Wisconsin Press, 1990. 311p. $25. ISBN 0-299-12664-1.

This collection of essays surveys the roots and effects of welfare programs on women, covering discrimination, racism, and activism.

Hastings Law Journal. **Symposium: Substance Use during Pregnancy: Legal and Social Responses.** Vol. 43, no. 3 (March 1992), University of California, Hastings College of Law.

This collection of articles covers one of the most controversial topics affecting poor women: What is the intersection of health, criminality, child welfare, and other issues in the case of women who use illegal drugs during pregnancy? Because of the shortage of treatment facilities—especially for women who already have children—this is a particularly important topic for those concerned about homeless women.

Hirsch, Kathleen. **Songs from the Alley.** New York: Ticknor & Fields, 1989. 420p. $22.95. ISBN 0-89919-488-5.

The lives of two homeless women in Boston—Wendy and Amanda—are traced from their beginnings to the harsh everyday life of homelessness. In an unusual format, this account runs side by side with the history of aid to homeless poor people during the 200 years of Massachusetts's history, including recent political activism for homeless people.

Liebow, Elliot. **Tell Them Who I Am.** New York: Free Press, 1993. 339p. $24.95. ISBN 0-02-919095-9.

The author wrote the ground-breaking and widely hailed *Tally's Corner* in 1967 to describe the life of so-called "street corner men" in a black neighborhood of Washington, D.C. After years of volunteering, observing, and interviewing homeless women in shelters in the Maryland suburbs of Washington, D.C., he provides this picture of the women's individual stories as homeless persons, as well as his own views of the broader economic, social, and political forces that cause and continue homelessness.

Miller, Dorothy C. **Women and Social Welfare.** New York: Praeger, 1992. 181p. $14.95. ISBN 0-275-94384-4.

This analysis of the roots and results of the public welfare system in the United States looks at the historic context for income, training, and assistance programs for poor women, in light of feminist theory. An extensive bibliography is included.

Rousseau, Ann Marie, and Alix K. Shulman. **Shopping Bag Ladies: Homeless Women Talk about Their Lives.** New York: Pilgrim Press, 1982. 160p. $9.95. ISBN 0-8298-0603-2.

This book of photographs depicts some of the rigors of life for homeless women in New York City. Some of the women tell their own stories, and the authors show homeless people in all aspects of their daily routine.

Schechter, Susan. **Women and Male Violence.** Boston: South End Press, 1982. 367p. $15. ISBN 0-89608-159-1.

The movement opposing violence against women began in this country in the mid-1970s; it is examined here along with the activism and individuals who helped create the issues and institutions for battered women in the United States.

Watson, Sophie. **Housing and Homelessness: A Feminist Perspective.** London and Boston: Routledge & Kegan Paul, 1986. 186p. $14.95. ISBN 0-7102-0400-0.

Although written from the point of view of British society, this is a worthwhile study of how Western society in general defines and provides for housing needs, with a particular emphasis on the impact of these policies on women.

Youth

Jarvis, Sara V., and Robert M. Robertson, Jr. **Transitional Living Programs for Homeless Adolescents.** Washington, DC: Georgetown University Child Development Center, Child and Adolescent Service System Program (CASSP), 1993. 122p. $10.

The William T. Grant Foundation Commission on Work, Family, and Citizenship. **The Forgotten Half: Pathways to Success for America's Youth and Young Families: Final Report.** Washington, DC: The William T. Grant Foundation (1001 Connecticut Avenue NW, Washington, DC 20036), 1988. 203p. $10.

Approximately 20 million 16- to 24-year-olds will not go on to college; this report examines the demographic facts about their lives, including the growth of poverty in this group, the decline of marriage rates, housing affordability problems, health needs, and employment prospects. A special examination is given to the chronically poor, youth at risk, rural youth, those in foster care, and runaways.

Bibliographies

Health Care for the Homeless. **Child Development and Developmental Delays: Homeless Children.** Boston: Health Care for the Homeless Information Resource Center, 1992. 9p. $5.

————. **Immunization Status of Homeless and Low Income Children.** Boston: Health Care for the Homeless Information Resource Center, 1992. 6p. $5.

Jarrett, Beth D., and Wes Daniels. **Law and the Homeless: An Annotated Bibliography.** Miami: University of Miami School of Law, 1992. 136p.

Kayne, Andrea. **Annotated Bibliography of Social Science Literature Concerning the Education of Homeless Children.** Cambridge, MA: Center for Law and Education, 1989. 12p.

Nordquist, Joan. **The Homeless in America: A Bibliography.** Santa Cruz, CA: Reference and Research Services, 1988. 64p.

Federal Government Documents and Reports

The following federal government publications can assist in learning more about homelessness and programs to combat it. Addresses for most agencies listed below can be found in Chapter 8.

Fannie Mae

Housing Policy Debate, Special Issue. "Counting the Homeless: The Methodologies, Policies, and Social Significance behind the Numbers." Fannie Mae Annual Housing Conference, 14 May 1991. 1,094p.

Fannie Mae is a "Government-Sponsored Enterprise (GSE)" that sponsors housing research and debate on issues affecting low-income people. This special issue of its journal contains papers presented at its annual conference by social scientists and policymakers examining the size and definition of homelessness. Contact Fannie Mae at 3900 Wisconsin Avenue NW, Washington, DC 20016.

Federal Emergency Management Agency

FEMA. **Checklist for Success: Programs To Help the Hungry and Homeless.** 1990.

Interagency Council on the Homeless

Burt, Martha. **Practical Methods for Counting the Homeless: A Manual for States and Local Jurisdictions.** Prepared for the Interagency Council. 1992.

Churches Conference on Shelter and Housing. **One Church: One Home.** Published by the Interagency Council. 1990.

Interagency Council on the Homeless. **The Annual Report of the Interagency Council on the Homeless.** Issued each year at the direction of Congress.

————. **Federal Programs To Help Homeless People.** 1993.

————. **Initiatives for the Homeless.** 1991.

————. **The McKinney Act: A Program Guide.** Revised periodically.

————. **A Nation Concerned: A Report to the President and the Congress on the Response to Homelessness in America.** 1988.

————. **Obtaining Federal Surplus Property To Help the Homeless.** 1991.

————. **Outcasts on Main Street.** Report of the Interagency Council Task Force on Homelessness and Severe Mental Illness. 1992.

————. **Reaching Out: A Guide for Service Providers.** 1991.

————. **Working To End Homelessness: A Manual for States.** 1991.

National Academy of Science

National Academy of Science, Institute of Medicine. **Homelessness, Health and Human Needs.** Washington, DC: National Academy Press (2101 Constitution Avenue NW, Washington, DC 20418). 1988. 165p. $19.95. ISBN 0-309-03832-4. Supplemental report from United Hospital Fund Publications Program (55 Fifth Avenue, New York, NY 10003).

This controversial report had a congressional mandate to assess the provision of health care services to homeless people. The resulting work provides background data and recommendations on housing, income, employment, mental illness, and deinstitutionalization, as these subjects relate to the problem. The document was debated on its release when 10 of the 13 experts who contributed to it published a dissenting report calling for national action on housing, wages, and benefits in order to fight homelessness.

National Institute of Mental Health

Mauch, D., and V. Mulkern. **The McKinney Health Services for the Homeless Block Grant.** 1991.

Morrissey, J. P., and D. Dennis, eds. **Homelessness and Mental Illness: Toward the Next Generation of Research Studies.** 1990. Conference proceedings.

NIMH. **Deinstitutionalization Policy and Homelessness.** 1990 Report to Congress.

――――. **The Homeless Mentally Ill: Reports Available from the National Institute of Mental Health.** 1987. DHHS Publication No. (ADM) 87-1520.
This annotated bibliography of NIMH reports on policy, research, and services summarizes papers, conference reports, and other documents that are available.

――――. **The Homeless Mentally Ill: Service Needs of the Population.** 1988. DHHS Publication No. (ADM) 88-1598.

This public information report gives an overview of issues in creating services for homeless mentally ill people.

――――. **A Synthesis of NIMH-Funded Research Concerning Persons Who Are Homeless and Mentally Ill.** February 1989. 71p.

The methodological considerations, findings, and implications of research projects on homeless mentally ill persons are described.

――――. **Two Generations of NIMH-Funded Research on Homelessness and Mental Illness, 1982–1990.** 1991.

Salem, D. A. **The Mental Health Services for the Homeless Block Grant Program: A Summary of the FY 1987/1988 Annual Reports.** 1990.

National Institute on Alcohol Abuse and Alcoholism (NIAAA)

Bassuk, Ellen. **Homeless Families with Children: Research Perspectives.** 1993. Conference proceedings. #HL60.

Bennett, G., and P. Shane. **Job Training and Employment Services for Homeless People with Alcohol and Drug Problems.** 1992. #HL63.

Fischer, P. **Alcohol and Drug Abuse and Mental Health Problems among Homeless Persons: A Review of the Literature.** 1991. #HL51. **Housing Initiatives for Homeless People with Alcohol and Other Drug Problems.** Proceedings of a National Conference. 1991. DHHS Publication No. (ADM) 92-1885.

This national conference heard from service providers and housing developers about some of the current thinking on creating and operating successful programs to meet the needs of various homeless people with histories of drug and/or alcohol use.

NIAAA. **Alcohol Health & Research World: Homelessness.** Vol. 2, no. 3 (Spring 1987). 92p. DHHS Publication No. (ADM) 87-151.

This special edition of NIAAA's monthly journal contains 20 articles and features on medical and nonmedical aspects of alcohol and homeless people. Long one of the most stereotyped problems of homeless people, alcohol dependence is increasingly being treated as a serious health problem that also requires housing as a solution.

————. **Alcohol Recovery Programs for Homeless People: A Survey of Current Programs in the U.S.** Washington, DC: U.S. Government Printing Office, 1988. 125p. GPO 201-875-83661.

The homeless alcoholic is one of the most enduring stereotypes of the unsheltered person. This survey of programs nominated by those who work with homeless people and alcoholics examines intake programs, primary and sustained recovery settings, comprehensive services, and alcohol-free housing models that are targeted to indigent alcoholics.

————. **Glossary of Service Activities for Alcohol and Other Drug Abuse Treatment of Homeless Persons.** 1991. #HL57.

U.S. Congress

Publications listed here are available from the U.S. Government Printing Office, Washington, DC 20402.

U.S. Congress. Select Committee on Aging. **Homeless Older Americans.** 98th Cong., 2d sess., 1984. 184p.

The number of older people is increasing across the nation, as is the number of homeless people, yet little attention is given to the older homeless person, whose extreme poverty is complicated by poor health, mental difficulties, and greater vulnerability. This hearing examined the physical, mental, and housing needs of this group.

————. Committee on Agriculture. **Review of Nutrition Programs Which Assist the Homeless.** 100th Cong., 1st sess., 1987. 337p.

Public officials, shelter providers, and homeless people present their views on how federal nutrition assistance serves the needs of homeless men, women, and children in the streets and in shelters, and the growing need for emergency food relief.

————. Committee on Banking, Commerce, and Urban Affairs. **Basic Laws on Housing and Community Development.** 102d Cong., 1st sess., 1991. 1,291p.

This periodically issued document collects all the operative statutory bases for federal housing programs.

————. House Committee on Banking, Commerce, and Urban Affairs. Subcommittee on Housing and Community Development. **Homelessness in America.** 97th Cong., 2d sess., 1982. 3 volumes. 4,107p.

The highly publicized first congressional hearings held on homelessness since the Great Depression gathered together shelter providers, homeless people, and local officials to create a powerful statement of a problem that was not yet widely recognized. The text of this hearing, together with the appendixes of submitted material, is an enduring and detailed record of the nature of homelessness as it burst into the national consciousness.

————. Committee on Banking, Finance, and Urban Affairs and the Committee on Government Operations. **Joint Hearing on the HUD Report on Homelessness.** 98th Cong. 2d sess., 1984. 418p.

The 1984 HUD report on homelessness was controversial for both its numerical conclusions about the size of the problem and the methodology used in reaching those conclusions. While much was written and said about the report, this hearing presented a range of testimony from those involved, including interviewers, interviewees, and social scientists who assessed the results.

————. House Select Committee on Children, Youth, and Families. **Federal Programs Affecting Children and Their Families.** 102d Cong., 2nd sess., 1992. 194p.

This report surveys the income, nutrition, social service, education and training, health, and housing assistance programs of the federal government.

————. Committee on Government Operations. **Homeless Families: A Neglected Crisis.** 99th Cong., 2d sess., 1986. H. Rept. 99-982. 24p.

This brief report, based on a congressional study, examines the causes of family homelessness, finds that the use of the Emergency Assistance Program shelter system is harmful for homeless families, and makes recommendations for change.

————. National Low Income Housing Preservation Commission. **Preventing the Disappearance of Low Income Housing.** The Report of the

National Low Income Housing Preservation Commission to the House Subcommittee on Housing and Community Development and the Senate Subcommittee on Housing and Urban Affairs, U.S. Congress, 1988. 135p.

This commission was formed as part of the congressional effort to re-examine the nation's housing policy, with an emphasis on the potential loss of subsidized units, the effects of such losses on low-income households, and possible solutions.

————. Select Committee on Hunger. **Hunger among the Homeless: A Survey of 140 Shelters, Food Stamp Participation and Recommendations.** 100th Cong., 1st sess., 1987. 108p.

Three national organizations working with homeless people surveyed shelters across the country to assess the food assistance needs of homeless people and look for long-term answers to hunger among the very poor.

————. Subcommittee on Public Assistance and Unemployment Compensation of the House Committee on Ways and Means and Subcommittee on Social Security and Family Policy of the Senate Committee on Finance. **Use of AFDC Funds for Homeless Families.** Joint Hearing, 100th Cong., 2d sess., 1988. 250p.

This hearing on-site in Brooklyn, New York, was convened to learn more about the use of AFDC Emergency Assistance funds for sheltering homeless families in welfare hotels.

U.S. Department of Agriculture

Study of the Child Nutrition Demonstration. February 1992.

U.S. Department of Commerce, Bureau of the Census

Taeuber, Cynthia M., ed. **Conference Proceedings for Enumerating Homeless Persons: Methods and Data Needs.** Data User Services, 1990.

This conference was sponsored by the Bureau of the Census, Interagency Council on the Homeless, and Department of Housing and Urban Development.

U.S. Bureau of the Census. **1990 Subject Report on Persons in Institutions and Other Group Quarters.** 1993.

This report covers counts of persons who are housed but not living in households: persons living in jails, nursing homes, juvenile homes, and hospitals.

U.S. Department of Education

Division of Adult Education and Literacy, Office of Vocational and Adult Education. **Education for Homeless Adults: The First Year.** 1990.

————. **Profiles of State Programs: Adult Education for the Homeless.** 1990.

U.S. Department of Health and Human Services

HHS. **Helping the Homeless: A Resource Guide.** 204p. GPO 1984 0-454-738.

Emergency feeding programs, emergency shelters, transitional housing, long-term housing, and multiservice programs are profiled. Special sections are provided on sources of funding and food; facilities and equipment; licensing, laws, and regulations; program design and operations; and common questions and answers on administrative and structural issues. An appendix explains how to seek government assistance.

Office of the Assistance Secretary for Planning and Evaluation. **Federal Programs Providing Funds or Services To Prevent Homelessness among Families at Risk.** 1991.

————. **Homeless Families with Children: Programmatic Responses of Five Communities.** 1991. Two volumes.

————. **Results from a Survey on State Initiatives on Behalf of Persons Who Are Homeless.** 1988.

————. **Survey of State Homeless Assistance Programs.** 1990.

Office of the Inspector General. **Alcohol, Drug, and Mental Health Services for Individuals.** 1992. OEI-05-91-00062.

————. **Homeless Prevention Programs.** 1991. OEI-07-90-00100.

————. **Medicaid and Homeless Individuals.** 1992. OEI-05-91-00063.

————. **State and Local Perspectives on the McKinney Act.** 1990. OEI-05-90-01090.

————. **Supplemental Security Income for Homeless Individuals.** 1992. OEI-05-91-00060.

Public Health Service. **Homeless and Runaway Youth: Public Health Issues and the Need for Action.** 1991.

Ridgely, M. S., C. T. McNeil, and H. H. Goldman. **Alcohol and Drugs among Homeless Individuals: An Annotated Bibliography.** 1990. #HL06.

Stefl, M., ed. **Helping Homeless People with Alcohol and Other Drug Problems: A Guide for Service Providers.** 1992. #HL68.

Tutunijan, B. A. **An Annotated Publications List on Homelessness.** 1992. #HL41.

Wright, J. D. **Executive Summary: Correlates and Consequences of Alcohol Abuse in the National Health Care of the Homeless Client Population.** 1990. #HL40.

U.S. Department of Housing and Urban Development

HUD. **Housing America: Freeing the Spirit of Enterprise—A Directory of Official U.S. IYSH Projects.** 1987. HUD-PDR-1075.

The United Nations General Assembly designated 1987 as the "International Year of Shelter for the Homeless (IYSH)." This event was intended to focus world attention and resources on new shelter strategies and policies for the poor. Homelessness in the United States takes a form different from many other parts of the world; HUD undertook this roster of 166 projects that met its criteria of serving the poor through private-sector cooperation with public agencies.

————. **Publications Relating to Homelessness: A Working Bibliography.** 1989. HUD-PDR-1240.

————. **Report on Homeless Assistance Policy and Practice in the Nation's Five Largest Cities.** 1989. HUD-PDR-1232.

————. **Report on the 1988 National Survey of Shelters for the Homeless.** 1989. HUD-PDR-1212.

————. **Report to Congress on SROs for the Homeless Section 8 Moderate Rehabilitation Program.** 1990. HUD-PDR-1247.

————. **A Report to the Secretary on the Homeless and Emergency Shelter.** 1984.

This initial effort by the federal government to assess the problem of homelessness resulted in enormous controversy. Focus was on this report's methodology, which used an obscure commercial marketing measurement of population as the basis for interviewing local shelter providers about the size of the homeless population. The result was a national estimate of 250,000–350,000 homeless.

U.S. Department of Labor

DOL. **Job Training for the Homeless: Report on the Demonstration's First Year.** 1991. #N-5637.

Employment and Training Administration. **Job Training for the Homeless.** Washington, DC: U.S. Department of Labor, Employment and Training Administration, 1991. 160p.

National Commission for Employment Policy. **Coordinating Federal Assistance Programs for the Economically Disadvantaged.** 1991. 71p. Washington, DC: National Commission for Employment Policy (1522 K Street NW, Suite 300, Washington, DC 20005).

————. **Helping the Homeless Be Choosers: The Role of JTPA in Improving Job Prospects.** 1990. 118p.

U.S. Department of Veterans Affairs

Leda, Cathy, et al. **The Third Progress Report on the Domiciliary Care for Homeless Veterans Program.** 1991.

Rosenheck, Robert, et al. **Progress Report on the Homeless Chronically Mentally Ill Veterans Program.** Annual Report.

VA. **Programs To Assist Homeless Veterans.** Washington, DC: U.S. Government Printing Office, January 1989. 129p.

This comprehensive listing of all federal programs that have provisions affecting homeless veterans offers a wide range of resources for their needs. Presented are services ranging from domiciliary care for mentally ill veterans to housing loans and counseling services.

U.S. General Accounting Office (GAO)

The GAO has published numerous reports on homelessness; some are undertaken by statutory mandate in legislation passed by Congress, which seeks to have periodic updates on various aspects of its programs. Others are undertaken by request of members of Congress. Contact GAO at P.O. Box 6015, Gaithersburg, MD 20877.

U.S. General Accounting Office. **AIDS Education: Issues Affecting Counseling and Testing Programs.** Washington, DC: U.S. General Accounting Office, 1989. 15p. GAO/HRD-89-39.

With neither a vaccine nor a cure available for AIDS, education is considered mandatory to control the spread of the epidemic. Testing, follow-up and long-term counseling, partner notification, outreach to intravenous drug users, and antidiscrimination protections are examined here for their effect on the need for and use of education about AIDS. Investigation revealed, for instance, that, while 34 percent of AIDS cases nationwide involve IV drug use, none of the health departments studied for this report had undertaken any outreach to drug users.

―――. **AIDS Forecasting: Undercount of Cases and Lack of Key Data Weaken Existing Estimates.** Washington, DC: U.S. General Accounting Office, 1989. 102p. GAO/PEMD-89-13.

An assessment of national forecasts of the future of the AIDS epidemic, this report offers a detailed explanation of the major models for predicting the spread of the fatal disease. An extensive bibliography of studies is provided.

―――. **Children and Youths: About 68,000 Homeless and 186,000 in Shared Housing at Any Given Time.** Washington, DC: U.S. General Accounting Office, 1989. 40p. GAO/PEMD-89-14.

One of several studies mandated by the McKinney Act, this report seeks to estimate the number of children and youths who are homeless. The study not only attempts to quantify those who are in shelters or on the streets, but also accepts the McKinney "homeless" definition to mean that those who are "precariously housed" include those living in doubled-up housing arrangements with friends or relatives.

―――. **D.C. Government: Information on the Homeless Family Program.** Washington, DC: U.S. General Accounting Office, 1991. 30p. GAO/GGD-91-108.

Welfare hotels are a major resource for family shelter in Washington, D.C.; this report examines the costs of these facilities, as well as the chronic nature of homelessness among the city's poorest families.

―――. **Homeless Mentally Ill: Problems and Options in Estimating Numbers and Trends.** Washington, DC: U.S. General Accounting Office, 1988. 122p. GAO/PEMD-88-24.

Finding that there is no sound national estimate, this report analyzes the various methods of attempts to count the homeless mentally ill. Although rather technical in its examination of the existing research methods, this analysis does offer a summary chart of the previous counting efforts.

————. **Homelessness: A Complex Problem and the Federal Response.** Washington, DC: U.S. General Accounting Office, 1985. 88p. GAO/ HRD-85-40.

This study examined dozens of local, state, and national reports on homelessness, interviewed people working on the issue, and studied federal programs for homeless people. The report enumerates factors affecting homelessness, as well as likely long-term strategies for solving the problem.

————. **Homelessness: Access to McKinney Act Programs Improved but Better Oversight Needed.** Washington, DC: U.S. General Accounting Office, 1990. 19p. GAO/RCED-91-29.

This report studies barriers to obtaining and using funds under 14 McKinney Act programs; these barriers were identified by service providers, state and local governments, and advocacy organizations.

————. **Homelessness: Action Needed To Make Surplus Federal Property Program More Effective.** Washington, DC: U.S. General Accounting Office, 1990. 44p. GAO/RCED-91-33.

Under the McKinney Act, federal surplus property (equipment, supplies, and buildings) is to be made available to help homeless people, but initially the government made little available. In this report, which followed federal litigation by homeless advocates, GAO evaluated barriers in the program and ways to improve it.

————. **Homelessness: Additional Information on the Interagency Council on the Homeless.** Washington, DC: U.S. General Accounting Office, 1989. GAO/RCED-89-208FS.

————. **Homelessness: Changes in the Interagency Council on the Homeless Make It More Effective.** Washington, DC: U.S. General Accounting Office, 1990. 16p. GAO/RCED-90-172.

The Interagency Council represents all federal agencies with programs or interests in homelessness; however, the council had been criticized for its response to the problem, and this report studies the efficacy of resulting changes.

————. **Homelessness: Federal Personal Property Donations Provide Limited Benefit to the Homeless.** Washington, DC: U.S. General Accounting Office, 1991. 39p. GAO/RCED-91-108.

Under the McKinney Act, federal surplus property (including equipment and buildings) is to be made available for use in helping homeless people. This report examines how extensively the donation program has helped, and how it might be modified.

————. **Homelessness: Homeless and Runaway Youth Receiving Services at Federally Funded Shelters.** Washington, DC: U.S. General Accounting Office, 1989. GAO/HRD-90-45.

————. **Homelessness: HUD Improperly Restricts Applicants for Supplemental Assistance Program.** Washington, DC: U.S. General Accounting Office, 1992. 36p. GAO/RCED-92-200.

The Supplemental Assistance for Facilities To Assist the Homeless (SAFAH) competitive grant program was evaluated in this report to determine whether it reached target populations and was managed effectively.

———— **Homelessness: HUD's and FEMA's Progress in Implementing the McKinney Act.** Washington, DC: U.S. General Accounting Office, 1989. 136p. GAO/RCED-89-50.

Congress mandated this evaluation of the HUD and FEMA McKinney programs that provide emergency shelter and various forms of housing assistance. The report not only analyzes the various funding formulas used to disperse this money, but also profiles those agencies receiving grants and their viewpoints on the causes of the problem they address.

————. **Homelessness: HUD's Interpretation of Homeless Excludes Previously Served Groups.** Washington, DC: U.S. General Accounting Office, 1992. 14p. GAO/RCED-92-226.

Eligibility for federal programs is set out in official definitions of relevant terms; the definition of homelessness has varied from program to program. This report examines the impact of this ambiguity and inconsistency for participation and operation of the McKinney Act programs.

————. **Homelessness: Implementation of Food and Shelter Programs under the McKinney Act.** Washington, DC: U.S. General Accounting Office, 1987. 40p. GAO/RCED-88-63.

Several federal programs for homeless people predate the 1987 passage of the McKinney Homeless Assistance Act. Both these and the subsequent emergency measures are examined here; numerous possible adjustments in program procedures are offered, as well as tables of funding statistics.

———. **Homelessness: McKinney Act Programs and Funding for Fiscal Year 1989.** Washington, DC: U.S. General Accounting Office, 1990. GAO/RCED-90-52.

———. **Homelessness: McKinney Act Programs and Funding through Fiscal Year 1990.** Washington, DC: U.S. General Accounting Office, 1991. 100p. GAO/RCED-91-126.

The status of and expenditures in programs authorized under the McKinney Act Amendments of 1988 are summarized in this report.

———. **Homelessness: McKinney Act Programs and Funding through Fiscal Year 1991.** Washington, DC: U.S. General Accounting Office, 1992. 100p. GAO/RCED-93-39.

The status of and expenditures in programs authorized under the McKinney Act Amendments of 1988 and carried out in fiscal years 1990 and 1991 are summarized in this report.

———. **Homelessness: McKinney Act Reports Could Improve Federal Assistance Efforts.** Washington, DC: U.S. General Accounting Office, 1990. 38p. GAO/RCED-90-121.

Reports on many topics are mandated by the McKinney Act to improve Congress's knowledge of the problem of homelessness, as well as its ability to identify problems and changes in federal programs. This report summarizes the report requirements.

———. **Homelessness: Policy and Liability Issues in Donating Prepared Food.** Washington, DC: U.S. General Accounting Office, 1991. 10p. GAO/RCED-92-62.

This report, mandated under the McKinney Act, examines the extent to which federal laws, regulations, or policies help or hinder federal facilities that might donate excess prepared food to help homeless people.

———. **Homelessness: Single Room Occupancy Program Achieves Goals, but HUD Can Increase Impact.** Washington, DC: U.S. General Accounting Office, 1992. 59p. GAO/RCED-92-215.

The SRO housing program attempts to meet permanent housing needs of single homeless people. This report looks at how successful the program has been in creating such housing and necessary support services.

———. **Homelessness: Too Early To Tell What Kinds of Prevention Assistance Work Best.** Washington, DC: U.S. General Accounting Office, 1990. 42p. GAO/RCED-90-89.

Some states have initiated programs to prevent homelessness before it happens; six federal programs support or supplement this work. This report examines eligibility requirements for such programs, as well as program limitations.

————. **Homelessness: Transitional Housing Shows Initial Success but Long-Term Effects Unknown.** Washington, DC: U.S. General Accounting Office, 1991. 68p. GAO/RCED-91-200.

Housing and supportive services are provided for some homeless people through the old Transitional Housing Program of the McKinney Act. This report examines the extent to which participants moved to independent living by finding permanent housing and a source of income.

————. **1990 Census: Limitations in Methods and Procedures To Include the Homeless.** Washington, DC: U.S. General Accounting Office, 1991. 19p. GAO/GGD-92-1.

The 1990 census included a controversial effort to count some of the nation's homeless people. This report resulted from a McKinney Act requirement that the methodology and procedures of the count be assessed.

————. **Pediatric AIDS: Health and Social Service Needs of Infants and Children.** Washington, DC: U.S. General Accounting Office, 1989. 20p. GAO/HRD-89-96.

With homelessness and drug use on the rise among the poor, also on the increase is pediatric AIDS, which operates medically in children in forms different from adults. Children with AIDS often have parents with a history of drug use, who in turn have a greater likelihood of having AIDS. AIDS is now the leading cause of death for children up to age four in New York City, for instance. Homelessness is a likely accompaniment or consequence of HIV infection.

————. **Welfare Hotels: Uses, Costs, and Alternatives.** Washington, DC: U.S. General Accounting Office, 1989. 63p. GAO/HRD-89-26BR.

The use of commercial hotels and motels to compensate for the lack of an emergency shelter system in a local area has become a well-known symbol of makeshift efforts to deal with growing homelessness. This government report examines hotels and their services, looks at their frequency of use as temporary and permanent housing, compares their rates to other types of housing, and explores alternatives.

Other Helpful Legal and Policy Materials

Federal

Code of Federal Regulations (CFR). These paperback books contain the regulations that govern the federal government's programs. Each CFR title is in one or more volumes; each contains "Parts." 45 CFR, for instance, covers the public welfare programs, and 27 CFR covers housing programs. Regulation 45 CFR, Part 233, for example, is "Coverage and Conditions of Eligibility in Financial Assistance Programs," and it explains all the rules and procedures for federal cash assistance programs. Section 233.120, for instance, explains the terms and conditions under which the federal government will make payments to eligible states for the Emergency Assistance program, which is the source of federal funds paying for welfare hotels for homeless families. The CFR is available through the Government Printing Office, which has stores nationwide [(202) 783-3238]. The CFR is revised periodically, and notice of revision is published in the *Federal Register,* where proposed, interim, and final regulations are routinely published.

Federal Register. Published daily, this newsprint book contains all the proposed, interim, and final rules for operation of the programs of the federal government, as well as announcements of meetings of national commissions (such as the Interagency Council on the Homeless) and notice of the availability and award of funds under federal programs. One could consult the *Federal Register,* for example, to find out how many dollars were awarded to one's state government for a particular McKinney Act program for homeless people, or to examine the proposed alcohol and drug policy for operation of emergency shelters funded with federal dollars. Available by subscription from the Government Printing Office, or in many libraries.

U.S.C.A. (United States Code Annotated). Various volumes of this publication cover all the federal laws pertaining to a specific subject. For instance, 42 U.S.C.A. contains 17 volumes and covers all the titles of the Social Security Act, including those laws governing the AFDC, or welfare program. They are available in some public libraries, law libraries, and the libraries of some public-interest organizations.

Other Material

Other relevant federal agency material is available by request from the appropriate agency. "Action Transmittals," which communicate program information from the Department of Health and Human Services to state agencies, can be requested for free, as can annual and other reports—on state welfare plans, for instance. Consult the regional office of the appropriate federal agency or a public library to find out what materials are available and how to request them.

State

State program manuals. Procedural manuals akin to the CFR are also available for many state programs. Contact the relevant state agency for information on manuals. In some cases, state agencies are compelled under federal law to make such materials available; individuals and groups working with public assistance recipients, for instance, have access to state AFDC manuals under federal law.

State statutes. State laws on various topics are available from commercial publishers. Contact a public library or a law library to find out where such statutes are available or the name of a publisher.

Periodicals

In addition to the references listed above, the following publications would be useful for staying current with new developments in homelessness and related policy. Some of these are key publications also listed in Chapter 8.

Access, a quarterly newsletter on research and government programs on the homeless mentally ill. Available free from National Resource Center on Homelessness and Mental Illness, 262 Delaware Avenue, Delmar, NY 12054; (800) 444-7415.

Alliance, the monthly newsletter of the National Alliance To End Homelessness. This publication covers federal government program and grant activity, future conferences, and new publications. Available from the National Alliance, 1518 K Street NW, Suite 206, Washington, DC 20005; (202) 638-1526.

Clearinghouse Review, the monthly legal services journal of poverty law developments. This publication includes substantive articles on legal developments in all areas of poverty law, short write-ups of developing cases, and reviews of relevant publications and reports. Most items in the journal are on deposit with the clearinghouse, and they can be obtained by non–Legal Services programs for a copying charge. The journal is free to Legal Services Corporation programs, and $75 per year for others.

Homewords, a quarterly newsletter of the Homelessness Information Exchange, highlighting programs and materials available through this program's database. Subscriptions available through membership in the

National Coalition for the Homeless, 1612 K Street NW, Suite 1004, Washington, DC 20005; (202) 775-1322.

Housing Affairs Letter, a weekly newsletter on affordable housing, fair housing, public housing, federal policy, and finance. Available by subscription from: CD Publications, 8204 Fenton Street, Silver Spring, MD 20910; (301) 588-6380. $339 per year.

Housing and Development Reporter, a weekly newsletter on all aspects of housing development, finance, and policy. Available by subscription from Housing and Development Reporter, 2300 M Street NW, Suite 100, Washington, DC 20037; (202) 973-7710. $830 per year.

Housing Law Bulletin, the bimonthly publication of the National Housing Law Project (NHLP), the legal services national support center on housing for poor people. The bulletin covers recent developments in all assisted-housing programs, and announcements of relevant publications. Available by subscription from NHLP, 2201 Broadway, Suite 815, Oakland, CA 94612; (510) 251-9400. Free to Legal Services Corporation programs; $50 per year to others.

In Just Times, the newsletter of the National Law Center on Homelessness and Poverty. This brief newsletter includes several short articles that cover highlights of its legislative and litigation activities, upcoming meetings, and recent publications. Available from the National Law Center, 918 F Street, Washington, DC 20004; (202) 638-2535. $10 donation requested.

Opening Doors, the newsletter of the Health Care for the Homeless programs, is published quarterly and contains a feature story on some aspect of homeless health care, as well as news of relevant publications and conferences. Available free to grantees from JSI, 210 Lincoln Street, Boston, MA 02111; (617) 482-9485. $7.50 per year for individuals.

Poverty and Race, the bimonthly newsletter of the Poverty and Race Research Action Council, publishes several feature articles on current-interest topics, as well as numerous announcements of publications, papers, research projects, and other programs on race and poverty. Available free from PRRAC, 1711 Connecticut Avenue NW, Washington, DC 20009; (202) 387-9887.

Roundup, the newsletter of the Low Income Housing Information Service (LIHIS), is issued ten times yearly. It covers federal legislative and regulatory activity on all low-income housing issues, as well as publications and conferences on housing and community development. Available from LIHIS, 1012 Fourteenth Street NW, Suite 1200, Washington, DC 20005; (202) 662-1530. $35 per year.

Safety Network, the monthly newsletter of the National Coalition for the Homeless (NCH), covers all federal homelessness activity, including grant announcements and legislative developments. A "Bulletin Board" announces publications, videos, and conferences. Available from NCH, 1612 K Street NW, Suite 1004, Washington, DC 20006. Free with membership.

Shelterforce, the monthly magazine of the National Housing Institute, contains longer general-interest articles about affordable housing, including stories about local programs and model projects as well as policy articles. Available from the National Housing Institute, 439 Main Street, Orange, NJ 07050. $18 per year for individuals.

10

Nonprint Resources

Films

The AIDS Movie
Type: 16mm film; video
Length: 26 min.
Purchase/rental cost: $390/$57
Distributor: Durrin Productions
                      1748 Kalorama Road NW
                      Washington, DC 20009
                      (800) 536-6843
Date: 1989

Three people with AIDS talk about what it's like to have the disease. An AIDS educator discusses awareness and prevention needs in the community.

Back Wards to Back Streets
Type: Video
Length: 55 min.
Purchase/rental cost: $445/$75
Distributor: Filmakers Library
                      124 East 40th Street
                      New York, NY 10016
                      (212) 808-4980
Date: 1981

Efforts to reintegrate former mental patients into the community are largely regarded as unsuccessful, inadequate, and a major contributing factor to homelessness. This investigative report, directed by Roger Weisberg for Public Policy Productions, looks at some successful community treatment programs, but also at the failures that resulted for the deinstitutionalized patient, including examinations of adult homes, the need for social services, and homelessness.

Bailey House: To Live as Long as You Can
Type: Video
Length: 55 min.
Purchase/rental cost: $295/$75
Distributor: Filmakers Library
                      124 East 40th Street
                      New York, NY 10016
                      (212) 808-4980
Date: 1989

Bailey House in New York City is a city-sponsored residence for homeless people with AIDS. This film tells the story of both residents and staff.

Both Sides of the Street
Type: 16mm film; video
Length: 18 min.
Purchase/rental cost: $300/$70 (16mm); $175/$55 (video)
Distributor: Onewest Media
                      P.O. Box 5766
                      Santa Fe, NM 87502
                      (505) 983-8685
Date: 1986

The Tenderloin area of San Francisco is under pressure from development that threatens many of the older and working residents, as well as homeless people and runaways who seek refuge there. Barbara Neal directed this film, which tells one woman's story as she sees her neighborhood change.

The Bronx: A Cry for Help
Type: Video
Length: 59 min.
Distributor: Filmakers Library
                      124 East 40th Street
                      New York, NY 10016
                      (212) 808-4980
Date: 1989

The South Bronx is often thought of as a wasteland, a place where people cannot live. This film shows what everyday life is like for those whose homes are in a neighborhood that has been left to violence, drugs, and lack of services.

Down and Out in America

Type:	Video
Length:	60 min.
Distributor:	Joseph Fuery Productions
	200 West 86th Street #11A
	New York, NY 10024
	(212) 877-7700
Date:	1986

Lee Grant directed this Academy Award–winning portrayal of people suffering from job loss, farm foreclosures, lack of housing, and other problems. Told through powerful interviews, the film examines the Los Angeles "Justiceville" encampment of homeless people and the notorious welfare hotels of New York City.

The Fall of the I Hotel

Type:	16mm film; video
Length:	57 min.
Purchase/rental cost:	$650/$100 (16mm); $250/$70 (video)
Distributor:	Onewest Media
	P.O. Box 5766
	Santa Fe, NM 87502
	(505) 983-8685

San Francisco's International Hotel was demolished in 1977 despite an eight-year struggle to save it by hotel residents, neighborhood churches, organized labor, and senior citizens groups. For several decades, the hotel had provided low-cost housing to many immigrant Filipinos, the last of whom waged an unsuccessful battle against developers who sought to build a parking garage on the site. This award-winning film combines interviews with residents, news film, and other resources to tell its story, culminating with the forcible removal of the last tenants.

Food Not Bombs

Type:	Video
Length:	25 min.
Purchase cost:	$20
Distributor:	Haight-Ashbury Free TV
	1827 Haight Street #201
	San Francisco, CA 94117
	(414) 995-2397
Date:	1988

Ninety-two volunteers of the "Food, Not Bombs" organization were arrested by police for serving free food to homeless people. This video documents the struggle between local authorities and members of the community.

Footage Sampler: Homelessness, the Unseen Dimensions

Type:	Video formats
Length:	21 min.
Purchase/rental cost:	Negotiable
Distributor:	Julia Keydel
	Homelessness Videotape Project
	131 West 87th Street #1B
	New York, NY 10024
Date:	1983

Through interviews, this film examines the controversy generated in an Upper West Side neighborhood by a proposal to expand outreach services for homeless people through the creation of a referral center. Homeless people and other community residents, as well as workers at the Goddard-Riverside Project Reach-Out program, are featured in this work, directed by Julia Keydel. The film shows homeless people on a human level and depicts solutions to the problems faced in the community.

Girltalk

Type:	Video
Length:	55 min.
Rental cost:	$75
Distributor:	Filmakers Library
	124 East 40th Street
	New York, NY 10016
	(212) 808-4980

The troubled lives of three teenage girls are depicted here; they offer virtually the entire range of problems faced by the young poor, problems that can all too easily result in homelessness. They are young veterans of juvenile courts, marginal jobs, foster homes, and teen pregnancy.

God Bless the Child

Type:	Video
Length:	96 min.
Purchase/rental cost:	Home video rental
Distributor:	Local video stores
Date:	1988

A single working mother is displaced from her home and cannot find affordable housing. Homeless, she loses her job and takes her child out of school. She is helped by an outreach worker, only to have her daughter suffer rat bites and lead paint poisoning in the run-down house they rent. Evicted, she makes the decision to abandon her child to foster care.

Hard Drugs

Type:	16mm film; video
Length:	16 min.
Purchase/rental cost:	$325 (16mm); $200/$50 (video)
Distributor:	The Cinema Guild
	1697 Broadway
	New York, NY 10019
	(212) 246-5522
Date:	1976

In this documentary, drug addicts talk about what led them to use drugs. People who are working to help them are also interviewed.

Heroism

Type:	Video
Length:	28 min.
Purchase/rental cost:	$250/$50
Distributor:	The Cinema Guild
	1697 Broadway
	New York, NY 10019
	(212) 246-5522
Date:	1987

An examination of some of the many people and organizations that have come together to offer services for people with AIDS in San Francisco. PWAs talk about how they help one another, and volunteer meal providers, artists, and medical researchers discuss their roles.

Home

Type:	Video
Length:	28 min.
Purchase/rental cost:	$295/$50
Distributor:	The Cinema Guild
	1697 Broadway
	New York, NY 10019
	(212) 246-5522
Date:	1986

A group of squatters in Brooklyn is the focus of this film, which documents the crisis of affordable housing in the nation and the possible solution offered by those reclaiming abandoned city-owned properties. Members of ACORN, a group advocating squatting, and community leaders are interviewed about the controversy generated by this tactic.

Homeless in America

Type:	Video
Length:	12 min.
Purchase cost:	$29.50
Distributor:	National Mental Health Association
	1021 Prince Street
	Alexandria, VA 22314
	(703) 684-7722
Date:	1988

Portions of the major national traveling exhibit on homelessness, assembled by the NMHA and Families for the Homeless, are presented here. Some of the nation's most prominent photographers participated in this project, which shows the human side of homelessness.

Homeless in Philadelphia

Type:	Video
Length:	48 min.
Purchase/rental cost:	$210/$50
Distributor:	Circulating Film Library
	Museum of Modern Art
	11 West 53rd Street
	New York, NY 10019
	(212) 708-9530
Date:	1986

The Committee for Dignity and Fairness for the Homeless sponsored this film; homeless people helped plan and produce the story, which depicts those homeless who are ready, willing, and able to work and speak out for themselves.

Housekeeping

Type:	Video
Length:	117 min.
Purchase/rental cost:	Home video rental
Distributor:	Local video stores
Date:	1987

Two teenage girls in the Northwest wind up being cared for by their aunt, who has been riding freight trains. Though the aunt, played by Christine Lahti, tries hard, she has brought with her the ways of the road, including insulating her clothes with newspapers and saving empty containers. The nieces grow in opposite directions, with one leaving to pursue a "normal" life, and the other so drawn to her aunt's ways that she and her aunt eventually leave to hop a train together.

Housing Court

Type:	16mm film; video
Length:	30 min.
Purchase/rental cost:	$425 (16mm); $295/$55 (video)
Distributor:	The Cinema Guild
	1697 Broadway
	New York, NY 10019
	(212) 246-5522
Date:	1985

The Bronx Housing Court in New York City is the setting for examining three buildings where tenants have sought relief in disputes with landlords. The court is viewed as the stage where the crisis in affordable decent housing is played out in 125,000 cases annually, dealing with evictions, code violations, and rent strikes.

Ironweed

Type:	Video
Length:	135 min.
Purchase/rental cost:	Home video rental
Distributor:	Local video stores
Date:	1987

Though not about homelessness in the 1980s, this film depicts the pain of that life in graphic terms. Based on William Kennedy's novel about Depression-era Albany, the story follows Jack Phelan (played by Jack Nicholson), an alcoholic who has left his family and is subsisting on the street with Helen Archer, also an alcoholic (played by Meryl Streep). As they scrounge for money for drink and places to sleep, witness the exposure death of a friend, and struggle with their pasts, they depict some of the enduring aspects of being homeless.

Locked Out of the American Dream

Type:	Video
Length:	60 min.
Distributor:	KERA-TV
	3000 Harry Hines Boulevard
	Dallas, TX 75201
	(214) 871-1390
Date:	1988

This examination of the growing shortage of affordable housing focuses on one Dallas family as it discusses the history of federal involvement in assisted housing for the poor. Profiles are offered of Boston and Baltimore, where nonprofit organizations have joined with developers and public agencies to create affordable housing. Developer James Rouse of Columbia, Maryland, and Boston's mayor Raymond Flynn are interviewed.

The Many Faces of Homelessness
Type: Video
Length: 35 min.
Purchase cost: $19.95 (½"); $49.95 (¾")
Distributor: Home Builders Institute
Fifteenth and M Streets NW
Washington, DC 20005
(800) 368-5242
Date: 1988

The home builders' industry prepared this film for its first industry event on homelessness; the film examines daily life for homeless people, as well as the builder's role in solving all aspects of the problem, from shelter to permanent housing.

Neighbors in Need
Type: Video
Length: 28 min.
Distributor: California Homeless and Housing Coalition
926 J Street, Suite 422
Sacramento, CA 95814
(916) 447-0390; (916) 447-0458 FAX
Date: 1990

The film examines some of the issues and difficulties in locating homeless housing programs, but shows how community effort and the work of volunteers can make a difference in how a project is received. Several California projects are profiled.

No Home on the Island
Type: 16mm; video
Length: 29 min.
Purchase/rental cost: $525 (16mm); $300/$55 (video)
Distributor: Filmakers Library
124 East 40th Street
New York, NY 10016
(212) 808-4980
Date: 1987

Homelessness on city streets is familiar to many Americans. Not so readily does the nation come to grips with homelessness in suburban areas. This film, directed by Mark Gross, shows a Long Island community where average, middle-class people experience the need for shelter when faced with job loss, social services cutbacks, recession, and escalating housing costs. Volunteer efforts to help those in need are spotlighted.

No Hunger in My Home

Type:	Video
Length:	26 min.
Purchase/rental cost:	$295/$55
Distributor:	Filmakers Library
	124 East 40th Street
	New York, NY 10016
	(212) 808-4980
Date:	1989

The stories of three women in a California suburb are told here to show the work of local communities helping hungry people.

Poverty

Type:	16 mm; video
Length:	18 min.
Purchase/rental cost:	$350 (16mm); $200/$50 (video)
Distributor:	The Cinema Guild
	1697 Broadway
	New York, NY 10019
	(212) 246-5522
Date:	1976

The late Michael Harrington, author of many works on poverty, including *The Other America* and *The New American Poverty,* comments on the continuing American problem of a growing gap between the nation's rich and poor.

Promises To Keep

Type:	Video
Length:	57 min.
Purchase/rental cost:	$250/$57 (nonprofits)
Distributor:	Durrin Productions
	1748 Kalorama Road NW
	Washington, DC 20009
	(800) 536-6843
Date:	1989

Directed by Ginny Durrin, this Oscar-nominated documentary tells the story of the four-year struggle by Mitch Snyder and the Washington, D.C.–based Community for Creative Non-Violence to hold onto a previously abandoned federal building they converted into an emergency shelter. Through film clips, press reports, and the words of homeless people themselves, the successful fight to secure the building as a model facility is shown. A discussion guide is available.

The Rebuilding of Mascot Flats

Type:	Video
Length:	59 min.
Distributor:	Filmakers Library
	124 East 40th Street
	New York, NY 10016
	(212) 808-4980
Date:	1991

A group of homeless New Yorkers plans to rebuild an abandoned building. With the help of Habitat for Humanity, they fight the odds: bureaucrats, lack of skills, no money. The film tells their story over a period of three years, as they turn their idea into a reality.

Samaritan: The Mitch Snyder Story

Type:	Video
Length:	104 min.
Purchase/rental cost:	Home video rental
Distributor:	Local video stores
Date:	1986

Martin Sheen stars as Mitch Snyder in this made-for-television film that was produced following the successful struggle to secure a federal building to shelter homeless people in Washington, D.C. True stories of several homeless people are included.

Shadow Children

Type:	Video
Length:	30 min.
Purchase/rental cost:	$250/$50
Distributor:	The Cinema Guild
	1697 Broadway
	New York, NY 10019
	(212) 246-5522
Date:	1991

Homeless young people living on the streets of the Bay Area in California are depicted here. Most of their families do not want them back, and the film shows the youths as they struggle with their need for food and shelter, the lure of drugs and prostitution as means of survival, and the unwanted attention of the police.

Shelter

Type:	Video
Length:	55 min.
Purchase/rental cost:	$445/$75
Distributor:	Filmakers Library
	124 East 40th Street
	New York, NY 10016
	(212) 808-4980
Date:	1986

This film uses interviews and portraits to show the variety of people who become homeless: the longtime jobless, former mental patients, families searching for work. Ideas on how to address the problem and who should bear the cost are shared by government officials, policymakers, and social service providers.

Shooting Back

Type:	Video
Length:	30 min.
Purchase cost:	$25
Distributor:	Video/Action Fund
	3034 Q Street NW
	Washington, DC 20005
	(202) 338-1094
Date:	1990

Homeless children and young people in Washington, D.C.–area shelters describe their lives and how they feel about learning documentary photography as a way of communicating their everyday lives to others. Their photos are shown in an international traveling exhibit, and they narrate opening-night events in this award-winning video.

Squatters: The Other Philadelphia Story

Type:	16mm; video
Length:	27 min.
Purchase/rental cost:	$425 (16mm); $300/$50 (video)
Distributor:	The Cinema Guild
	1697 Broadway
	New York, NY 10019
	(212) 246-5522
Date:	1984

This story of squatters reclaiming buildings in Philadelphia traces not only their need for housing, but also their personal and political transformation as they lobby officials, testify before Congress, and raise funds for their cause.

Streetwise

Type:	Video
Length:	92 min.
Purchase/rental cost:	Home video rental
Distributor:	Local video stores
Date:	1985

This film examines the pain and courage of homeless teenagers on the streets of Seattle, watching closely as they survive by forming their own community, supporting themselves by panhandling, dealing drugs, and working as prostitutes. Martin Bell directed this story, which was nominated for an Academy Award for Best Documentary in 1984.

Takeover

Type:	Video
Length:	57 min.
Purchase/rental cost:	Varies for organizations and homeless groups
Distributor:	Skylight Pictures
	330 West 42nd Street
	New York, NY 10036
	(212) 947-5333
Date:	1992

The film chronicles the efforts of homeless people in Minneapolis, Tucson, Philadelphia, Detroit, Chicago, and Los Angeles as they act in a national effort to occupy vacant government-owned housing.

Temporary Dwellings

Type:	Video
Length:	28 min.
Purchase/rental cost:	$295/$55
Distributor:	Filmakers Library
	124 East 40th Street
	New York, NY 10016
	(212) 808-4980
Date:	1989

This story of homeless people in Seattle depicts Tent City, an encampment where homeless people could live and run their own lives. The effort achieved its purpose, as the city's mayor provided a shelter where homeless people could stay and build a community.

Uninvited: The Homeless of Phoenix

Type:	Video
Length:	28 min.
Rental cost:	$50
Distributor:	Films Incorporated
	5547 North Ravenswood Avenue
	Chicago, IL 60640
	(800) 323-4222

Thousands of homeless people settled in a tent city around Phoenix; this film, directed by Herbert Danska, tells their story, as well as the views of members of the advocacy organization, the Consortium of the Homeless, government officials, and others. The presence of homeless people in Phoenix raised enormous hostility in the local community.

We Are Not Who You Think We Are

Type:	Video
Length:	12 min.
Purchase cost:	$15
Distributor:	Video/Action Fund
	1077 30th Street NW
	Washington, DC 20007
	(202) 338-1094

Women prisoners tell about the roots and rootlessness of their lives, and, in the telling, relate stories of economic hardship, child abuse, and enormous personal difficulties. Filmed on location at Bedford Hills Corrections Facility in New York, this is a story of those who are increasingly the next generation of homeless people: the nation's huge prison population.

Who's Going To Care for These Children?

Type:	Video
Length:	14 min.
Purchase/rental cost:	$99/$50
Distributor:	Filmakers Library
	124 East 40th Street
	New York, NY 10016
	(212) 808-4980
Date:	1991

Boarder babies are infants who cannot go home with their birth mothers, either because of the mother's homelessness, drug use, or HIV/AIDS illness, or because of the baby's HIV illness. Increasing numbers of these babies know no home but a hospital, except for the care of foster parents and volunteers. This film tells the story of some of them.

Women of Substance

Type:	Video
Length:	12 min.
Purchase cost:	$15
Distributor:	Video/Action Fund
	1077 30th Street NW
	Washington, DC 20007
	(202) 338-1094

Women grapple with drug addiction in this brief but intense video, which highlights the obstacles facing those who want drug treatment, who have children or are separated from them because of homelessness or addiction, and who need the total family treatment that is so unavailable. A discussion guide is available.

Databases and Computer Networks

Bibliographic Databases

The National Clearinghouse on Alcohol Information (NCALI)

Source:	Data Base Search Service
	P.O. Box 2345
	Rockville, MD 20852
	(301) 468-2600
Cost:	None

Annotated references from over 200 alcohol-related information sources are available through this service. Custom searches are performed for subjects, authors, keywords, or year of publication.

The National Resource Center on Homelessness and Mental Illness

Source:	Policy Research Associates, Inc.
	262 Delaware Avenue
	Delmar, NY 12054
	(800) 444-7415
Cost:	Variable

Both standard and customized bibliographic searches are available from this database, covering dual diagnosis, epidemiology, ethnographic research, families and children, general issues, health and health care, housing, legal issues, and outreach.

City Databases

COMSEARCH Foundation Funding

Source: The Foundation Center
         1001 Connecticut Avenue NW
         Washington, DC 20036
         (800) 424-9836
Cost: Variable

Computerized database searches can be performed to locate foundations that provide support for specific subject area or geographic area efforts. Four major categories for which printouts are available: broad topics ($38), including health care, families, children, services; subjects ($18), for program areas such as health care, volunteer programs, rural issues; geographic ($30), providing an analysis by region or states receiving the greatest share of funds; special topics ($18), including the most frequently requested foundation listings.

Federal Funds Information for States (FFIS)

Source: National Conference of State Legislatures
         1560 Broadway, Suite 700
         Denver, CO 80202
         (303) 830-2054
Cost: Annual subscription basis

NCSL operates this database jointly with the National Governors' Association. Detailed computerized information and projections are available on about 90 percent of the federal funds distributed in each state for more than 240 programs. Subscribers receive three reports annually with this service.

HandsNet

Source: HandsNet
         20195 Stevens Creek Boulevard, Suite 120
         Cupertino, CA 95014
         (408) 257-4500; (408) 257-4560
Cost: $25 monthly or $270 annually, plus one-time
         fee for software and fees for on-line time
System: Macintosh, IBM PCs

This national computer network of advocates for low-income people— including homeless people—counts many state coalitions and key research organizations as subscribers. Groups can access daily news briefs, post inquiries or news on policy issues, scan federal regulation updates, and use electronic mail to communicate rapidly and on a 24-hour basis.

Homeless Programs Database

Source:	Homelessness Information Exchange National Coalition for the Homeless 1612 K Street NW, Suite 1004 Washington, DC 20006 (202) 775-1322; (202) 775-1316 FAX
Cost:	Custom and standard searches are available, as well as prepared packets of information.

This database carries information on homeless shelter, housing, education, and health programs, as well as organizational information and funding research.

HUD USER

Source:	HUD USER P.O. Box 6091 Rockville, MD 20850 (800) 245-2691
Cost:	$10 (standard); $20 (custom)

Standard searches on housing topics are available from the on-line services of the Department of Housing and Urban Development. Standard searches are available on federal housing assistance programs, Community Development Block Grants, affordable housing, and housing for the elderly. Custom searches are also performed for other up-to-date information.

LEGISNET

Source:	National Conference of State Legislatures 1560 Broadway, Suite 700 Denver, CO 80202 (303) 830-2054
Cost:	None

This system abstracts thousands of legislative research reports, public policy documents, state surveys, and statistical information. The database is available for all state legislators and their staff.

Local Government Information Network (LOGIN)

Source:	National League of Cities (NLC) 1301 Pennsylvania Avenue NW Washington, DC 20004
Cost:	Various subscription packages
System:	Almost any personal computer, word processor, or data terminal

Local officials can communicate with their colleagues via this system, as well as access a 25,000-unit database on local government programs. Services are provided for both large and small communities.

Local Information Network for Universal Service (LINUS)

Source:	National League of Cities (NLC)
	1301 Pennsylvania Avenue NW
	Washington, DC 20004
Cost:	Actual time used
System:	Almost any personal computer, word
	processor, or data terminal

Local officials can access all information offered by the NLC, the International City Management Association, and their counterparts in other jurisdictions, as well as services provided by some participating public-interest groups.

National League of Cities Database

Source:	National League of Cities (NLC)
	1301 Pennsylvania Avenue NW
	Washington, DC 20004
Cost:	Subscription

Customized printouts of various databases about city officials and cities are available through this service. The City Officials Data Base provides contact information on mayors, council members, and selected department heads; individual terms of office are available for some officials. The City Information Data Base offers facts on government structure, elections, terms of office, and the jurisdiction itself. City Information is available for all cities over 10,000 population and for smaller cities if they belong to the NLC.

YOUTHNET

Source:	National Network of Runaway and
	Youth Services
	1319 F Street NW, Suite 401
	Washington, DC 20004
	(202) 783-7949; (202) 783-7955 FAX
Cost:	Actual time used
System:	Almost any personal computer, word
	processor, or data terminal

Over 130 agencies working with homeless, runaway, and atrisk youth subscribe to this network, which offers e-mail, funding alerts, federal policy updates, research reviews, conference announcements, and more.

boarder babies contracted HIV from their mothers; in some cases, the baby's mother has died. In other cases, the baby cannot go home because of a mother's drug use, homelessness, or illness. In some communities, litigation compels a search for a foster home so that the baby does not remain in the hospital.

case definition The official Centers for Disease Control (CDC) definition of AIDS. A finding of case definition AIDS is necessary for access to some services and programs.

Centers for Disease Control (CDC) A federal government agency responsible for infectious disease control. The agency is located in Atlanta and operates under the U.S. Public Health Services, a part of the U.S. Department of Health and Human Services. CDC monitors tuberculosis and HIV/AIDS.

CHAS Comprehensive Housing Affordability Strategies. This document superseded the CHAP; it is a five-year housing plan required of state and local governments seeking federal housing funds. Under the CHAS, governments are to identify and prioritize their housing needs, and identify the resources and programs for reaching their housing goals.

chronically mentally ill A state of severe and persistent mental disorder (schizophrenia, depression) that interferes with function and requires long-term psychiatric care.

clean needles Usually refers to syringes used for injection of drugs. Clean needles reduce the chance of passing HIV via blood that accumulates in the syringe. A clean needle can also be one that has been sterilized with bleach after being used.

commodities Surplus agricultural products purchased under the Price Support Program by the federal government and distributed through two basic outlets. One is to mass meal programs, including school lunch programs, large soup kitchens, and other congregate feeding sites. The second disbursement is through food banks and social service programs that provide food packages to individuals and families.

Comprehensive Homeless Assistance Plan (CHAP) A document required of all cities, counties, and states eligible for early McKinney program funds. CHAPs were superceded by CHAS (see above).

creaming The practice by service providers or program operators of selecting as program participants, or tenants, those candidates whose profiles make it likely that they will achieve success in the program with relatively less difficulty than other candidates. This practice renders programs freer of "problem" participants and also gives the program a higher apparent success rate.

criminalization   The trend toward attaching criminal charges and penalties to common acts of homeless people, such as sleeping in public places (parks, etc.) and begging. Numerous jurisdictions have passed laws of this sort in an effort to push downtown-area homeless people away from businesses and restaurants. In the South and West, laws have been enacted against sleeping or camping on beaches or in parks or having one's belongings in such areas. Many of these laws are found in areas with large tourist industries.

day labor   Usually manual-labor jobs that are available to homeless and poor workers on a temporary basis. Job seekers wait on designated street corners or appear at a for-profit labor center in hopes of being assigned to a job, such as loading trucks or cleaning out abandoned buildings. Workers are paid low wages, charged for the necessities of their job (such as rides, shovels, gloves), and are not protected from unsafe conditions or unfair practices.

deinstitutionalization   Officially defined by the National Institute of Mental Health as the prevention of inappropriate mental hospital admissions through the provision of community alternatives for treatment, the release to the community of all institutionalized patients who have been given adequate preparation for such discharge, and the establishment and maintenance of community support systems for noninstitutionalized people receiving mental health services in the community.

doubling up   An accommodation to the housing crisis in which one household shares its housing with at least one other household, related or unrelated. An arrangement frequently found among the poor, their breakdown is a leading cause of homelessness.

drug-resistant tuberculosis   Recent strains of tuberculosis that are impervious to one or more of the 13 commonly used antibiotics employed to treat the disease.

dual diagnosis   A person with both a drug and/or alcohol problem and a mental health problem.

Emergency Assistance to Families (EAF)   A short-term federal emergency-aid entitlement program under which states elect to participate in a 50-50 match to provide services, including temporary shelter, for needy families.

expiring subsidies   Under the Section 8 certificate program, private owners contract with the federal government to reserve their housing units for low- and moderate-income people in exchange for a guaranteed long-term rent. When these contracts expire, the subsidies are lost, and owners can elect to charge a higher rent or convert the building to another use.

Fair Market Rent   A cost assigned by HUD to a typical rental unit in a given geographic area for households of differing sizes. Fair market rents are then used to calculate payments for low-income tenants using assisted housing programs, where HUD will pay the difference between 30 percent of a person's income and the fair market rent.

federal preferences   Priority cases for federal housing assistance, as established for applicants for HUD rental-assistance programs. Preferences are given to people who are involuntarily displaced, living in substandard housing or homeless, or paying more than 50 percent of income for rent.

fiscal year   A 12-month period for budget purposes. In most states, the fiscal year (FY) runs from 1 July to 30 June. The fiscal year that begins 1 July 1994 is referred to as FY 95. Some states and the federal government use a fiscal year that begins on 1 October and ends 30 September.

flops or flophouses   Hotels in which rooms are generally cheaply rented by the night; usually only a bed is provided, often in a space just big enough to accommodate it.

food bank   A nonprofit clearinghouse for surplus or salvaged food. Producers, markets, and food outlets such as restaurants can donate food, which is stored, if necessary, and redistributed to soup kitchens, shelters, and social service agencies. Food banks generally charge a nominal cost to recipients (such as 10 cents a pound) to cover operations.

food stamps   In 1961, the USDA enacted the food stamp program, technically known as the Family Nutrition Program. It extends to all 50 states and is administered by welfare or social service departments. The USDA pays the full value of the stamps and half the administrative costs. Free stamps are made available to families who lack the cash to purchase them; a family's allotment is determined by subtracting 30 percent of its monthly income from the Thrifty Food Plan cost for a family of that size. The balance is given to the family in free stamps.

general assistance (GA)   State and local welfare programs for people who do not qualify for federal benefits are typically called general assistance, general relief, or home relief. These programs offer income supports to needy people who meet financial eligibility rules. GA programs exist in about two-thirds of the states, although very short-term or one-time aid is available in some of these. Some programs restrict coverage to "temporarily disabled" persons who are awaiting SSI coverage. Some programs offer a specific shelter payment; others pay consolidated benefits.

gentrification The purposeful transformation of a neighborhood to one that will attract higher income residents through the displacement of lower income tenants, the renovation of vacant buildings, and the opening of higher price businesses.

Good Samaritan laws Also known as donor liability laws, these statutes, enacted by virtually all the states, protect food donors. The laws provide that excess food donated to food banks, soup kitchens, or similar outlets is given in good faith, with regard to its condition, and that the donor is not responsible after the act of giving.

Greyhound therapy The often officially sanctioned practice of providing one-way bus tickets to homeless persons or others seeking shelter or benefits, if the applicant cannot prove local ties or is deemed otherwise undesirable in the local community. Also a practice used upon discharge of mental patients or just-released prisoners to move them to another community.

HIV or HIV-1 Human immunodeficiency virus, the virus that causes AIDS.

HOME A federal housing program authorized under the National Affordable Housing Act. HOME is basically a block grant program for low-income housing, and states can use it for new construction, rental subsidies, or rehabilitation. HOME is not an acronym or abbreviation for any other term.

homeless person The McKinney Homeless Assistance Act, first passed in 1987, defines a homeless person as: "1) an individual who lacks a fixed, regular, and adequate nighttime residence; and 2) an individual who has a primary nighttime residence that is: a) a supervised publicly or privately operated shelter designed to provide temporary living accommodations (including welfare hotels, congregate shelters, and transitional housing for the mentally ill); b) an institution that provides a temporary residence for individuals intended to be institutionalized; or c) a public or private place not designed for, or ordinarily used as, a regular sleeping accommodation for human beings." The law specifically excludes from the definition "any individual imprisoned or otherwise detained pursuant to" federal or state law. Not everyone considers this definition to cover all those who are without guaranteed adequate housing. HUD, in implementing the McKinney Act programs, has used other standards to determine whether a person is eligible for a specific homeless program.

homeless youth   A youth who lacks parental care, foster care, or institutional care.

housing problems   Households are defined as having housing problems if they occupy units that (1) have "physical defects," (2) are overcrowded, or (3) have a cost burden.

housing trust fund   A revenue pool for the creation of low- and moderate-income housing. Trust funds are created by state legislation or voter initiative, and generally are fueled by real estate–related revenues such as developers' contributions, taxes, fees, or grants.

in rem **housing**   Residential property taken by a local jurisdiction in a tax foreclosure proceeding. These units often cannot be reoccupied because local governments do not have the funds to rehabilitate them after seizure.

inclusionary zoning   A requirement for developers to create affordable housing in exchange for certain development rights or bonus allowances.

intravenous drugs   Chemical substances used in the body by means of inserting a syringe or needle into a vein.

IVDU   Intravenous drug user.

linkage   A development requirement under which for-profit building at one location is related to development at another site involving low- or moderate-income housing.

low-income   HUD defines low-income people as those whose household income is between 50 and 80 percent of the area median income, adjusted for household size; very low income is defined as below 50 percent.

McKinney Act   Any of a number of programs under the most significant piece of federal legislation to address homelessness: the "Stewart B. McKinney Homeless Assistance Act," first passed in 1987 as PL 100-77. The act is named for the late representative Stewart B. McKinney (R-CT), a member of the Housing Subcommittee who was concerned about the problems of homeless people.

magnet theory   The idea, proposed by public officials or residents opposed to measures that assist homeless people in their community, that the availability of this assistance will attract homeless people from other areas.

multidrug-resistant tuberculosis (MDR TB)   Recent strains of tuberculosis that are impervious to two or more of the 13 commonly used antibiotics employed to treat the disease.

NAHA   The National Affordable Housing Act of 1990, a major new piece of housing legislation that reauthorized many existing housing programs and created CHAS, HOME, and HOPE, among others.

needle exchange   The practice of providing clean syringes to intravenous drug users in an effort to reduce the incidence of transmission of HIV.

NIMBY   Acronym for the "not in my backyard" syndrome, which refers to the resistance of residential areas to the siting of any facility perceived as undesirable and affecting neighborhood quality and property values. The term includes, but is not limited to, the presence of shelters, drug-treatment facilities, community residences for the mentally ill, halfway houses, sewage treatment plants, jails, and toxic-waste facilities.

opportunistic infection   A general term for the variety of diseases and infections that can surface and become problematic when the immune system is depressed as the result of HIV infection. The infections would not have an effect in a healthy person.

overcrowding   A housing unit is classified as overcrowded by HUD if more than one person per room is housed there.

poverty line   An official measure of the income needed to provide basic necessities; the 1993 poverty line for a family of three was $11,890.

prepayment   Owners ending their subsidized use of buildings as low- or moderate-income housing. Owners of buildings who use federal mortgage subsidies to develop projects where some or all of the units are rented to low- or moderate-income persons for a period of 20 years may elect to end their obligation to the subsidy program by paying off the mortgage before its due date, thus jeopardizing the tenancy of the lower income people, who may be forced to seek other housing if the use of the building is changed.

project-based rental assistance   Rental assistance that is attached to a dwelling unit.

rental assistance Financial assistance to a low-income household to help meet housing costs.

runaway A child or youth under the age of 18 who is away from home for at least one night. The federal government adds the phrase "without parental or caretaker permission" to this definition.

Section 8 A HUD program that provides low-income housing by giving certificates or vouchers to low-income people to help pay for existing housing.

skid row The traditional name given to downtown areas where the homeless people of earlier decades could be found. The name supposedly originated in Seattle, from the road where logs were "skidded" to the waterfront. Such areas have been wiped out by development in many cities, taking with them the marginal commercial enterprises and cheap housing that were supported by their low-income residents.

soup kitchen Typically places where one or more meals are served on a regular schedule, generally at no cost to the recipient. Many soup kitchens are in churches, shelters, or other community facilities; they are usually staffed by volunteers, and the food is procured from donations and food banks.

SROs Single room occupancy dwellings are inexpensive rental living accommodations, often in a hotel setting. Residents have private rooms but share bathrooms and kitchen space, if available. SROs are usually found in older downtown areas; hundreds of thousands of such affordable units were destroyed during the last decade of redevelopment projects. A few nonprofit groups have begun to develop such projects; some units are also funded by the McKinney Act.

street youths Young people who have been on their own for some period of time; they may originally have been homeless, throwaway, or runaway youths. To survive, street youths may support themselves through illegal means, such as selling drugs or sex.

substandard Housing is considered substandard by HUD and the Bureau of the Census if it has certain physical or structural deficiencies such as an absence of plumbing or heating equipment, holes in the walls, or rats or mice.

Supplemental Security Income (SSI) A federal benefit program, authorized under the Social Security Act and begun in 1974, that makes cash payments to the aged, blind, and disabled. Eligibility is determined on the basis of need, using nationwide standards based on the poverty threshold and related to the consumer price index with the same formula used for Social Security benefits. Nonrecipients of Social Security can receive SSI if they qualify.

supportive services Programs provided in conjunction with housing, and sometimes as a condition to having access to housing. These include job training, health care, drug or alcohol treatment, and education programs.

system youths Young people who have been in the custody of the state for reasons such as child abuse, neglect, or other family difficulties. Subsequently these young people may have been put into multiple foster-care placements. Such youths frequently become homeless.

tenant-based rental assistance Financial assistance provided to a low-income household to help meet housing costs. The tenant or tenant household may use the aid to move to another location.

throwaway youths Young people who have been put out of their own homes by their parents or guardians, often for behavioral reasons.

transitional housing A second stage of shelter for homeless people, usually smaller in scale than emergency facilities, but often a multifamily residence. Residents generally stay in transitional programs for flexible but not indefinite periods of up to two years, with supportive services available to prepare them for greater self-sufficiency and independent living. Such services include counseling, job training, parenting classes, and budgeting.

tuberculosis (TB) Acute or chronic infection that is being seen more frequently in HIV-positive people, homeless people, and poor people generally. It is caused by an airborne pathogen, and passed through inhalation, thus contributing to its spread in physically crowded situations such as overcrowded housing or shelters. TB was once believed to be all but wiped out in this country, but case numbers have been rising in recent years.

vouchers A federal assistance program for housing in which the government pays the difference between 30 percent of a tenant's income and a "payment standard" for a unit selected by the tenant. Unlike Section 8 certificates, vouchers may be used at any rent level where tenants have selected units, not just at "fair market rent."

warehousing (1) The practice of holding off the rental market habitable dwelling units, in order to have enough vacant units in a building to meet legal requirements for selling or converting it to a condominium or cooperative. (2) The practice of providing emergency shelter in minimal surroundings, generally in a mass shelter, where homeless people are offered little besides a cot or a mat for the night.

welfare hotels   Commercially owned hotels or motels used to provide shelter to homeless families, generally those on public assistance. Physical conditions and services are often inadequate; cooking facilities are generally not provided.

Index

Mary Ellen Hombs has long been an advocate for poor people. From 1971 to 1988 she lived and worked with homeless people in Washington, D.C.'s Community for Creative Non-Violence, helping create and operate emergency, medical, and housing services, as well as being involved in national and local policy advocacy. She worked for over ten years with the National Coalition for the Homeless; she presently directs the Legal Services Homelessness Task Force in Washington, D.C.